DATE DUE

DEC 1 '78			
JAN 31 '78			
JUN 11 '90			
NOV 7 '90			
NOV 11 '94			
JAN 14 '97			

THE AMERICAN EXPLORATION AND TRAVEL SERIES

*Palenque: The Walker–Caddy Expedition
to the Ancient Maya City, 1839–1840*

palenque

the walker-caddy expedition to the ancient maya city, 1839-1840

Collected and Edited by
david m. pendergast

University of Oklahoma Press : Norman

Library of Congress Catalog Card Number: 66–22722

Copyright 1967 by the University of Oklahoma Press, Publishing Division of the University. Composed and printed at Norman, Oklahoma, U.S.A., by the University of Oklahoma Press. First edition.

To J.H.C. and P.W.

foreword

IN THE CENTURY AND A QUARTER separating the year 1840 from the present, the ever repeated cycle of sun, rain, and jungle growth, often aided by human activity, has accelerated the gnawing decay which began more than a millenium ago at the ancient Maya ceremonial center of Palenque, in the state of Chiapas, Mexico. Accompanying this decay, time and technology have joined forces to alter old ways of life and occasionally to obliterate whole villages, leaving only the memory of a name enshrouded in the tropical forest. Consequently, both John Herbert Caddy's limning, in words and in pictures, of British Honduras, the Petén of Guatemala, the towns of Yucatán, and especially the ruined grandeur of Palenque, as they were in 1840, and Patrick Walker's report of the Palenque Expedition are of interest to archaeologist, historian, and traveler alike.

As time and the elements have altered the scene of Caddy and Walker's era, so also have they ravaged the records of the Palenque expedition and the men who made it. Foremost among the remaining documents of the expedition is the diary kept by John Caddy, then lieutenant in the Royal Artillery. This I encountered through a series of coincidences which commenced in British Honduras and led me to Caddy's great-granddaughter, Mrs. E. G. Pullen, of Oakville, Canada. Through her, the diary, a number of preliminary drawings of Palenque, and several related notes and papers, as well as biographical data on Caddy, have been brought to light. Walker's official report, thought at first to have been lost, was discovered in the Colonial Office archives in England, although the paintings which accompanied it have vanished. For every scrap of evidence which has appeared during a year-long search, countless others are missing, and the story presented here is therefore something of a patchwork.

The sole published description of Caddy's report of the expedition, a brief note by Marshall Saville in a bibliography of Palenque, mentions a manuscript evidently similar to Caddy's description in Section V, accompanied by a series of paintings. These were obtained from Alice Caddy (Mrs. Ben Lucien Burman) of New York City, a granddaughter of John Caddy. Fortunately Saville, in the hope of publishing the report, had had photographs made of the paintings at the Museum of the American Indian, for after the return of the materials to the Caddy family, both report and paintings were destroyed. The photographs alone survive today, and were provided through the kindness of Frederick Dockstader, director of the Museum of the American Indian, to serve as illustrations for this book. I am grateful to Mr. Dockstader and to the Museum of the American Indian, Heye Foundation, for allowing me to use them.

Additional information on the expedition has been derived from a far-flung range of sources, the primary ones being the archives of British Honduras, the records of the Colonial Office in England, and files of the *Belize Advertiser* in the collections of the Bancroft Library at the University of California, Berkeley. Even in these records there are gaps; no complete file of the *Belize Advertiser* exists, to my knowledge, for the period in question, and several relevant letters and other documents are missing from the mouldering volumes of the archives of British Honduras. In addition, as will be seen later in this volume, many data on the life of Patrick Walker have successfully defied all efforts to root them out of English records.

I have elected to reproduce the texts of Caddy's diary, Walker's official report, and dispatches and other documents, as well as newspaper accounts, just as they were written; idiosyncratic usage and spelling have been preserved, without corrections or the obtrusive [*sic*] which often interrupts the continuity of a tale. Except for the rare insertion without notice of punctuation marks for the convenience of the reader and arbitrary division of the diary into parts or sections, the story stands as it was written 125 years ago. The explanatory notes are mine.

In carrying out the research for this volume, I have been aided, as is every delver into ancient records, by many people to whom I fear I cannot give adequate thanks. Foremost among those whose efforts have contributed to the telling of the tale are Mrs. E. G. Pullen and other descendants of Captain Caddy, a lineage which stands as a far better monument to the man than this poor report of his deeds. I am deeply indebted also to the Hon. A. A. Hunter, minister of natural resources and trades for British Honduras, for his assistance and interest, and to the staff of the Registry in Belize City for aiding me in clambering through their shelves to disturb the dust of the nineteenth century. To Leo Bradley, librarian of British Honduras, go my thanks for making available the resources of the National Collection in the Bliss Library and for suggesting sources in England. My especial gratitude goes also to A. H. Anderson, archaeological commissioner of British Honduras, and to Mrs. Anderson, both of whom have taught me much about British Honduras, past and present.

In England, B. Cheeseman, librarian of the Colonial Office in London, went to great effort to provide answers to my many difficult and often vague questions, and the staff of the Public Records Office kindly provided copies of documents which Mr. Cheeseman had searched out. To the Keeper of Public Records I am indebted for permission to quote directly from, and to reproduce, dispatches and other materials protected by Crown Copyright. A list of all such materials included in this work is given in Appendix II. I have also been assisted by Mr. Philip Wright, librarian of the Society of Antiquaries of London, and Major R. St. G. G. Bartelot, of the Royal Artillery Institution, Woolwich. Mr. Patrick Gordon Walker, then foreign secretary to Her Majesty's government, although not a descendant of the earlier Patrick Walker, answered my query regarding possible relationship by requesting a search of files in the Foreign Office, and C. J. Child, deputy librarian of the Foreign

Office, provided a most helpful clue to Patrick Walker's marriage date and place.

I have left for last an acknowledgment which should have stood near the top. For his willingness to follow up fragmentary leads, to check at great length for sources which sometimes finally proved to be nonexistent, and to provide answers to questions which I suspected, even in posing them, might be unanswerable, I owe a great debt to my brother James.

Should there be others whose contributions ought here to be cited but who remain unnamed, I trust they will take solace from the fact that their efforts have helped to bring the long-forgotten journey to light at last.

It is curious how events have come full circle after so long a time. As I write this, the pages of John Caddy's diary lie spread before me in a thatched house not unlike the houses which gave shelter to Caddy and Walker on their journey. Around me stands the bush— the rain forest which Caddy's words depict so well—and I note the occasional flight overhead of one of the birds whose long-dead ancestors were the fruits of Caddy's hunting. The writing of this book was begun in the place from which the expedition set out a bit over 125 years ago, and completed at a Maya ceremonial center not altogether unlike the one whose features were recorded by Caddy's brush. Today, a modern road replaces the tortuous Belize River passage, and one can travel from Belize to Old Bank, or Benque Viejo, in less than three hours rather than the eighteen days required by Walker and Caddy. But despite the many changes, much remains the same; the bush, the birds, the houses, the people, and many of the places are altered little, if at all. As I see these things now, I see them in part through Caddy's eyes, and my enjoyment of them is deepened. It is my hope that this book may also bring enjoyment even to those who have never seen the land through which the forgotten journey was made.

David M. Pendergast

Altun Ha, British Honduras
May 25, 1966

contents

plates

Palenque: The Walker–Caddy Expedition
to the Ancient Maya City, 1839–1840

1. a time of discovery

THE EARLY DECADES of the nineteenth century were unsettled times in tropical America—times of growth and unrest, of excitement and discovery. New lands were explored, and new resources exploited, and the spirit of adventure ran strong in the rugged mountains, on the verdant lowland carpet beneath the high rain forest, and down the many ribbons of water joining the land to the sea. New people, many of them colonists from Europe, brought new skills and ideas, linking the traditions of the Old World to the dynamic expansion of the New.

With the ferment of these years came frequent political upheaval, which in the late 1830's was stirring much of Central America. The Central American Federation, which had briefly offered hope of stability by uniting several republics, had been constructed on a weak foundation, and by 1839 the mortar had crumbled and the shaky structure was gone. Guatemala in particular seethed with unrest; now under the control of General Morazán and the forces of federalism, now swayed by Carrera and his rebels, the country offered little in the way of safety either for natives or for travelers. Nowhere in the area was government likely to be stable, and in fact it often happened that those who sought to present credentials, petitions, or even their support found no government at all as control shifted from one group to the other, and officials, with the papers and sometimes the funds of government in their valises, simply disappeared.

In Yucatán, the people, feeling themselves physically and politically set apart from Mexico, were often restive. Shortly before 1840,

3

political and economic ties between Yucatán and Mexico were severed, and the peninsula began a brief existence as a separate nation.

Planted squarely in the midst of the turmoil stood British Honduras—"The Settlement," as it was sometimes known—then the lone English colony in Central America, and often in those days the only country in which stability of government was assured. Situated at the eastern base of the Yucatán Peninsula, British Honduras comprised only a tiny strip of Caribbean coastline backed by extensive mangrove swamps, dense tropical forests, and a few areas of modest elevation, especially in the south, which served to relieve the sameness of the jungle-clad lowlands.

Under Superintendent Colonel Alexander MacDonald and earlier administrators, The Settlement had grown from its supposed late seventeenth century beginnings, when the area was occupied by shipwrecked English mariners, to a position of considerable importance, stemming not so much from the country's natural resources (which could largely be duplicated elsewhere with the exception of hardwoods) as from the existence of a shallow-water port at the capital, Belize. The railroad-building boom in Europe during the 1830's had created a market for the mahogany and other hardwoods which flourished in the vastness of The Settlement's western reaches, and through Belize flowed raw materials destined for the mills of the world, while to it came ships laden with the finery which that world produced. Parisian fashions in hats and gowns, gentlemen's furnishings, pianos, furniture from England, fine foods and wines, whisky— all these and much more passed through Belize, some to remain in The Settlement, but the major portion ultimately to appear in the homes of the leaders of society in neighboring nations. In these years, Belize was the commercial hub of the area, and its merchants frequently served as bankers for the wealthy of those republics where neither banks nor governments could be depended on for long; The Settlement was then to Central America what Hong Kong later became to Asia.

As the 1830's were a time of political and economic change and development, so also was this decade a time of awakening interest in the mysterious ruins of ancient civilizations, known largely from the tales of travelers who in penetrating the jungle depths had suddenly found themselves at the feet of pyramids atop which, thrust upward with the tallest trees, stood the remains of what many supposed to have been temples or palaces. Travelers' tales, embellished as they so often are in the telling and retelling, spoke of buildings rank with vegetation, inhabited only by bats and snakes, but smelling somehow of great age and of a forgotten people. Stories there were, too, of monuments carved with the figures of strangely garbed human beings, and of animals, seemingly including the elephant.

Among the ancient sites which had attracted the attention of those journeying through the land of the ancient Maya, Palenque in the state of Chiapas was one of the more important. The site was first discovered by the Spaniards in the middle or latter part of the eighteenth century, and between 1784 and 1834 a number of brief accounts appeared, including those of Ramón de Ordóñez y Aguiar, in 1784; Domingo Juarros, in 1808; Pablo Félix Cabrera, in 1822, the first to contain an extensive series of illustrations of the site; the work of Dupaix, also illustrated, published by Lord Kingsborough in 1831; and the works of Juan Galindo, 1832–34. Most of these descriptions of Palenque were largely or wholly based on brief explorations of the ruins, and none was characterized by illustrations of striking accuracy. This difficulty was not remedied by the sojourn of Comte Jean de Waldeck at Palenque in 1832 and 1833, for although he was a skilled lithographer, Waldeck allowed his imagination to run riot in illustrating the ruins, as had others before him. However, Waldeck's work, together with Lord Kingsborough's earlier publication, served more than any others to excite the imaginations of scholars and explorers. Speculation increased, often taking wildly fanciful turns, and debates were held in the United States and England, even by those whose acquaintance with Central America was limited to a highly foggy notion of where the area might be, and whose learned treatises on subjects antiquarian were chiefly distinguished by the purest of theory supported by the poorest of facts. Clearly the time was at hand, and the intellectual climate propitious, for an expedition of a more scientific nature, better equipped to explore, record, and bring back for the world to examine, the true nature of the fabled ruins.

Two such expeditions were mounted in 1839, one with the semi-official support of the government of the United States; the other the earliest-known official government archaeological expedition organized solely for the purpose of exploring Palenque, originating in British Honduras. For their exploits in the former, the two participants achieved immediate and lasting fame; the names of John Lloyd Stephens and Frederick Catherwood became irrevocably linked with the beginnings of scientific archaeology in the Maya area. The latter expedition, although equally momentous, was no more than a brief incident in the lives of the two men whose effort it was, and it brought to them no more than passing recognition of their contribution to knowledge of ancient Maya civilization. Neither Lieutenant John Herbert Caddy, Royal Artillery, artist and diarist of the expedition, nor Patrick Walker, the expedition's leader, had been an antiquarian by inclination or experience before the journey to Palenque, and this pattern was little altered by their Palenque experiences. For these and other reasons, the light shed by the Walker-Caddy expedition on the nature of Palenque was no stronger than a feeble candle-flame, too weak to be seen by more than a handful of persons, and it soon flickered out in the blaze of Stephens' *Incidents of Travel in Central America, Chiapas, and Yucatán*, published in 1841.

Thus it is that the lives of Stephens and Catherwood are painted with clear, bold strokes on the canvas of time,[1] while those of Caddy and Walker have receded into the shadows beyond all hope of full recounting. So far as it is now possible, these pages contain a reconstruction of the lives and times of the two men, a patchwork of dry documents, of their own words, and of those written about them by

[1] See Victor W. Von Hagen, *Frederick Catherwood, Archt.* (New York, Oxford University Press, 1950) and *Maya Explorer: John Lloyd Stephens and the Lost Cities of Central America and Yucatán* (Norman, University of Oklahoma Press, 1947).

6

others. Perhaps, knowing these men in the only way they can be known, with some understanding of the circumstances which joined them for a brief period and cast them in the role of explorers, we shall be able to relive, at least in part, their long-forgotten journey to Palenque.

II. the participants
–caddy and walker

OVER THE SIGNATURE of Salter Jehosaphat Mountain, deputy chaplain to the Garrison of Quebec, there appears the following entry in the Quebec City baptismal records: "John Herbert, son of John Caddy, Esq. Captain in the Royal Regiment of Artillery, and his wife Hannah, was born June 28th and baptized July the 12th in the Year of Our Lord One Thousand, eight hundred and one." The second child and first son born to the Caddys, John Herbert began life in the military setting which was to shape most of the years to come. Captain, later Colonel, John T. Caddy had come to Canada from Kent, England, about 1796, probably with military units posted in Quebec to control Indian uprisings and other difficulties in what was still generally a frontier area. In October of 1798, at the age of twenty-four, Caddy took as his wife Hannah Goddard, eight years his junior, the daughter of a Quebec brewer. Their life revolved around military posts, and from the beginning there seems to have been little question that their first son would continue his father's tradition of service with the Royal Artillery.

By 1808, Colonel John Caddy had been transferred to Fort Malden, at Amherstburg, Ontario, where he and his family were to spend the next decade. John Herbert began school in that year and continued his education in the classes at Amherstburg until 1815, despite the disruption occasioned by the War of 1812, in which Fort Malden played a significant role. It may have been during these years that John's interest in drawing, which was later to be so important a part of his life, was first awakened, perhaps by Mathew Donavon, one of his several early teachers.

8

Early in 1815 young John left Canada for England, where he entered the Royal Military Academy. Having completed his basic education, he was enlisted as a gentleman cadet in the Royal Artillery on March 26, 1816, and trained as an engineer and cannoneer, also receiving instruction in sketching and painting from the academy drawing master. While in England, Caddy spent much of his time at No. 5 Chatham Place, Woolwich Common, Kent, the home of Richard Hamilton, a colonel in the Royal Artillery and a family friend. Hamilton, who had served in the West Indies, may have directed Caddy's interest toward service in the Caribbean. More important than Hamilton's influence, though, was that of his daughter Georgiana, three years Caddy's junior; for in 1828 she and Caddy were married at St. Clements Dane, London.

John Caddy received his commission as a second lieutenant, Royal Artillery, on July 29, 1825, and his promotion to first lieutenant occurred only two years later, although the commission is dated December 31, 1830, and was not entered at the Office of Ordnance until May of 1832. For much of this period, beginning in 1828, John was serving the first of several tours of duty in the West Indies, holding for a time in 1830 the position of secretary to General Blackwell in Tobago. Georgiana was introduced almost at once to the life of an army wife, for she was left behind in England at the home of her now-widowed mother.

What manner of man was John Caddy at the age of twenty-seven, when he began his long association with the West Indies? It is difficult to say, since at this time apparently he had not yet been smitten by the urge to record his experiences in a diary. Certain it is, however, that he was an artist of considerable talent, rising far above the "recording artists" trained as a matter of course to draw, however crudely, military installations and other scenes of potential strategic interest. Caddy's ability in the use of watercolors extended to scenery, structures, and even to detailed paintings of flowers, but was weak in the area of the human figure, a limitation never overcome, which probably made him all the better as a landscape painter.

In one other respect, Caddy's personality was almost surely fully formed by this time. Indeed, he had one trait so characteristic that it probably existed from his very early years. Although he was to write at a later date, "A hasty scribble shows more what immediately emanates from the heart, than a letter studied and written in well pointed sentences," John Caddy was never one to dash off a quick bit of work, whether written or painted, and be satisfied with it. He was inclined, rather, to make a note, or a sketch, and from this work up a preliminary statement or a rough version of the work. The next step was frequently an intermediate form (perhaps a sepia rendering of a scene), and thence onward to the final version, which, apart from the application of Caddy's talent to the undertaking, should have been perfection itself simply from the number of transformations through which it had passed. This Caddy characteristic, a sort of combination of perfectionism and procrastination, was at once John's greatest problem and a very useful asset. It meant that many projects were left unfinished, and many more probably were considered but not begun. On the other hand, the reworking of a thing time and time again meant that several copies of it existed. Hence the record of a journey or the painted impression of a scene was more likely to survive, in one form or another, the ravages of time.

Caddy returned from his first West Indian duty in 1831, and spent two years at the Hamilton home in Woolwich with his family and his mother-in-law. This peaceful interlude was interrupted by a second posting to the West Indies in 1833. That year, on the fourth day of July, Caddy left home, wife, and young daughters Anna and Elizabeth behind him and set out once more for the Caribbean, this time to the island of St. Lucia. On the second tour of duty, Caddy kept a diary, of which a fragment remains. From his description of his departure and a few passages from the diary itself, we can learn something not only of the life of a young artillery officer in the 1830's, but also of the nature of Caddy himself.

"On the 4th day of July 1833 I left per steamer for Gravesend (the vessel in which I was to embark for the West Indies having dropped down the day previous) and my precious existence was placed in some little jeopardy on my first outset, in consequence of an opposition Boat passing at the very moment the wherry in which I had most of my light marching order baggage came alongside the Steamer in which I proposed embarking, causing such a hubbub in the muddy Thames, as very nearly capsized the boat—half filling it at the same time with water—however I got on board without the benefit of a sousing & the only inconvenience I sustained was that part of my traps got a little wet.

"The Captain of the vessel who seemed a better class of person than one generally meets in this station of life, advised me to keep a sharp look out for my baggage, as some gentlemanly fellow might, quite by accident, mistake one of my trunks for the one which his servant unluckily forgot to put on board. I thanked him for his hint, and lost nothing—but judging by the appearance of most of the company, both cabin & steerage I should say I was particularly lucky.

"Off Woolwich a party of Ladies & Gentlemen joined the vessel on a Pic Nic—to most of whom I was known, they very politely requested I would join them, but as I was not exactly in condition to add to the hilarity of a party of pleasure, I declined with all due acknowledgement of their kindness. The Musicians, who had been endeavouring with all their might to impress upon our imaginations, that they had some pretty considerable idea of the art they professed, and one would fancy they were emminently successful from the manner in which the young Ladies & their beaux promenaded along the deck—about to commence a Waltz—to that tune from Der Freishutz—and the blowsy looking elderly ladies with their various coloured bonnets befeathered and beflowered to the very acme of what they call fashion, vainly endeavouring to keep time with their paddles, to the tune, making it very manifest to a spectator that the effect produced on their different tympanums was not at all unanimous. When we approached Gravesend one of the Fiddles went round with a saucer to collect whatever the generosity of the Passengers might think adequate to the exertions they had made for their amusement. I observed the smallest donations were thankfully received, as copper formed the principal part of what the saucer contained—on their counting over the money I heard one exclaim 'What only sixpence from that one gay party from Woolwich—well I'm blow'd!!!'—

"On arriving at Gravesend the Capt. of the Ship in which I had taken my passage came alongside the steamer, & had my baggage put into his boat informing me that the Custom House officer would not allow it to be embarked until it had been overhauled at the Custom House. I thought this rather hard, that an officer proceeding to a foreign station should be obliged to have his trunks ransacked—to see that he had no merchandize amongst them—after uncording & examining part of my baggage, the rascal came to me with a sneaking sort of smirk upon his ugly visage & said 'I should not think of putting you to the least inconvenience Sir, you must know our Principal is rather particular'—I suppose he expected me to give a fee for this insinuation that his superior was the cause of inconvenience. I put my keys which he handed me into my Pocket & he watched the withdrawing of my hand, as a hungering dog watches his master when he opens the basket containing their joint meal—however this Custom House Asst. came off minus."

As the coast of England slipped away into the mist, Caddy's desire to record his adventures seems also to have vanished. Perhaps he found his shipboard existence too unvarying and colorless to warrant description; in any case, his diary is blank until September 14, 1833, the rain-dampened day of his arrival in St. Lucia. On the fifteenth and the days following, Caddy, after taking over command of the detachment of the Royal Artillery, found himself some rather soggy quarters, and began to acquaint himself with the island, its people, and the food of the artillery mess. Of the last, he noted on November 2nd, "dined at mess—d—— bad dinner, as usual—" surely a comment echoed by soldiers round the world.

In November, Caddy settled into the routine which would be characteristic of much of his tour on St. Lucia: travel around the island, dinner and social engagements with the upper elements of local society, and frequent hunting tours. The shooting of birds was partly sport, but it had a practical side as well; to pay off debts owed to a variety of tradesmen and agents in England, Caddy shot and stuffed birds and shipped them to his mother-in-law, who sold them at about three shillings each. It appears from this that the pay of a military man in the 1830's was no less inadequate for the support of a family than it was earlier and later.

Amidst the daily notations of places visited and things done, the diary for November 13 nicely reflects Caddy's ability at observation in a realm other than that of flora and fauna: "Heavy rain. Sun made an attempt to appear about two o'clock—upon which I sallied out for a walk—climbed the hills that overhang the Baron's residence— went through a considerable quantity of wood & at the embouchment of the path, came upon a small house, the residence of a French family—the daughter, rather good-looking girl, was leaning over a gallery, talking to her brother, in somewhat an indecent posture— upon my making my appearance she gave a hop, skip and jump & disappeared—her dress or undress being nothing more than a—— oh, no, we never mention it—her hair dishevelled, no stockings, no shoes—got a devil of a ducking—bed early."

November and December were largely filled with local amusements, with an occasional bit of military duty interspersed for variety. A fishing trip on the nineteenth of December is typical of the pastimes which filled Caddy's days in late 1833: "Up at six—Baron d'Yvolez called for me to go to his brothers on a fishing excursion— on arriving at the estate of the Souci de Grand Cul de Sac—we had a cup of coffee and some toast, when we sallied out to see the negroes catch fish in the canal, which had been previously drained—but as I expect they had an interest in not letting their master know that there were any large fish—allowed them to escape or else bagged them for their own particular purpose. Young de Bernard, a Gent by the name of Bistin and myself went to the river in hopes of improving our sport and after endeavouring to catch the mullet in their holes for some time, wading up to our armpits—de Bernard and myself pressed a canoe into our service and commenced rod fishing— killed about a dozen and a half of fish, called Bouger—very like the perch in shape but of a red colour—returned to dinner at d'Yvolez's about six—Madame looked very interesting—returned home about 10 o'clock."

With all the activities open to a young officer, life could still be lonely and unpleasant, especially at holiday time. More than a tinge of bitterness colors Caddy's entry for December 25, which closes: "—dined at mess—had dinner & pudding—not eatable—Merry Christmas!!" The burden of existence on St. Lucia was not lightened by a siege of fever, and the diary entries for December 30 and 31 are an eloquent expression of the feelings of all who have been felled by the scourge of the tropics: "—dined at Pongo—on a Pepper Pot— bed early, woke in the night about 12 suffering excessively from head ache and fever, accompanied by intolerable heartburn—my intestines felt as if on fire and that the hot flame rose through the medium of my throat as a chimney—fancied myself tumbling over precipices—holding on by tufts of grass, which gave to my weight, until I awakened with a jump—dozed again & fancied all kinds of heads, commencing with small thin features & gradually enlarging until they became immence, & then a jumble of large eyes, noses, mouths, without any regard to unity—31st. Servant called me at six, after getting the better of my fever by keeping the clothing well tucked round my head & all except a breathing place until a profuse perspiration & had just dozed off into a comfortable nap, when my servant came to inform me I was on duty, and had to visit the issue of the bread to the troops—I damned him, the Baker and all concerned without remorse—turned to the other side & slept again, praying he would not 'call again'—I wish my duns would as easily acquiesce in my request—mustered my detachment at 10—very seedy."

Recovering from his bout with fever, Caddy resumed the round of parties, hunting, and travels. We can only hope for the sake of his health that the events of January 8 were not typical of each day. "Shepherd & I went out shooting pigeons—Killed none—a black day—capital dinner—8 sat down—8 bottles Champaigne at dinner, & 8 Madeira—pretty well for a small tea party—everyone exceedingly intoxicated—steered the boat home with a flowing sail—8 miles by sea—Grant so drunk fell from his horse—and was lodged up at Mrs. Pilages, on the delicate bosom of Mademoiselle Celice—stopped at Chipchace's on our way home, had a sigar—stayed at Dalrymples for some time in expectation of rest of party coming home—came on rain hard—introduced our horses to same room, where they stood very quiet—fed Butterfield off a clean plate—he left his 'card' with Dal in grateful remembrance of his hospitable entertainment—Dal forgot what had happened and when he arose in the morning, thought he had found a mare's nest—bed by 3 P.M."

The diary continues, with occasional gaps, through April 22, 1834, with most of the days filled with games of whist, military tasks and minutiae, and frequent grumblings about the failure of mail packets to arrive on schedule. Interspersed with the other activities, and apparently becoming one of the more important pursuits by 1834, were many sessions of drawing and painting, indicating that Caddy had returned to an activity which had always held great attraction for him and which now, to judge by correspondence from his mother-in-law, was also a means of discharging more of the debt which had piled up in England. Drawing and hunting filled many days, and Caddy's views of the latter, as well as an observation on the quality of St. Lucia's atmosphere, are contained in a letter directed to a friend in England: "Although in a climate which is, I believe, noted as one of the most unhealthy of the Antilles; at least it is so nominated at the Insurance offices, hence the enormous premiums charged; I cannot divest myself of that kind of sport, which must have been innate in my composition—and in very defiance of all advice—given gratuitously by most officers—with the terror of deadly venomous serpents, and as deadly fevers—pointed out to me, in as glowing colours as the snakes themselves are clad withal, or as the blue and yellow melancholy hue, which fever imparts to the complexion—still in despite of all this have I traversed the woods and waded the streams in search of sport and not without success." Whatever suffering he may have endured by being separated from home and family, it cannot be said that Caddy was seriously strained by overwork. However, the leisurely life is not always the most enjoyable, and even for John Caddy, with his naturalistic bent, the hunting and the social round must have seemed at times more wearing than military routine, for he wrote, "A man lengthens his life by remaining in this country—because a month here is as long as 12 in England."

The abrupt termination of the diary in April reflects the fact that in May of 1834 Caddy relinquished command of the detachment in St. Lucia and was transferred to St. Vincent, where he was stationed at Fort Charlotte. Here his routine was altered for a time, for in late summer he was joined by his wife and daughter Anna. In April, 1835, the family was enlarged by the arrival of a son, John Hamilton, but later that year the Caddys sorrowfully filed away among their papers the bills for coffin manufacture and burial charges for their short-lived first son. The following year saw the birth of a second son, John St. Vincent. The family remained together at Fort Charlotte until July, 1837, when they returned to Woolwich, to the deathbed of Georgianna's mother.

Caddy had begun as early as 1831 to sketch and paint West Indian scenes, and in 1835 he sent a number of paintings to England in the hope that their publication might aid in removing the burden of debt from the family. A publishing house having expressed reluctance to enter upon such an undertaking without a guarantee of profit, Caddy took it upon himself to produce a set of twelve smaller drawings and to get up a list of potential subscribers. As a result of an advertisement in St. Vincent and of his personal solicitations, he was able to provide an estimate of 210 interested persons, which apparently was sufficient augury of income to bring a gleam to the publisher's eye. The first in a projected series of four folios, engraved by Westall, Fielding and Company and printed by Ackermann, London, in 1837, included scenes of St. Lucia, St. Vincent, St. Kitts, and Dominica. Arriving in St. Vincent early in 1838, some months after the Caddy's departure from the island, the volume was advertised in the *St. Vincent Gazette and Weekly Advertiser* of February 17 at a "price, the set, to subscribers £3.10s, Sterling, or Seventeen Dollars, CASH." The remaining three volumes never saw the light of day, and the financial success of the venture or lack thereof is not a matter of record. Nevertheless, it is clear that Caddy's artistic activities, as well as his interest in natural history, contributed to the quality of both the written and the painted record of the Palenque journey four years later.

The return of the Caddy family to England was followed by over a year of relaxation for John, out of the heat and humidity of the tropics and among the friendly and familiar scenes of home. His enjoyment of this life was once again interrupted in December of 1838 by orders posting him to the small Royal Artillery garrison in British Honduras. The move may have been ordered simply to bring the British Honduras detachment up to strength or to provide a trained gunnery officer; in any case, the move was clearly not connected with archaeological matters or Caddy's talent with a brush. In an action surely typical of all armies everywhere, Caddy's engineering ability was considered, as was his total lack of familiarity with matters nautical, and he was forthwith appointed harbour master for The Settlement. Here, as in the Caribbean, boredom seems to have been a main feature of Caddy's life, and at times it gave way to homesickness. He wrote: "I thought to myself whilst swinging in my hammock last night and enjoying the fumes of a real Havannah—after a mess dinner & a bottle of Old Madeira—of infinite merit—that perhaps the description of a days sport amongst the finny tribes in the rivers of this Colony might not be unacceptable to some of my friends of the Croft—at home—what recollections this little word brings into my mind—none can have the most distant idea, except those who have been exiled to some such place as this, the value attached to the word home.—kind relations—loved friends— directed to that home from whence no days of happiness passed in their society—the lovely scenes traversed in our angling excursions. I almost feel the try of a noble Trout and hear the line rattling thro the reel as he dashes up the stream and endeavours to gain his hiding place under the bank on the opposite side, where the pendant branches of many-foliaged trees & bushes hang over the slow, deep, cooling eddy which laves the aged trunk & roots of an ash filling out—forming a shelter from the sun & a hiding place from the eye of his destroyer—all are pictured in the mind surely, as plain as reality to my imagination, and makes it sure that any description of scenery or sport here will fall far short of what it is at home."

While carrying out his duties as harbour master of Belize, Caddy had the opportunity of setting down in his diary a brief description of The Settlement and its capital and "fort" as they were about 1839. In addition, he made several sketches, and probably some paintings, of local scenes, perhaps thereby attracting the attention of Superintendent MacDonald to the presence in The Settlement of an accomplished artist. Only two of Caddy's efforts from this period, both views of Belize, have survived. The diary, however, provides a good picture of the nature of The Settlement and its people at this time; following some notes on the coast and rivers of the colony, the description continues:

"The largest lagoon in the country is the Manati, before mentioned—it is about 9 miles in length and from 3 to 4 in breadth; with a depth varying from 2 to 6 feet. At a short distance from its Western shore a series of conical hills rise, composed of limestone, and contain caverns of some extent; they are covered from base to summit with a most luxuriant growth of forest trees of large size, and great variety, giving to the lagoon a most picturesque appearance as you emerge from the dense mass of monotonous mangroves, with their extraordinary looking roots, through which the lower river meanders to the sea. There are some plantations on the borders of the lagoon, but the soil immediately on its margin is sandy and unproductive; but in the valleys formed by the hills at a short distance inland it becomes rich in the extreme. I several times visited the Plantations (on its margin) of Mr. McDonald, Lieut. Patten, and Mr. Matheson. They all had commenced on the margin of the lagoon but found it labor in vain, and were obliged to fell trees and clear in the vallies, where I saw rice, Indian corn, plantains, yams, with some cotton, and many other articles of tropical produce growing most luxuriantly. I also saw the rice and tasted it, it was large grained and very white and as good in flavor as any I ever met with.

18

The Indian corn was also excellent; and the few cotton plants were as they well could be of pods but they were in a green state and consequently the quality could not be ascertained.

"The water in this lagoon is almost salt, something more than brackish, except in the height of the wet season when from the number of tributary creeks which flow into it, it becomes nearly quite fresh. The water is never very clear—it abounds in fish, and the Manati or Sea Cow is occasionally killed in it. There are many fresh water lagoons in the interior, particularly to the northward of the Belize River. They are generally surrounded by marsh and logwood swamp and consequently exceedingly detrimental to the health of the European. These lagoons actually swarm with fish, and were I to relate the wonderful accounts I have heard, with regard to the quantity taken in a given time, I fear I might be accused of using too freely what has been termed a travellers license, and trenching considerably on the prerogative of Baron Munchausen, of long bow notoriety.

"The whole country is intersected by extensive Pine Ridges. On the Pine Ridges there are ponds of water in the wet season, but which entirely dry up in dry weather. These ponds teem with quantities of a species of fish called the Fresh water Snook. It would be difficult to account for their appearance in such miriads in these ponds unless lodged there by the receding floods—as most of these plains are overflown periodically, Forming the natural pasturage of which there is sufficient for the maintenance of an almost unlimited number of horses and cattle; but sheep do not thrive well in consequence of the pasture being long and the ground too moist.

"These tracts of country are nearly useless in an agricultural point of view, altho' I saw the sweet potato produced on a patch at Mr. McDonald's at Manati, which were large and of a less watery nature than they generally are—various productions have been tried on these but failed.

"The Pine from which these ridges take their name is a species of the American Pitch Pine, and is almost the only tree of any magnitude which thrives on these barrens, it grows to a large size and when dry is one of the most durable woods of the Country and is much used where exposed to the influence of the atmosphere, or even to the deteriorating properties of salt water, which it resists for many years. As piles for wharves it is much esteemed. This tree contains a quantity of resinous matter, which exudes freely at a certain time of the year when notched with an axe—and a piece of wood lit, burns with a strong flame like a torch—I have not a doubt this Resin might be extracted as an article of commerce. The Cahoon—a species of Palm—also run in ridges through the country but these ridges are the reverse of the pine ridges—the Cahoon grows in the richest soil, generally a black vegetable mould of some depth. It bears large bunches of nuts from which an excellent oil is produced, useful when fresh instead of butter or lard in culinary—and also for burning. It is produced in small quantities, but might be made to almost any extent.

"The high land commences about the Manati Lagoon and extends to the S.W., ridge rising above ridge until the Cockscomb in the Ahama range crowns the whole, having an elevation of 3000 feet above the level of the sea. I had a great wish to explore this mountainous district and climb to the summit of the Cockscomb, but was unable to do so during my sojourn in the Country. A spur of this range runs towards the Belize River, about Roaring Creek one of its tributary streams.

"All the rivers of this country are subject to periodical floods, which rise to an astonishing height but seldom last for any length of time causing some inconvenience to the inhabitants—but little actual damage to their plantations. The natives call these inundations when very high 'Top gallant floods.'[1]

"The town of Belize is the only one in the settlement. It is situated at one of the mouths of the old River and takes its name from a Buccaneer chief named Wallace who established himself here, taking refuge from the vengeance of the Spaniards on whom he had com-

---

[1] That is, a flood of sufficient depth to submerge the top gallant (flags atop the mainmast of a sailing vessel).

mited depredations.[2] The site perhaps is the best that could be chosen as far as its central position goes, as it is about midway between Yucatan and Guatemala in which countries most of the British goods imported into Belize find a ready market. The trade with Yucatan was entirely contraband until very lately when the Yucatans declared themselves independent of Mexico and opened their ports to the importation from other countries at a very reduced scale of duties. It is built on each side of the River the communications being by an excellent wooden bridge and is laid out in streets running at right angles to each other, the principal one being close to the sea; at the southern end of which stands the Government House, the residence of Her Majesty's Superintendent. It is a handsome building of wood, on a foundation and above ground cellarage of brick, having a veranda running completely round it at each storey. On the opposite side of the street stands the Church[3] a brick structure of neat appearance, having a tower and spire; the interior is handsomely fitted up, and contains an excellent organ. The court house stands at the other end of this street near the mouth of the River. It contains a convenient court room, as well as the offices of the Clerk of Courts, Provost Marshal, Treasurer, Port Master, etc. and a store for Militia clothing. The Jail is also a creditable building. The prisoners are made to work on the roads, filling them in with sand procured from the shallow part of the sea in front of the Town, rather severe labor standing in the burning sun up to the waist in water shovelling the sand and mud into scows kept by the Settlement for this purpose. Nearly the whole town has been reclaimed from a swamp in this manner.

"The remaining public buildings are the Hospital, and free school. In the former, Patients are admitted by an order from a Magistrate and if poor, have the benefit of Medical attendance and nursing at

[2] This is perhaps the most popular of several explanations of the derivation of the name Belize; equally likely is that it derives from the Yucatecan Maya word *belize*, meaning "muddy water."

[3] St. John's Church, later Cathedral (Church of England), constructed in 1812; it and Government House, built in 1814, still stand.

the expense of the Public. The free school is under the immediate superintendence of the Rector. The Clerk of the Church being the schoolmaster to the male children. The females are under the care of a schoolmistress. Upwards of a hundred children are thus given the rudiments of a Religious education. There is also a school attached to both the Wesleyan and Baptist missions.

"The houses in the front street face the sea and consequently have all the advantage of a 'Sea Breeze' which is tolerably regular for eight months of the year. They are chiefly of wood, with a lower storey of brick, the latter being used as stores and the upper part as the dwelling—some are handsomely finished and well furnished. Polished mahogany is profusely used for the doors and pannelling and often in the building itself.

"The Barracks are situated about half a mile north of the Bridge at Newtown, on land reclaimed from Mangrove swamp. They face the sea at about 150 yards from the shore—the water is very shallow for some distance out—they are built of wood and have been very good buildings but are at present in a sad state of disrepair. They consist of seven houses, detached, for Officers; a Messroom and Barrack Rooms for the men capable of containing about 400 with a Hospital. The vicinity is swamp for miles back, and very unhealthy to the European's constitution. The Black soldiers however suffer little from this circumstance but are dreadfully annoyed by the mosquito and sandfly; each man is obliged to be provided with a mosquito net or Pavilion as it is called by the inhabitants. It is generally made of coloured calico in the shape of an oblong bag and is hung up at night by strings tied to the beams and rafters. The sandflys at some seasons are so troublesome that the men on guard actually carry a brush made by splitting a piece of Bamboo into very fine strips leaving a part for a handle.

"About half a mile from the Town at the entrance of the River there is a small Island misnamed a Fort and called Fort George. It has been formed chiefly from the Ballast of vessels from Great Britain and is therefore British ground—it is 350 feet long and 120 feet broad—on it are the Artillery Barracks. There are 11 guns mounted but only three on serviceable platforms—ten 24 P[ound] and one 6 P Iron gun, used for firing the morning, mid-day, and evening guns, at daylight, 12 o'clock, and 8 in the evening.

"The Island is not more than a foot above the high water level of the sea, whose tide does not rise or fall more than 10 inches generally. The guns are completely exposed as there is not even a breastwork. I commenced one with the assistance of the Prisoners from the Jail, and raised about 18 or 20 inches on the sea side with a breadth of about 12 feet but could not continue it, as they were withdrawn. The Island stands in an excellent position for the protection of the Town, commanding completely the channel through which vessels or craft must enter the Harbour—but in its present condition would be next to useless. About 3½ miles to the eastward of the Town are a number of low Islands called the Sunken Cays, in fact they are mere clumps of mangrove swamp. Between these are channels called Bogues, in one of which ships load with mahogany brought from the Northward.

"St. Georges Cay is about 9 miles to the North East of Belize and was at one time the residence of many of the Mahogany cutters. It is now a convalescent Post. It contains many tolerable cottages, one belonging to the Government. Persons suffering from the effects of fever quickly recover from its harmful influence when removed here, where the pure sea breeze almost constantly refreshes the atmosphere. There is excellent sea bathing here, several baths having been built. The Cay is also a convenient careening place for the broghens.[4]

"A small Cay about three miles to the Northward, called Frenchmans Cay, is a celebrated spot for Pigeon shooting, it being covered with wild Fig, and another tree bearing bunches of red berries on which they feed (The Fiddle wood so called by the natives). The mode generally adopted is for the party to separate, each taking up a position under a tree with a tolerably clear space above you through which a few yards of blue sky may be seen—having a boy or two with you to look out for the birds when they drop—others are then

[4] Cargo vessels.

sent round the Island to beat the bushes, and by this means you may have as many snap shots as you wish. It is quick work—and the mosquitos are dreadfully annoying—settling on your hands and face in swarms. The pigeons are the white headed and as Ollapod[5] says "are pleasant cooing in the wood, and pretty pricking in a pie."

"On one of the Cays at the entrance to the channel leading to Belize there is an excellent Lighthouse supported by the Colony and a signal post on English Cay from which all vessels are signalled to another Port in the Cupola of the Court House at Belize. Also a very good House occasionally occupied by the superintendent.

"There is little society in Belize at the present time, the Principal people being merchants or Mahogany cutters have little time for amusement. However about Christmas when the Militia and Flotilla turn out for a fortnights drilling, there is a round of gaiety. At this season of the year nearly the whole Population assemble in the Town of Belize, which becomes a scene of noisy mirth."

Such was the setting in which John Caddy found himself in 1839, and such were his observations on the natural surroundings, resources, and specifics of the settlement and the military installations, and his notes on the people, their annoyances and amusements. Caddy had the eye of an artist combined with that of a military engineer, well suited to the task which was soon to confront him. The presence of an artist-draftsman-engineer-diarist in The Settlement provided one of the two elements vital to the success of the Palenque venture. The other, an energetic, competent public servant capable of leading an official government expedition, stood at hand in the person of Patrick Walker.

Late in the year 1836, Mr. Thomas Miller, keeper of records and clerk of the courts for British Honduras, succumbed to an attack of the ever-present tropical scourge, fever. Lord Glenelg, then secretary of state for the colonies, recommended in February, 1837, that one James Walker, who had for some years held a position in the

---

[5] A contraction of the Spanish *olla podrida*, a pot pourri or mixture. The reference here is apparently to a literary character, perhaps one given to ollapodisms (sayings formed of a mixture of several languages).

Colonial Office, be appointed Miller's successor. Walker arrived in Belize on April 15, 1837, bearing his appointment and a number of testimonials to his abilities as a public servant and accompanied by his younger brother, Patrick. James was immediately sworn in as clerk of the courts of British Honduras and keeper of the public records, in which offices, together with that of "one of the Judges of the Supreme Court," he served with distinction until April of the following year.

On April 28, 1838, Colonel MacDonald posted a dispatch to Lord Glenelg which read, in part: "Mr. Walker Clerk of the Courts and Keeper of the Public Records, having applied to me for leave of absence on urgent private affairs; I have consented to his return to England for a few months time. I trust he will be able to execute his affairs in such a way as to enable him to return to this Settlement as soon as possible." James Walker departed The Settlement by schooner a few days later, bound for England with dispatches for the Colonial Office, although in August a dispatch from Lord Glenelg was to arrive at Belize refusing to sanction Walker's leave of absence after so short a period of service. Walker met with Glenelg late in August to discuss matters relevant to the governing of the colony from which he had recently come, and there was no suggestion in Walker's letter following the conversation that he entertained thoughts of remaining in England. Nevertheless, something, perhaps the "urgent private affairs" referred to in the dispatch from MacDonald, dictated that James Walker would never again cross the seas to British Honduras.

Prior to his departure from The Settlement, Walker seems to have felt the pressure of his duties to be rather too much to bear without help; consequently, Patrick Walker was sworn in as assistant keeper of the public records on January 30, 1838, at which time he also commenced service as assistant clerk of the Supreme and lower courts. Patrick, then in his early twenties, brought to his first posts no background of public service, but this lack was more than balanced by generous measures of talent and energy, which sufficed in less than three months to mark him as the logical successor to his brother, whose duties he assumed as keeper of records and clerk of courts pro tempore on May 8.

Walker's zeal in office soon had the effect of increasing the number of positions which he held. On June 25, 1838, he was made one of the judges of the Supreme Court, an office which must have made simultaneous service as clerk of the courts just a trifle difficult. Patrick had by this time filled all of the posts formerly held by his brother in The Settlement, but the pro tempore status of the major positions suggests that it was fully expected that James would return, perhaps by the end of the year. However, Patrick already had become an indispensable member of the government; Colonel MacDonald, in a dispatch to the Secretary of State for the Colonies in August, 1838, wrote of Walker: "Talented and energetic, I have ever found him a firm friend and faithful counsellor." Significantly for his later career, Walker undertook at about this time an inspection trip to the Mosquito Coast, on the eastern shores of Central America. On his return he provided Her Majesty's government with a report covering the habits, dress, customs, and economy of the Mosquito Indians, a people with whom he was later more closely associated.

When it became clear that the elder Walker was never to return, Patrick became, in 1839, acting clerk of the courts and keeper of the public records, retaining his position as a judge of the Supreme Court. A grant of a parcel of land on New River Lagoon, made to Walker by MacDonald on February 13, 1839, suggests that Walker recognized his future in The Settlement and had decided to become a landed gentleman. Later in the same year Walker acquired a second grant, on the south bank of Deep River.

With a positive passion for expanding his activities, Walker assumed one post after another in 1839. In January, he was appointed a member of the general staff of the Prince Regent's Royal Honduras Militia, a local organization of much pomp and little circumstance, serving as "Inspector and Keeper of Arms, Clothing, and Accoutrements." In the following month he was given the rank of major, taking on the additional task of serving as aide-de-camp to the commander-in-chief, Colonel MacDonald. In June, Walker became both the advocate for the Crown in The Settlement and the magistrate of the Bay of Honduras, thereby compounding the complexity of his legal duties, but saving space in the courtroom; one chair sufficed to seat the clerk, magistrate, Crown advocate, and one of the judges.

Not satisfied with his offices in the military and legal spheres, Walker became, for a brief period, public treasurer as well, and by mid-1839 had also taken on the title of colonial secretary, a position in The Settlement second in importance only to that of superintendent. With spare time weighing heavily on his hands, Walker turned to membership on the committee of management of the Belize Regatta Club and service as rector, and later churchwarden, of St. John's Church (and hence probably superintendent of the church's free school).

MacDonald again found occasion in 1839 to commend Walker's qualities to the Colonial Office, writing: "From the testimony I have already borne of the value of Mr. Walker's services I need not now repeat any thing in his praise in a public point of view—as for his private conduct I may with safety add that he is one of the most exemplary young men I have ever met." It appears that the Superintendent's appraisal of Walker reflected the opinion of most residents in The Settlement, although Walker's drive for position and power had undoubtedly earned him some enemies as well. Documents reaching the Colonial Office from time to time suggest that there was some confusion and disagreement among residents of The Settlement regarding who was the official holder of which titles, and who might be entitled to take over certain positions in the local government; considering the proliferation of Walker's titles and duties, such confusion and disagreement is hardly surprising.

In noting the exemplary nature of Walker's private life, MacDonald hit on an important point. While it is true that time has obscured much of Walker's personality, his main flaw seems to have been that he was altogether too energetic, too businesslike, to be believable. Few young men of his or any other time would have been willing to sacrifice most of the pleasures of life for the sake of meteoric rise in government service or would have been marked by as little self-effacement as Walker seems to have been. In his acquisition of government positions, Walker appears to have set aside the normal diversions of life in the drive which brought him from a position of minor importance in the courts to a point at which it could be said that wherever he went, about two-thirds of the government of British Honduras went also. John Lloyd Stephens, who met Walker at the end of October, 1839, just before the offices of acting clerk of the courts and acting keeper of the public records were shed from the gargantuan list, later put the matter quite succinctly, describing Mr. Walker as "Secretary of government, and holding, besides, such a list of offices as would make the greatest pluralist among us feel insignificant." Two men less alike than Caddy and Walker can scarcely be imagined: the one inclined to frivolity, interested in the people and the things in the world around him, the other efficient, hard-driving, and not given to diversions. Yet with his superabundant energy and his position in government to lend authority to the undertaking, Patrick Walker was obviously well qualified to represent Her Majesty as leader of the Palenque Expedition.

iii. the race to palenque

In October, 1839, two men shortly to be joined in an historic under-taking were blissfully unaware of the travail which lay ahead. John Caddy, with perhaps a tiny spark of interest in ancient peoples kindled by his drawing, about 1836, of the petroglyphs on "Carib Rock" in St. Vincent, pursued his light duties as a Royal Artillery officer, possibly sometimes making repairs to the antiquated cannons of Fort George, which had been salvaged from the wreck of the armed English merchantman *Yeldham* after it had foundered on the reef off Ambergris Cay in 1800. More often, however, Caddy's time was devoted to hunting, sketching and painting, and dreaming of home.

Patrick Walker, like Caddy almost surely possessed of little interest in the relics of lost civilizations, found much to occupy his working hours, with management of the Belize Regatta Club seem-ingly the closest thing to recreation which he enjoyed. Walker's official status in The Settlement occasionally may have brought him into contact with citizens who knew something of the ancient ruins, but he could scarcely have foreseen that such things would soon become, however briefly, the main object of his interests and actions.

For The Settlement as a whole, interest in and knowledge of former inhabitants of the land may have been a trifle more intense than it was for Caddy and Walker. The arduous life of the mahogany cutter frequently led him into the little-traveled and unknown reaches of the interior of the colony, where his livelihood depended upon intensive searching of the terrain for suitable trees, often scat-tered so widely that the average distribution was about two to the

29

acre. In his searches, the cutter occasionally came across the overgrown remains of what he took to be ancient cities, possibly, in the idiom of the day, antediluvian. When he returned to Belize, and the warmth of companionship or of the local corrosive rum brought forth tales of the interior, the ruins often figured prominently in his magnified recollections of things done and seen. Such tales had been told and retold by others who had trod the same ground, so that there existed in Belize a considerable store of information on the location, size, and general nature of several mysterious, abandoned ruins within the confines of English territory and elsewhere in neighboring lands.

In such a situation, a catalyst was needed to transform the existing body of knowledge and interest into something more forceful. The catalyst was provided on October 30, 1839, by the arrival of the brig *Mary Ann* at Belize harbor, bearing two travelers, John Lloyd Stephens and Frederick Catherwood, lately come from the United States with the purpose of conducting a scientific examination of ancient Maya cities known and yet unreported.

Stephens, recently appointed chargé d'affaires for the United States and given the mission of representing that country to the government in Guatemala, intended to use his official mission as a means of making the first thorough investigation of the antiquities of the Maya area. In this undertaking he was to be aided by Catherwood, an English architect and artist who had had considerable experience in the depiction of ancient structures in other parts of the world.

On their arrival, the two explorers were met by Walker and Mac-Donald, with whom the plans for the expedition were fully discussed. MacDonald must have decided immediately that England, despite her reputation for scientific research, was about to be outdone by a representative of that upstart former colony to the north. Clearly, the resources of British Honduras were insufficient to support an expedition of a scale and duration equal to that planned by Stephens, but might it not be possible to precede Stephens and Catherwood to Palenque? After all, the site lay not too far distant from Belize in the state of Chiapa, and hence could be reached quickly and with relatively little expense. Besides, the American team had indicated that the first object of their investigations was to be Copán, which was situated well off in the opposite direction. With the honor of English science at stake, MacDonald acted without prior sanction from Belize in the state of Chiapa and hence could be reached quickly to the ruins of Palenque. On the ninth day of November, Mac-Donald apprised Lord Russell of the undertaking, bending the truth of the matter just a bit now and then to make the expedition seem less a spur-of-the-moment entry into competition with Stephens:

MY LORD,

It is not unknown to Your Lordship that in the Province of Tabasco, a portion of the Mexican Republic in Central America, there exist some far-famed remnants of ancient architecture called "the Ruins of Polenki." These ruins, I believe, form now a great object of interest among the enlightened in the United States, and I am led to understand that similar sentiments pervade the curious in Europe.

It has been my intention for some considerable time past to bring the subject before the Secretary of State and to suggest that an attempt should be made to explore Polenki with the view of deciding satisfactorily whether those ruins from their huge and extraordinary nature are such as to justify the reports concerning them, or whether these reports are exaggeration and the place unworthy of the notice of the modern traveller.

In recent American Papers I observe that the Government of the United States has determined on undertaking the task and has actually appointed Mr. Stevens a well known American traveller with a competent artist and engineer to proceed to Polenki.

The want of a capable draughtsman has been an insuperable obstacle to my accomplishing the purpose which I had contemplated. This obstacle being now removed by the presence of Lieut. Caddy of the Royal Artillery who is an artist of first rate ability, I have organised a small expedition which will proceed on the 13th Instant up the River Belize via Peten on the Lake of Itza to Polenki—By adopting this route, the actual position of the Lake of Itza will be ascertained by observations taken on the spot.

I have entrusted the guidance and direction of the expedition to Mr. Patrick Walker, a gentleman whose name I have had frequently to bring most favourably before the notice of the Secretary of State, and in whose enterprise and perserverance I have every confidence.

The pencil of Lieut. Caddy will illustrate the journey and I am fully assured that the views taken by him will convey to Your Lordship's mind a perfect idea of the appearance of Polenki.

Thus Patrick Walker and John Caddy had been thrown together by circumstance in what was to be the first official government expedition to "Polenki." Stephens and Catherwood were made fully aware of the purpose of the trip, and Stephens was later to write that he feared that the earlier arrival of Walker and Caddy at Palenque might result in exclusion of the American expedition from the site, but this proved not to be the case.

From a cursory interest in things archaeological in The Settlement, there had developed something of a contest between two rival expeditions. The Settlement's weekly newspaper, the *Belize Advertiser*, carried the following paragraph in its issue of November 16:

We have to announce to our readers the departures of Patrick Walker and Lieut. Caddy of the Royal Artillery, on Wednesday last. The object of these gentlemen's mission, is, we believe, to inquire into the truth of the destruction of the province of Palanque, as also to visit the river Tobasco, and to make themselves acquainted with the political and commercial aspects of the new republic of Central America. From the talented pen of Mr. Walker we expect to have a solution to our doubts respecting places of which there have been so many extraordinary reports. There is no doubt that this gentleman will carry along with him that energy of mind and activity of body, which distinguished him in the various public situations he filled, as a man of no ordinary acquirements.

This announcement was followed in the issues of November 23 and December 21 by two front-page articles which, in addition to reprinting excerpts from Del Río's description of Palenque, make clear the attitude of the people of The Settlement toward the contest between the two expeditions:

Plate 1. *John Herbert Caddy, from a painting by Henry Hoppner Meyer (c. 1782–1847), probably painted in Canada in 1842 or 1843.*

Plate 2. *City of Belize, British Honduras, 1839, from a painting by Lieutenant John H. Caddy, R. A.*

Plate 3. *Pencil sketch by Caddy of Belize, probably in 1839. The mouth of the Belize River is seen at left, with Fort George in the foreground.*

Plate 4. *The town of Flores in the Petén, as seen from the shore of Lake Petén Itzá. Pencil sketch made by Caddy during the expedition's protracted stay in the area.*

Plate 5. *Sepia rendering of a scene in the central plaza of Mérida, Yucatán, produced by Caddy from a sketch made in 1840.*

Plate 6. *John Caddy in his later years; probably taken in the 1870's.*

Plate 7. *Georgiana Caddy, probably after her husband's death. Note that she holds the photograph reproduced in Plate 6.*

few yards I saw a most disgusting looking serpent about six feet long stretched in a gleam of sunshine directly in the path with his head towards us. I fired and killed the beast cutting off his head. which I think was the ugliest I ever saw. leaving his body in the path. I dissected it. the two fangs in use at the time were nearly an inch long, curved backwards, with a hollow slit about the 10th of an inch towards from the point upwards. along the jaw on each side were six fangs in successive stages of perfection, the one next to that in use being almost as hard and perfect as the other and the rest became softer as they were more distant. the roots entered a bag web attached to the upper gums which on being opened contained a brownish matter which passed thro' the tooth into the wound made by the bite. the head was very flat and broad. and the body instead of tapering off gradually from the middle to the end of the tail had an abrupt decrease at about 8 inches from the extremity. the back was very dark coloured streaked with black belly dirty lead colour with a yellowish tinge

Plate 8. *Page 185 of Caddy's diary, describing the killing of the snake* sketched.

PALANQUE—We announced lately that an American gentleman,
Mr. Catherwood, accompanied by Mr. Stephens, Charge de Affairs
from the States, to Guatemala, with the design of visiting the remains
of the ancient city of Palenque, situated (to us) several days' journey
beyond the Peten, to the North of the province of Chiapa.

We are happy to find the design of Mr. Catherwood has roused the
jealousy of our Settlement, and induced a visit with a like object, to
the same place by a different rout—We fear the two gentlemen from
this, who have taken the direction of the Old River, and on by way of
Peten, have chosen an unseasonable period, and will be greatly retarded both by water and by land, but "a stout heart to a stey brae"[1]
gets over many difficulties, and may add to their personal adventures.
Instead of the *remaining* part of the city also being reduced to ruins,
we expect to find this report greatly exaggerated...

We trust that Lieutenant Caddy's graphic pencil, amongst the
many other objects, will give fac-simile copies of the hieroglyphics;
which we conceive will be found to resemble the pictoral characters of
the Mexicans, some of which we believe to have been received and
are preserved at Madrid.

Although a trifle confused in the facts of the case, the newspaper
statement of the reasons behind the Palenque expedition was somewhat more straightforward than MacDonald's dispatch. Rivalry
there was, then, but not real race; Stephens and Catherwood embarked for Copán knowing that Walker and Caddy had, at about
the same time, set course for Palenque.

Stephens and Catherwood had planned their expedition well in
advance, and were able to acquire the necessary equipment at comparative leisure. Walker and Caddy, with the expedition suddenly
thrust upon them, made haste to bring themselves to full readiness in
the few days available. Although the first leg of the trip was to be
made with a force of twenty-nine men, the necessity of traveling by
river dictated that the amount of food to be carried would not be
great, and the expedition was begun in the expectation that produce
and other comestibles would be available along the way.

[1] "A stout heart to a steep hill."

33

Walker set out to purchase the necessary food, including a few easily portable groceries, plus barrels of pork and flour. To these were added a barrel of the basic staple, rum, and a quantity of brandy, the latter to be substituted for rum in the daily ration of the expedition's leaders, to whose palates the cheaper decoction was more than disagreeable. Saddles, knives, pots, canvas for tarpaulins, medicines, red cloth shirts for the soldiers and servants, hats, moccasins, paddles, cordage, oil and wicks, and a myriad of other essentials were quickly collected; while boxes were made and fitted with locks, to contain the expedition supplies. Finally, Walker procured from the estate of a recently deceased citizen two azimuth compasses, and some ornamental jewelry to be distributed as presents to the natives encountered en route.

Caddy, in addition to assisting with the amassing of supplies, provided himself with paper, paints, pencils, brushes, and the other items necessary to his function as expedition artist. He also purchased a brown, paper-bound notebook, similar to those he had used while in the West Indies, in which he proposed to record the passage of each day's adventures. While traveling, he made brief notes of people, places, and happenings, thus: "Nov. 16th—Big Haulover—Peteneros—Snake—specimens of oratory—ducking. Dec. 1st—in woods! Old Bank on the river side—Picturesque Rapid—Jocko & Tiger with antelope—Wild Hunter shot Warry—Ticks Mosquitos, Flies etc. Dec. 13th—Remained all day—Carnick very ill & obstinate— brought on disentary by drinking quantities of cold water—stayed here 3 nights." And so it went, probably for each day of the expedition. On his return, Caddy expanded on the notes, drawing from them a full and lively account of the historic venture, which he penned in his difficult script on more than 250 oversize sheets of paper.

It was the worst of times for an expedition to the uncharted bush of the interior, especially for one which was to commence with the difficult passage up the Belize River. In November, the rainy season was on in full force, and a deluge could be expected to lash the land at any time. The river was in flood, making travel difficult because of strong currents and hazardous because of the brush, trees, and other flotsam and jetsam in the stream. Had prior arrival at Palenque not been a matter of urgency, Walker and Caddy would have been well advised to await abatement of the rains in December or early January. With the race on in earnest, they could do little else but push off and trust to luck, weather or no. On November 13, 1839, the party set out on what proved to be a long and difficult road to Palenque.

Now, through the words of John Caddy and occasional comments from others, let us be off on this long-forgotten journey.

IV. Belize to palenque
–Caddy's Diary

ON THE MORNING of the 13th November, 1839 our Party assembled at the Wharf in front of Government House. It consisted besides Mr. Walker and I, of one N.C. Officer and 14 men of the 2nd West India Reg't. 1 man of the Royal Artillery, my servant, Mr. Nod interpreter and nine hired Pitpan men. A squabble arose among the latter for the honourable post of Captain of the awning Pitpan in which we were to travel; and after a good deal of difficulty the choice fell upon one Jim Sutherland a man of colour, one of the best steersmen in the settlement and about the greatest scamp withal. After stowing away our heavy baggage in the large Pitpan, and settling the crews of each we were detained by the unexpected absence of our Interpreter; however sending a messenger after him, whilst we partook of a hasty lunch with Colonel Macdonald, we embarked after bidding adieu to His Excellency and a few friends who were present. We called at the Court House wharf for our Interpreter, whom we found in charge of two Policemen in a very comfortable state of inebriety, nevertheless we took him into the Pitpan, and again launched into the stream, and passing beneath the Bridge, which was crowded with persons to see us off, we were going ahead at a rapid pace when Mr. Walker recollected that a Box containing presents for the natives was left behind, we had therefore to return a short distance and sent Antonio one of the 2nd. West India Reg't. to Gov't. House for them, while we were entertained with the lively conversation of Mrs. R and sister. Antonio soon made his appearance with box on head, when bidding farewell to our fair friends we once more put off.

The vehicle in which we travelled, called a Pitpan, was one of the

36

largest of that description of boat—about 40 feet in length and nearly 5′ in extreme breadth, cut from one tree (it was not so flat bottomed as most of them are, having more of the dory[1] shape in it with the exception of the Head and stern which terminated as they all do, square). At about six feet distance from the stern an awning eight feet long fixed upon neat staunchions was erected, having painted canvas sides which could be rolled up or let down as circumstances might require. We had Mr. Nod and my servant under one end, our canteen and portable kitchen in the centre and ourselves on the seat next the stern, with our carpet bags and portmanteaux stowed away in the stern sheets. Eight paddlers in front of the awning, one besides the steersman at the stern—and thus propelled we passed rapidly through the water.

The branch of the river from Belize to the Haulover—so called from its being the place where the cattle taken to Belize are driven across—runs through a mangrove swamp for the distance of 4 miles; a road has been cleared on the right hand side which is passable in the dry season; and indeed cattle are driven along it at all times of the year. Nothing can be more monotonous than this part of the River until you arrive at the Haulover where its principal mouth opens to the sea, having besides the two channels already mentioned several smaller ones. The quantity of alluvial deposit from the River causes great shallowness of water for miles continuous to its outlet, and it appears that the whole of that part of the coast from Haulover to Belize is a deltic island, which is evidently increasing, and others forming. It is astonishing how quickly the Mangrove springs up—as soon as the alluvial has increased to within a foot or so of the surface of the water you will see a few twigs of this bush with some leaves showing their heads above water and in a few years from this commencement an island is formed. Entering the main river at the Haulover you lose the monotony of the scene and a variety of trees beautify the banks. We found the current very strong from there being a

[1] A small- to medium-size dugout with both ends usually brought to a point. The river dory has a rounded bottom to facilitate slipping across currents, while the seagoing dory is keeled.

flood in the river, and from the quantity of Plantain and other trees which passed us at the rate of four miles an hour, the Plantations must have suffered—our course was mainly due West until we arrived at Ripley Bank where we proposed remaining for the night in order to have time to set all things to rights, so that we might have no delays after making a start from this place.

The property belongs to Dr. Young a gentleman of colour, educated in England, where he took his degree as M.D. He is also one of the Magistrates of the Settlement, who from his acknowledged ability, united to independence of character, has gained the esteem of his fellow Colonists. We disembarked the whole of our traps about 4 o'clock in the afternoon and after serving our provisions to our men, made arrangements for an early start in the morning; apportioning the baggage more equally between the two Pitpans and changing some of the crew. After which we made ourselves comfortable for the night in the neat cottage on Gov't. property—which is a very pretty spot on an elbow of the river where there is a considerable portion of land cleared and tastefully planted with fruit trees, having a very orchardlike appearance. The Old River Mahogany cutters generally construct a boom at this spot to prevent their mahogany going out to sea—but unfortunately it sometimes gives way and much trouble and expense is thus entailed on the owners, who have to pay so much a log to the dorymen who are quickly on the look out and frequently succeed in bringing in the greater part.

Nov. 14th—We were on the alert at daylight, and soon embarked, as we did not remain to breakfast, preferring making some chocolate in the Pitpan with our portable kitchen, boiling the water with spirits of wine. The flies were dreadfully annoying particularly a small black fly which inhabitants call the Bottlerump, from the circumstance of the nether end of this little tormentor having a strong resemblance to a black soda water bottle. It draws the blood to the surface of the skin, leaving a small blood spot whenever it bites. Another called the doctor fly is as large as the cow dung fly so well known to fly fishers at home, and very much resembles it in appearance, it draws blood copiously leaving a stream issuing from the wound. There are many

38

others some of the wasp and hornet species whose sting often causes fever.

We landed about 12 o'clock at a place called Burrells Bank—having only accomplished about 9 miles in consequence of the strength of the current against us—in order to allow our men time to cook their days provisions. This is a celebrated spot for snipe shooting and I anticipated a couple of hours good sport, but never was a person so grievously disappointed, not from the scarcity of game for there was abundance of Teal, snipe, and Plover—but I had unfortunately entrusted my gun to my servant at Belize to clean after having used it for a day—I had not had occasion for it since, and as it appeared quite dry and clean, I loaded both barrels and sallied forth vowing vengeance on the feathered race. I had not proceeded 50 yards from the house, when up got one snipe after another—snap—snap—both barrells missed fire—pricked the nipples, inserted some powder and put on fresh caps, walked on toward a small pond when I espied 6 or 7 Teal nestling in a small nook among the reeds—sent my boy on a few yards to rouse them, up they rose—snap went one barrel, and the other hung fire so long that I was very near shooting my black boy, as it went off after I had lowered it from my shoulder. (Sporting dogs of the English breeds do not thrive well in this country and consequently a boy or two beat the country). How I blessed my careful domestic! I should like to have put a charge of dust shot into the most fleshy part of his unworthy carcass—I went on with one barrel and got a few birds—but was so disgusted that I returned to the House making a vow never to trust my gun to the care of a domestic again—and set to work to clean it thoroughly. After taking some lunch, and again consigning my servant to the hottest place I could wish him (which could scarcely be hotter than the spot we were now quitting) I lit a genuine Havana as the only means of soothing my ruffled spirit, and embarking puffed away all thoughts of my disappointment—wishing like Jacob Faithful "better luck next time." About three quarters of a mile above Burrells Bank the river takes a sharp turn from W to N.E. The banks become higher and the trees of larger growth—the current also becomes stronger. At about half

39

past 4 we put up at Bakers bank, where we hung our hammocks for the night. The mosquitos were insufferable and had it not been for our Pavillions we should have been remarkably well phlebotomized. As it was, their constant humming almost deprived me of sleep. Shakespeare could never have experienced the nuisance of these nocturnal musicians when he says "and hush'd with buzzing nightflies to thy slumber." I confess they had a contrary effect with me. All the Plantations along the river are called Banks, and where Mahogany is "manufactured," a curious expression for squaring—are called Barcadiers. This place belongs to Mr. Tillet who has a stock farm here and is owner of a large herd of cattle.

Nov. 15th—We started as early as possible breakfasting in the Pitpan—very heavy work for the Padlers. The river takes a bend from Westward then runs due north until you arrive at Mexico creek about four miles from Tillets when it trends almost due west again for about three miles when you come to the little falls—which we passed over and should never have known of their existence had we not been told we were passing them—so high was the water. We landed to allow the men to cook about 12 o'clock, on a bank that had been completely overflown. I here got some snipe and Teal and killed several very fine specimen of the sheer winged Gallinule. In the season after a flood snipe abound in the clearances along the river—a shiny alluvial deposit being left after the subsiding of the water to which they appear extremely partial. We espied an alligator taking his repose with his enormous mouth wide open; he was laying on a mud bank in a sunny nook on the margin of the river and was so very like a dirty log of wood, which the Negro says he tries to emulate in appearance that if he had not been silly enough to open his mouth, we might have proceeded on our way without noticing him—however as it was he was doomed to have his palate tickled in a very different manner from what he anticipated, when he set his trap for the unwary insects that should have the temerity to venture between his insatiate jaws. One of my gun barrels was loaded with snipe and the other with what is termed BB or Bristol Blue, my single Barrel was also loaded with the latter which my companion took, and paddling very gently until we got within twenty yards of him I gave the word and the whole three barrells told in his gullet; he gave a convulsive jump and seemed for a moment to stand on his tail, on being saluted in this unexpected manner and threw himself with a tremendous splash into the stream, however being wounded unto death he could not long keep under water and we saw his horrid looking eyes peering above it a few yards ahead of us, and then the horny ridge along his back was visible and he moved slowly along the bank until he made his way into a small creek through some reeds and we lost sight of him.

The scenery of the River increases in beauty as you ascend, the banks are now becoming much higher, and the trees of more luxuriant growth—particularly the wild fig tree of which there are several varieties, one called by the natives the bow fig bearing a fruit as large as a middling sized pear, having a thick skin or rather rind filled with pulp containing seeds. It is very tasteless. The other is the same known through the West India Islands and which gave Barbados its name. The Barbadian (so called from the circumstance of the branches throwing out beard like fibres which grow downwards and take root in a similar way to the Banyan) bearing a small fruit the size of a cherry of a sweet taste of which the feathered tribe are particularly fond—and wherever the fruit was ripe, the trees were alive with birds among which were several of the Toucan tribe with their enormous bills snapping together like the sounds of castinets and their crimson and orange coloured breasts shining in the sun, also the orange and black oriole were very plentiful, and in the mornings and evenings we heard the melancholy cooings of the Pigeons of which there are several varieties—the most common is the white headed. We killed two or three Guanas one of which we cooked and most excellent it was, it resembles the chicken in taste, more than any other meat kind that I know. The 3 were different in colour, the largest which was four feet long from snout to tail, was of dingy brown, slightly mottled with a blackish shade; the next in size was of a bright green and proved to be full of eggs (as we found when dressing it for our meal, as we chose it from its more pleasing appearance than the others)—the other was not above two feet long, of a bright brown and dark marks down the sides.

In passing around an elbow of the river our men were obliged to take to their sitting poles, which appeared rather hard work. Six men standing on the seats in the fore part of the boat two abreast and one in the stern sheets near the steersman, place thin sitting poles against the bottom of the stream so as to have command of them when reaching forward as much as possible, and after pushing the pitpan ahead as far as the poles allow them, they shift with such dexterity and quickness as not to allow the force of the current to cause a retrograde motion before they again have a purchase. The steersman has a rather difficult task, as from the great length of the Pitpan if he does not keep her head directly against the stream, the current takes effect and turns her broadside on, to the great loss of time and labour, and to the risk of being upset—which is not at all an infrequent occurrance. The steersman of the baggage Pitpan shot across the river at the foot of the rapid, for the purpose of trying to beat us, paddles versus poles, however they were too heavily laden or they certainly would have given us the go by. The Pitpan men made the woods echo again with their cheers as either boat appeared to gain a slight advantage, and the taunts, talked at each other in a sort of chant, were rather amusing. During this contest we past through a very picturesque part of the river with some of the largest fig trees we had yet seen, growing from the waters edge with their knotted and twisted roots projecting half way across the river—covered with Parasitic plants and creepers or vines the flowers of which were exceedingly beautiful. One very curious looking creeper of a bright orange colour which covered the bush and low wood like a net. Also some fine specimens of Convolvoli of various colours.

We put up for the night at Mudian Landing a bank belonging to Mr. Forte—where we were kindly received. We hung our hammocks in the hall, with our Pavillions over them and slept tolerably, although the mosquitos managed to insinuate themselves under my canopy and cause me some annoyance.

Nov. 16th—We were off soon after daylight, having partaken of what the natives call a "Doctor," being a compound of new milk, sugar and a spoonful of Brandy, the quantum intended by this measure being perfectly ad libitum, as the liquor is generally poured over the bottom of the spoon instead of into its bowl.

The river had fallen considerably during the night. Its rise and fall is generally very sudden and we were told some extraordinary cases connected with this circumstance. One of a Mahogany cutter whose bank is one of the most elevated in the river, having retired to rest at the usual hour, found on awakening in the morning that the water had risen to the very door of his house, at least 40 feet above the level of the night before—and that he might have taken a short cut to Belize over the overflown country.

We passed a Pitpan, that had been washed away from some bank, stuck upside down in the Bush rope of an enormous tree like Mahomets coffin suspended between heaven and earth at least 20 feet above our heads as we passed beneath it. We landed about half past 4 o'clock at another haulover, a high bank with a few cottages picturesquely situated occupied by two or three families of black people from Peten, who gave us one of them very civilly—but we encountered a regular virago in the person of a black *Lady* from Belize who owned a house here which was unoccupied, and our men took possession of it. She lived on the opposite side of the River, but seeing some arrivals she came across evidently to prevent a temporary occupancy of her mansion; and finding the men making preparations to that effect, she gave tongue in the most vociferous manner, however she saw that all her rhetoric was thrown away, the soldiers only advising her in the most delicate manner possible to "hush her mouth." She descended the bank calling them whilst foaming at the aforesaid "a parcel of d——d goodfornoting kings niggers" stepping into her frail vehicle, which trembled in sympathetic unison with its mistress' feelings who handled her paddle most dexterously shooting across the river with great rapidity, but still keeping up a continued abuse of the "Kings niggers" even some time after she had arrived at her domicile on the opposite bank—however in cleaning the rubbish

43

from her hut an effectual preventative was given to its occupancy by one of the most venomous snakes being discovered amongst it, which operated much more on the fears of the men than all the threats of the virago—nothing would induce them to sleep in the hut although the snake was killed. It was one of that kind called by the natives the Tommy Goff—of a light brown colour with dark spots on its back, belly a dingy lead colour—it was four feet in length. Its bite is exceedingly dangerous, if not mortal, although every gang of negroes has a snake doctor attached to it who pretend to cure its bite, and I am told that some are successful. They make use of a plant which they call the Guaco, and which is plentiful throughout the forest. It was pointed out to me, and is so remarkable that having seen it once a person could not mistake it afterwards. It grows something like an English nettle, the leaves are larger but of similar form, with serrated edges, of dullish green with a red tinge running into the green in stripes and has a downy appearance. They use it pounded as a poultice applied to the affected part, and also a decoction as a drink.

Rather a ludicrous scene took place here soon after the departure of our heroine of loquacious propensity. The Corporal of the party who rejoiced in the cognomen of Sisambo, and who possessed all the excessive vanity inherent in the negro character, set to work to adorn himself, producing his box on the bank from which he took a variety of articles, displaying the whole to the wondering eyes of the natives in a pompous sort of manner—looking at himself now and then in a small looking glass with great complacency—at last having completed his toilet he looked around exclaiming in a half authoritative manner "come, who go put me cross de River?" At which a huge fellow, one of the Kings or rather the Queens niggers, who had been observing the equipment of Sisambo, with a sort of malicious grin, offered his services. The smirk on this fellows swarthy countenance betokened mischief, which became more visible as he descended the bank to the margin of the water armed with a paddle—followed by Sisambo picking his way so as not to soil his snow white trousers—a small Pitpan which required the greatest steadiness in the parties to enable them to embark, was to be their conveyance, and as soon as

Sisambo was squatted on his heels in the centre, balancing himself with a hand on each gunwale, Potts the ferryman sat himself down on the flat stern of the Pitpan which resembled a Butchers tray placing his legs out before him, and pushed off, shipping a small quantity of water, and purposely giving his huge body a rolling motion, at last upsetting his conceited superior in as apparently accidental a manner as possible—much to the amusement of the party on the bank who set up a most hearty roar of laughter, in which Sisambo had the good sense to join. The delinquent plunged about in the current getting into the Pitpan and upsetting it several times in order to persuade us that it was purely accidental, exclaiming every time "Ah cha! de dam ting no work" at last he landed with as demure a face as he could get up for the occasion. The Petencros procured us some fowls, and were otherwise obliging, and we hung out our hammocks as usual, but were dreadfully bitten by flies.

Nov. 17th—Started at daylight, the men having prepared their breakfast the night before to save time—we cooked ours under the awning of the Pitpan—making a capital stew in our Periss unit. We smoked nearly all day to keep away the flies, but they seemed to care little about smoke, except those which had the temerity to attack our faces, and which were now and then brought down by a well directed puff.

We picked up a quantity of Hucati eggs as we went along, our boatmen detecting where they were buried most quickly; and although to our unpracticed eyes there appeared no difference in the sandy bank, yet wherever they pointed out there were sure to be eggs. They are about the size of a Hens egg, but quite oval, and are very delicate when fresh, which is ascertained by the transparency of the shell, as it becomes more opaque the older it is. The Hucati itself is considered by many men more delicious than the Green Turtle—it certainly is more delicate, but whether that would be considered an advantage over its rival of the Briny deep, must be decided by a common council of turtle loving aldermen. The Hucati instead of fins have feet with claws—they grow to the size of 30 lbs.—lay about 60 or 70 eggs which they conceal with great sagacity having many

45

enemies independent of man. Fired two balls into an alligator but did not kill him although one took effect about 2 inches behind the shoulder. We got several Guanas; they are very tenacious of life, and unless you kill them outright generally manage to escape. I had always heard that if this animal by any accident was curtailed in its fair proportions by the loss of a foot or so of tail, that another grew immediately, I had the opportunity of witnessing this in one I shot, the new tail having sprouted from the upper part of the old one, thus [*blank space*] and was about 4 inches long—we passed Labouring Creek which runs into the old river from the north taking its rise in a Lagoon at no great distance from the margin of Belize river. The banks here are low, and immediately behind them is an extensive marsh. This creek has a petrifying property and many fine specimens of different woods have been found perfectly agatized. We arrived about 4 o'clock at the Mahogany work belonging to Mr. Turnbull where we were hospitably received by himself and his amiable wife an English lady. Although their habitation is 60 feet above the dry season level of the water, yet during the last floods they were driven out, and obliged to make use of the fire place in the kitchen a sort of square platform raised about 3 feet from the ground in the centre of the apartment, as a place of refuge for Mrs. T and her children. What a situation for a delicate female which this lady appeared to be, altho' she made light of these little annoyances. We discussed a capital dinner in which the Hucati formed a prominent portion. The liver of this animal is very large in proportion to its size and is considered a great delicacy. In the middle of the night we were all disturbed by an awful shouting from my companion, who had hung his cot in the hall which was open in front and had awakened fancying the water had made its way into the house. It was some time before he was persuaded to the contrary, and only when he heard the Lady of the house laughing most heartily was he convinced of this illusion. After a desultory conversation carried on for a few moments we again composed ourselves to sleep and were "a pied" at daylight.

The life of a Mahogany cutter is one of excitement partaking in a great measure of the Gipsey style, with a dash of sans agisse. The mode of proceeding generally speaking is this. If the person about to become a cutter has not capital of his own, he gets a merchant to disburse him, to whom, of course, he is pledged to deliver his Mahogany, making the best bargain he can as to the price per thousand feet, he is to be credited with. After procuring a grant from the Superintendent which is merely for cutting Mahogany or Logwood and not giving him any title to the land; or else by purchasing the right of cutting in some old work, he then hires a confidential negro whom he makes what is called Captain of the gang, whose duty it becomes to look out for negroes, who enter into a written agreement with the Cutter which is duly registered in the office of Clerk of Courts, and an infringement of this agreement is brought before the magistrates who award a punishment according to the nature of the offense. Having collected the number of men required, the merchant is obliged to make advances to them, and it is his interest to induce them to take the greater part of goods at about one hundred percent above prime cost, or as much more as they can get. The cutter is also obliged to take the provisions for his gang from the Merchant in question. These consist of salt pork, flour, and spirit, with impliments for cutting and trucking the wood. Having made all these preparations and procured conveyance by either broghen, dory or Pitpan according to the situation of the work, it is sometimes difficult to get all hands together, for as long as any money remains, they make merry, being about the most improvident people in the world. Many of the cutters have their Pitpans very comfortably fitted and travel with every convenience. Protected from the sun by handsome fixed awnings—cushioned seats—canteens fitted with silver drinking cups &c. They frequently sleep under their awnings at night in preference to taking the chance of bed ashore and with a good mosquito pavilion this may be done with impunity. Having arrived at the locality for the Bank or Barkadier, the first thing undertaken is the construction of huts which is soon accomplished as the materials generally speaking are close at hand. The posts, rafters, &c being strongly bound together with a vine called Bush Rope or more emphatically by the negroes "Tie Tie." The roof is thatched with either the Bay thatch or Cohoun leaf. These are both palms but in the former the leaves grow from a centre like radii whereas on the latter they grow from a long branch very like those of the Cocoa nut. The sides and ends are closed in with the straight stem of a small Palmetto placed upright and tied together. Should there be no natural pasturage in the vicinity, ground is cleared for the purpose, (as a number of oxen are required for truckery) as well as for a plantation.

The hunters having formed out the best place to commence cutting mahogany, a truck path is cleared to the work, and then the business of selecting and felling commences. The Mahogany tree is not cut close to the ground, the spurs preventing this, which run up to a considerable height and project some distance from the trunk a description of natural Buttress for the support of the enormous bulk and lofty branches of this beautiful tree. In consequence of these a platform, or what the cutters term a Barbacue, is erected round the tree high enough to allow it to be cut as close as possible to the junction of the spurs with the trunk. Two men work at the same tree and I believe sometimes more—cutting as much as possible parallel to one another so that the part cut may be wedge shaped, in order that the tree may fall in the direction opposite the cuts which it generally does. The fall of a large mahogany tree I have been told, for I had not an opportunity of seeing one felled—is perfectly astonishing as it comes down with a crash which shakes the whole Forest, tearing away from the large vines which for years have twisted round its stem, among its huge branches and from them to the neighbouring trees, forming stays for its support from the effects of the hurricanes which occasionally sweep through these wilds—however nothing can withstand the enormous weight of this hercathon of the Forest, the vines snap in all directions, except where a longer one has twisted itself round a younger tree, and enfolding it like the embrace of a Boa Constrictor, tears it up by the roots. Hundreds of smaller trees are crushed; and unfortunately accidents now and then occur. Not very long ago a young man of great promise was crushed to pieces by the branch of a tree.

The Trunk and Branches, of a certain girth, are cut into lengths,

48

and roughly squared, and are then transported on strong Bullock Trucks, the whole of which are made of junks cut from a Mahogany tree after being made circular—to the Barkadier.

The negroes cut the spurs from the tree in their spare time, making large bowls and small Pitpans of them, or take slabs made from them to Belize where they have a ready market. The branches of the Mahogany tree are considered equal if not superior to any wood for timbers of vessels and when well seasoned are most durable. The large broghens employed for the transport of Mahogany and log wood from the different distant Rivers are entirely built of this wood. The logs are often floated down to Belize without squaring and are then hauled up and manufactured, measured, marked, and again turned into the water, made into rafts, and floated along side the vessels destined to convey them to England. Should the locality turn out a good one likely to give several years cutting, a regular village springs up and the wives and families of the gang take up their abode during the season, which commences soon after Christmas or after the termination of the wet weather. And at last it becomes the home of many, who take advantage of the Plantations and clearances. After this digression we must return to bid adieu to our hospitable friends of Beaver Dam, whom we left with regret after partaking of Breakfast.

Nov. 18th—We made a very short days journey in consequence of the extreme strong current from the rapidly decreasing flood. Our paddlers had the greatest difficulty in keeping their own in some turns of the river, and were obliged to take to the sitting poles where the depth of water would permit them. We were compelled to put up about 4 o'clock at Saturday creek where there were a few huts one of which we got possession of for the night and miserable enough it was, for the water had been inside of it and made a puddle of the floor— however we procured eatables, and consoled ourselves with a Bottle of capital Madeira keeping out of the mud by swinging in hammocks, enjoying that soother of annoyances a good cigar. The grey vapours of the night were still houvering over the rapid stream, making the dawn scarcely perceptible when we, nothing loth, emerged from

49

under our pavilions and soon as possible were on board our Pitpans. A short distance above Saturday creek we disembarked on a low sandy island where the water was so shallow as to oblige the men to haul the Pitpans over it. I observed many pebbles here some of which were very transparent—also some small pieces of Jasper. We arrived at 4 o'clock at the Bank of Mr. W. Usher one of the oldest Mahogany cutters in the settlement; and had we not been acquainted with this gentlemen, the name he had given to his bank, would at least have augured well of our reception—Society Hall could scarcely be supposed to have an inhospitable owner.

Mr. Usher was in the bush with his gang when we arrived, but his housekeeper very quickly had the table spread with an excellent lunch to which we paid our respects, while a Flibbertigibbet was dispatched for the host who soon made his appearance which took my fancy as being picturesque and brigandish from the dress he wore—this consisted of a broad brimmed Panama hat, a red flannel shirt over his usual under garments and white trousers, with mocassins of tanned leather on his feet—a belt round his waist to which was appended a negro cutlas or Machete in scabbard, a painted leather bag a sort of omnium gatherum containing besides Powder and shot, a variety of articles too numerous to mention; a light single Barrel in his hand the butt resting on his thigh—he was mounted on a rough and ready nag from which after dismounting the saddle and bridle was taken, and with an impetus given from the niggers foot, had permission to help himself until again called for.

Mr. Usher has for many years carried on the business of a Mahogany cutter with various success, at one time amassing large sums, but at present scarcely getting a remunerating price for his wood; however nothing seems to daunt his spirit of enterprize, and bad times, which have caused many to withdraw from the business only give a zest to his exertions and year after year he worked away nothing dejected, living most of his time in the bush. He is one of the magistrates of Belize and Admiral of the Prince of Wales Honduras Flotilla, which honorable title was gained by the gallant manner in which the Bay men, as they call themselves, manned the broghens during the various attempts of the Spaniards to gain possession of Belize.

The house is beautifully situated on a bank about a hundred feet above the river, and commands a view of it for some distance both up and down. The hills (until we arrived here we could discern no high ground behind the forest trees that skirt the banks) are high in this vicinity some 1,000 feet above the low water level of the river, and are composed of limestone covered to their summits with primeval forest trees. There is a good plantation belonging to Mr. Usher on the opposite bank containing every tropical vegetable, and some sugar cane from which he makes sufficient sugar for his own consumption and that of his gang, and has erected a small cattle mill for the purpose of grinding the canes. We remained with Mr. Usher for the night and about 10 o'clock next morning went on to Tiger Run where we arrived about 3 o'clock. There is a considerable village here and the people appear comfortably off, having Provision grounds and some cattle, but they might be much better circumstanced were they industrious which is seldom the case.

Wishing to get the people together we gave them a dance or rather endeavoured to do so, but the show of females was very small, and their performance on the light fantastic anything but graceful. The instrument to which they danced was called a Mirimba, and is of a very primitive nature. It consists of a frame about four feet in length by 15 inches in breadth, made of cane, or bamboo, across the length of which are placed a number of thin slips of the hard part or outer rind of the palm, strung, and kept about an inch apart, beneath which are placed a corresponding number of hollow gourd shaped tubes open at top, and having an orifice near the lower end, which is covered by a thin film taken from the inside of a Pig, resembling gold beater's skin; these tubes are suspended vertically so that each slip of the hard wood, shall be immediately above one of them, which decrease in size from base to treble. It is placed in front of the Musician being retained in its position by a half hoop round his waist, and is played upon with a pair of sticks having a ball of Indian Rubber at one end of each. The sound is pleasing, but their tunes are monotonous and few in number. There was a "tom tom" or negro dance got up in a hut opposite the one we occupied, which prevented our sleeping for a long time after we had stretched ourselves in our Hammocks which ended in a squabble between Sisambo and the Captain of the Baggage Pitpan. A wordy war continued until I was obliged to interfere, and having sent master Sisambo into another hut, the rumpus gradually subsided, although the Pitpan Captain kept up a sort of running soliloquy for about an hour. This is very common among the negroes; after quarelling and using all manner of unheard of epithets towards each other, they separate and turn round at intervals making gestures of defiance and bawling out at the top of their voices, and continuing to abuse themselves for hours after being out of hail of their adversary.

We went on to Duck run a few miles up the River, the highest inhabited spot, and took up our quarters in the hut of a Portuguese Jew of the name of Fonseca—who was endeavouring to gain a livelihood by retailing a few articles of merchandize such as he denominated "Shoap, Kanttles, cotton shtoffs, &c"; his stock in trade was exceedingly low at the time we arrived. From this place which is about 150 miles from Belize we sent back the Pitpans, and a letter informing Colonel Macdonald of our safe arrival this far on our journey, which we accomplished in seven days, contrary to the expectations of many of our acquaintances in Belize who prognosticated the almost utter impossibility of our getting up the river during the heavy flood. We retained four men of the 2nd W.I.R. to go on with us, and set to work to procure horses for our journey.

The banks here are high 60 or 70 feet above the river, the soil rich in the extreme and abundance of pasturage. At about half a mile back from the river an extensive Pine ridge commences and as far as the eye can reach is like an open Park. There are some horses and cattle still here altho the greater number have been taken away by the owner who formerly had a mahogany work in this neighbourhood. On our passage up the river we were told that a species of madness had broken out among the dogs, and many had been destroyed in consequence. We saw several tied up which were in a rabid state, foaming at the mouth and howling most piteously. They attribute it to their eating the bones of the curaco, which it is stated by the Indians, are poisonous at this time of the year. The Indian Rubber tree was pointed out to me, one species of it at least—it does not grow to a very large size—the largest I saw was not more than three feet in circumference; cutting through the bark with a machete a buff coloured substance about the consistence of sour cream exudes, and after being exposed to the influence of the atmosphere becomes dark coloured as we see it in use. This might be collected in great abundance as the trees are plentiful.

We removed from Fonseca's whose Casa was not the most comfortable kind, independent of its smallness, to one of larger dimensions on a more elevated spot. It belongs to an old Yanky negro named Charly Cuff who had been on board a man of war in the British Service of which he was very proud. Charly was exceedingly loquacious, particularly after having imbibed any potent liquor. He has the credit of being a miser by his neighbours who say he has a considerable sum buried in his Plantation. He gave us no very favourable account of the Petenero revolutionists who had made his house their halting place on their way to Belize. There were several of these gentry idling about his premises when we were there, one fellow, a white man, walking about with a long sword with a silver belt and mountings, however they were of use to us and I doubt whether we should have been able to procure horses and mules sufficient had we not hired and pressed into service those upon which they had fled to Belize.

We were detained at Duck Run until the 29th first from not being able to procure horses, and afterwards from heavy rains, but on that day we packed our baggage on mules and had horses sufficient. The party now consisted of—I shall give their names and avocations and the order of march—Mr. Walker and I, Mr. Nod, Interpreter; Gunner Carnick Royal Artillery, my servant; Antonio 2nd W.I. Regiment, servant to Mr. Walker; Jocko 2nd W.I. Regiment; Potts Do. Robinson Crusoe Do. Ambrosio an athletic negro hired at

Tiger Run as arriero;[2] Manuel Moralez a run away Petenero assistant arriero (a villainous looking fellow with a long lank hair, and a
most sinister expression of countenance, but a good hunter)—and two
woebegone fellows who asked us to allow them to accompany us to
Peten, 3 Indians procured from an old Black man who lived in the
left hand branch of the River, and who acts as a sort of Padre, he can
read and write, and was much pleased at being presented with a
Testament and Prayer Book in the Spanish Language, he was brought
up in Peten, the Indians seemed very much attached to him; he paid
us a visit whilst at this place. We were a long time getting off as the
mules were obstreperous and would not be loaded, one fellow in
particular the finest of the lot kicked our Portmanteaus into the air
several times with every mark of disrespect; at last we were ready and
progressed. As I was to provide game for the party I took the lead
with Mendoza as guide carrying a light load and my single barrel gun
and Jocko carrying a compass and some et ceteras. My nag was a
gallant grey cob, who showed some tricks at first but became docile as
possible in the course of a few hours. I carried a double barrel and
had a pair of Pistols in my holsters with a Machete by my side. My
dress consisted of a broad brimmed Panama well stretched down a
green shooting jacket with capacious pockets and blue serge trousers
and mocassins and I carried an old Pea Jacket on my saddle in case
of rain—my companions dress was pretty nearly the same as my own,
and our soldiers had blue shirts (serge) and trousers. They were
each armed with one Pistol and a machete or Cutlas. The Indians
were nearly in a state of nudity having nothing on but a pair of loose
cotton trousers tied round the waist and tucked or rolled up as high
as possible. They carried their loads by a band of bark of the Maho
tree, which is very strong, round their foreheads, squatting on their
heels and lifting it up with them. They lean very much forward,
always having a long stick to support them. A load is about 70 lbs.

The creeks were very much swollen by the heavy rains, and we had
a great many of them to pass, which made our days journey though
short, exceedingly troublesome, the banks of some of the creeks being

[2] Muleteer.

high, full of fissures, and very slippery being a sort of blue clay. The country through which we passed was partially clear, as there had been a Mahogany work here, and we followed its truck path for some distance. We commenced forming our first encampment about 4 o'clock and as this will be an every day business I shall give a description of our camp. The first things to be considered in selecting the spot are water, and fodder for our horses and mules. The Peteneros who travel this path generally know the places where these are to be found. The leaves of a tree called by the natives the Ramoon and Pin (and by the Belize people the bread nut totally distinct from that of the Sandwich Ids.) a most superb evergreen, is the best. The tree grows to a large size, the leaves are small, dark coloured, of an ovate shape, and very full the under side being of a light brownish tinge. The cattle are extremely fond of these leaves, and even eat the smaller twigs. They also feed upon the leaves of the Cahoon Palm, but do not like them so well as the Ramoon, nor are they so nutritious—but still they serve as fodder when the other cannot be easily obtained. Our huts were very expeditiously constructed, as we carried a good sized tarpauline with us which saved much time in cutting Cahoon or Bay thatch for a roof; our encampment consisted of four huts, the largest made sufficiently commodious to swing three hammocks, and contain the greater part of our baggage in case of rain, the black soldiers built one for themselves, the Indians another and the Spaniards one at a little distance. Our horses and mules were tethered close to our hut in front of which a large fire was kept up. The soldiers kept watch by turns 4 hours each. The flies were most annoying and seemed to have particular times for their appearance, the mosquitos coming out about dusk in miriads and lasting the whole night, a short time after sunrise they retired and the Bottle rumps made their appearance and continued to torment us during the day, with an occasional visit from a few doctor flies. The dew was very heavy during the night, and the morning was damp and chilly when we turned out at dawn. We soon had our mules laden and broke up our encampment taking some chocolate and a biscuit prior to starting.

The country through which we passed was flat and cut up by

innumerable creeks which evidently had their rise in a mountainous district, as they contained large masses of limestone, with pebbles, and Jasper in abundance. I picked up several very beautiful specimens and placed them where I might get them coming back.

We encamped on a rising ground, at an angle where a rapid, and clear brook, falls into the river Belize, near the mountain cave falls whose roar we heard distinctly. I had a shot at a water dog or otter as he swam rapidly down the stream and must have hit him hard, as I stopped the rapidity of his movements, and the water was discoloured with his blood; but he crept into a hole before my man could stop him, and we could not dislodge him from his place of refuge—we indulged in a delicious bath in a clear pool of the Brook which after our hard days labour was most refreshing. Although there had been no rain, we were perfectly wet through up to our hips from passing the creeks and wet bushes—and were glad to get on dry clothes. We saw no game the whole day, nor indeed did we see any yesterday, this gave us some annoyance, as from the representations given by our Interpreter and others, we expected to get abundance for our party, and consequently, with the exception of some biscuit and flour and a small quantity of oatmeal in cannisters, we had laid in no provisions, and if we were equally unsuccessful for a few days we should very soon demolish what we had. This idea caused some little uneasyness, but the "wild huntsman" cheered us by saying that a little farther on we were sure to meet "muchos pajaros, muchos warrishe."[3] The main river at this spot was deep and about 70 yards broad but in the dry season there is very little water and Pitpans have great difficulty in ascending so high.

Nov. 30th—The next morning soon after daylight we were en route again, and had a much easier day's journey although I got as complete a sousing in the early part of it, as one could ever wish for. We had one very bad creek to pass with steep muddy banks, I gave my nag the rein and descended into it, the water coming about half way up the saddle flaps. I was taking particular care of my gun, which I held aloft in my right hand when unfortunately my horse got his

[3] "Many birds, many warris (bush pigs)."

foot through the rein, and reared up, shaking his feet to rid himself of it, as if he was aware of not being able to mount the steep bank in that condition, this movement over balanced me and I was obliged to slip into the water up to my arm pits. My nag scrambled up the bank, shook himself and turned round to see how I faired, however I was not far behind him. One of our mules fell down in the creek, and wetted most of our things. We came suddenly upon a drove of Warri, but I was so anxious that I fired at one too soon, and thus lost a chance of getting two or three. About 3 o'clock we came to a place called Old Bank on the side of the Belize River a very picturesque spot, with a cleared space, and some fine old trees one of which had been washed down by the flood and laid directly out into the stream.

Soon after we arrived I sent the huntsman out to endeavour to get some game, and I went another way in expectation of meeting with something also. As I strolled along I heard the report of a gun ahead of me, and after proceeding a short distance, Jocko came running up to me with a small deer, or rather antelope, bellowing out directly he saw me "Hi Captain Tiger, Tiger." It appeared that Jocko had strolled out and had come upon a Tiger in the act of commencing a meal upon the antelope one of the hind quarters of which he had attacked; Jocko fired his pistol at him which had the effect of driving him from his prey of which he possessed himself and was running to the Camp when I met him. A hunt was instituted for the tiger but we saw nothing of him, but the marks of his paws, and those of the deer also. The latter animal is the same as the one described by Stedman in his description of Surinam. Our Huntsman was successful returning with a Warri. This animal resembles a pig, its skin was so full of ticks, which take their name from it being called the Warri tick, that we were obliged to skin it, which operation is seldom performed by the natives, who directly they kill one, light a fire and singe it well, taking off all the hair and ticks also. When I returned to the camp I was rather annoyed at my servants exposing himself very much to the sun by swimming across the river twice, and remaining on the opposite bank endeavouring to get some plantains, from an abandoned plantation, across the river, which was very rapid and full of sunken trees, and branches. The cord broke several times, and we were obliged to abandon them for the night. We had now sufficient meat for a day or two, and determined to remain to endeavour to procure a supply for some time longer. We portioned out a mess to our people with some biscuit. And we made a meal off the antelope, which was indifferent eating, being dry and tasteless, the Warri was much better. We tried to catch fish but were very unsuccessful only taking one snook of about a pound and a half weight, and a few small fish resembling perch. It was a fine starlight night, and our encampment had a most picturesque effect. Our horses tethered on a small clearance near a bright fire reflected on the rapidly rushing stream, with the huge trunk and limbs of the trees in bright relief against the dark distance, and our people grouped about the fire which threw a red glare on the swarthy countenances. The wild huntsman would have made a capital study as a bandit. We swung in our hammocks enjoying the scene until nine o'clock when we set our watch and hanging our Pavilions under which we ensconsed ourselves were soon as fast asleep as if we had been on beds of down.

Dec. 1st—The suns bright rays were shining into our tent before we awoke from a comfortable snooze. I do not think I ever saw so many butterflies together as were disporting their bright colours in the sun about midday; the greater number were of a light buff, but there were some of all hues of the rainbow. Now and then I observed several very large mottled grey ones, which made a short flight, and returned to the branches of a large tree. I watched them for some time and when I found out where they perched, they were so identified with the grey moss that I could scarcely distinguish them from it. There were also some magnificent parasitic plants, and many orchidious, some in full bloom of a bright violet colour.

2nd—We remained here all this day as it was the last place where we were likely to get plantains, and as our biscuit had got wet, it was requisite to procure something as a substitute.

Dec. 3—Made a last attempt before starting to get a cord across the water, which we accomplished and the plantains were made fast to some Tie Tie, and launched tolerably high up the stream but the cord broke and we had the mortification to see them float away from us, and at last stick among the branches of a fallen tree on the opposite side. We persuaded one of the Indians to go across which he did swimming like a dog, striking downwards, instead of out, in the manner we swim. I am informed that this is the usual mode among all the Indian Tribes. The string by which he was to haul over the Tie Tie broke, and the fellow was either afraid to try the river again, or did not wish to accompany us, for he made off, and we saw no more of him. We started into the forest again with very little provision as we had shot nothing, trusting to what we might fall in with in our path. We had three of the most villainous days marches through swamps nearly the whole time. The horses and mules up to their girths, frequently falling into holes so deep that we were obliged to dismount in places above our knees in mud to assist in taking the loads off the mules and drag them out by main force. On the last of the three days we were obliged to abandon one unfortunate mule to its fate dividing the load in the best manner we could amongst us. The places where we were compelled to encamp were actually in the swamp, the dryest place was inch deep in mud, over which we had to place a thick layer of branches and leaves and then our Tarpauline as a floor cloth.

The mosquitos and flies were intolerable, and settled on us in swarms. I was driven under my pavilion before I could smoke my cigar, and I continued puffing away to keep them off my face. The dew was so heavy at night that it fell upon our tents like rain, and when we awoke in the morning we could with difficulty discern one another from the density of the fog. I recommend this place strongly to those who would wish to experimentalize on the effect of miasma on the human frame. We could scarcely get dry wood sufficient to keep up a fire, which was useless as far as cooking was concerned, for we saw neither bird nor animal in this dismal swamp and the Barbacued Warri, which we brought from Butterfly bank, had been doled out in small quantities to our people, and the last day they had nothing but a very little mouldy biscuit, however we were enabled to give them an extra glass of spirit, which consoled them in a measure. The first day's route was through a Logwood swamp which would have delighted the eyes of the most covetous cutter of that wood, for the trees were very large and had they been within a transportable distance from a place of shipment would have been exceedingly valuable. We then got amongst Wild Plantain, and the thorny stemmed Palmetto, of which there are several varieties all equally disagreeable to the horsemen, and it was with the greatest difficulty we avoided having our legs lacerated by them, some as sharp as lancets, and of the same shape sticking out perpendicularly from the straight stems. It required a degree of braveurism, with a horse stumbling and his feet sinking into mud holes of a narrow path intersected by the roots of trees, to keep our legs clear of wounds, having at the same time to look out for the upper part of our bodies and face from the prickly creepers that hang over head; for one might have the luck of being hauled off ones horse by some of these which the natives with their usual felicitous adaptation of names call the "haul back." They have long pendant shoots, leafless, but armed at intervals of 6 or 7 inches with sharp thorns turned back, which act like hooks taking a strong hold. Another called the cockspur having bunches of thorns on its stem resembling the pedal defense of Chanticleer.

Dec. 7—We got out of the swamp into a better path among fine trees, many of Mahogany, Cedar and Santa Maria a wood something resembling mahogany, and growing to nearly as large a size. Our men started without having a meal all yesterday the only thing we had to give them was some oatmeal and very little of that, made into gruel. Towards midday I killed a curacoa, and soon after fell in with some Qualm, and killed a brace of them—this timely supply raised our spirits and we looked forward with some degree of pleasure to our nights encampment, especially as we were in expectation of getting good water which we had not had since we left the river, being obliged to drink that water taken from the holes along side the path, which was the colour of Tar, and somewhat of the same consistence. At about four o'clock we came to a spot called Santa Maria, where there was a small clearance made some years ago by run away slaves from Honduras, and which had been long abandoned. Our people

60

immediately went for water, and we took advantage of a sunny spot to dry our baggage which had been rolled about in the swamp. I was much annoyed to find that the box of ammunition had got very wet, and with the exception of the pound cannisters of powder was considerably damaged.

I had just time to perform my ablutions and put on dry clothes, and was comfortably swinging in my hammock, watching Antonio preparing one of the Qualm for our repast, when Manuel came running breathless into the camp with the joyful intelligence that he had discovered a cow drinking at the place where he had gone for water. I had just cleaned and reloaded my guns so I let him have the double barrell and soon after heard him fire both as quickly as they could be fired one after the other, and in a very short space of time the unfortunate baca was brought piecemeal to the encampment, looking any thing but enticing, being some half starved creature that had not had strength to proceed with its companions driven along this path from Peten to Belize and consequently was abandoned by the cattle drivers. A barbacue was forthwith erected and extra fire kindled beneath it, and the meat placed under this process of curing. What the natives call a Barbacue, is used for a variety of purposes, and consists of forked sticks driven into the ground and others placed on the forks and again across the latter, forming a platform. The meat is placed on this and fire kept underneath it until it becomes almost black, when it will keep for sometime, being partially cooked and well smoked and exceedingly disagreeable in flavour. However it is the only mode of preserving meat for any time in this hot climate—and we had the whole of the unfortunate animal, a striking representative of Pharoahs lean kine, dressed in this way, with the exception of a mess served out to the people which was unlimited, and they were cooking, eating, jabbering or chewing sugar cane, which they procured from an old plantation, the whole night. I endeavoured to find out when these canes were planted but the only answer I got was "muchos años,"[4] they were of excellent quality, and although growing wild without having been replanted for upwards of twenty years, some

---

[4] "Many years (ago)."

of them were 20 feet long and nearly 3 inches in diameter. The whole country through which we passed from Duck Run to this place was low and swampy scarcely partaking of an undulating character. Our path laid nearly due west the whole way—and except when in the Logwood and Palmetto swamp, was through a forest of magnificent trees. We once or twice were within sound of the different falls of the Belize River.

Dec. 8—This being Sunday Mr. Walker read prayers to our people, at the conclusion of which Antonio favoured us with an Amen which would have done credit to the most orthodox parish clerk, and it came so unexpectedly that it deranged the gravity of nearly the whole party Parson included. My servant Carnick taken very ill with fever, administered Calomel Pills at night and dose of salts this morning, giving him hot gruel to induce perspiration, and remained for a day.

Dec. 9—Carnick considerably better and able to proceed. I fell in with no game but killed a mountain fox called a Zorilla by the Spaniards. It was a fierce little animal, and stood at bay in the path disputing with one of the men. It is not half the size of the English fox, of a greyish colour the hair tanned at the roots—legs tanned as also the face with a black muzzle and long bushy tail. I skinned it and dried the moisture of the skin with wood ashes, which I have often used with success when preparing specimens of ornithology, and could not procure the necessary preservative. The best is the corrosive sublimate dissolved in spirits of wine, or high wines—which has the advantage of being cleaner than any other preparation. Night was closing in, and we had arrived at our place of encampment some time, but a portion of our party were still absent, which caused me great uneasiness, particularly as my sick servant was one of the absentees. I kept up a discharge at intervals from the fire arms but got no return signal, which we had agreed upon in case of separation, at last I was obliged to dispatch a party with a light, and fire arms in the direction we had come, but it was near ten o'clock before they returned with the missing who had take a wrong direction, and I found Carnick much exhausted. The spot where we encamped was called San Pedro, why I am not aware, but from the circumstance of all these stages being named after some saintly person, I had fancied that at least we should find a few huts in the shape of a village, but was mistaken as they are merely spots which have been partially cleared by the Peteneros travelling to Belize, and there was generally a cattle pen, which caused us some annoyance from the quantities of Warri ticks that abound in them. These insects, called Garapatas by the Spaniards, are much more troublesome than the flies, they are of all sizes from the most imperceptible mite to the size of a Castor oil bean which the larger ones very much resemble. The smaller ones hang in clusters on the bushes, and as you pass along thousands get upon your clothes and on to your skin, into which they insert their heads causing great irritation and consequent sores, as it is next to impossible to resist scratching. In removing them they give great pain as they hold on like grim death.

Our encampment was by the side of a muddy creek, into which ran a clear sparkling rill of the most delicious water flowing rapidly over pebbles, some of great beauty. We cooked some of the Cahoon cabbage[5] which was very good—some of our party would not eat it in consequence of an idea that it caused sore throat. It makes a good salad.

Dec. 10—Broke up our encampment early and had exceedingly heavy travelling. Carnick very ill, and consequently we were obliged to halt for the night in nearly as bad a place as we had before encountered. Our horses and mules were very much fatigued and were looking exceedingly miserable. Came to a place where we could not pass and had to take a detour of some distance where we crossed a very deep creek which we were told was the main river—obliged to take the loads from the mules and horses and swim them across, taking advantage of a tree placed for ourselves.

Dec. 11—Off as early as possible. Carnick so weak that I was obliged to have his horse led and a man to walk along side of him to prevent his falling. The path was much better today leading over some high ground, and rocky eminences of limestone formation,

[5] The tender heart of the young cohune palm.

about 3 o'clock we descended to the bed of a river running over rocks. We were again obliged to stop here in consequence of the illness of my servant, and as there were some huts built on a rocky island in the stream we took possession of them. This place is called Los Enquentros. The river which is one of the extreme branches of the Belize is beautifully clear and full of deep holes or rather basins, in one of which we had a most refreshing bath; the water was quite as cold as I could wish it. We took advantage of a patch of greensward to dry our clothes and the turn out would have graced rag fair. I basked in the hot sun for some time as a luxury for in the forest you scarcely get a glimpse of his glorious face. A king of the Vultures, in a gorged state, sat with out spread wings on the highest branch of a blighted tree; whilst his subjects—known in the Antilles and Jamaica under the names of Johnny Crow, Corbeau and called by the Spaniards Zopilot—were seen at a respectful distance on the neighbouring trees. We soon had a nasal demonstration, that their savory meal was not far distant. An unfortunate cow left in pretty much the same plight as the one we had killed, as Paddy said to save its life, had gathered together this flock of foul feeders. It is astonishing with what quickness these birds find out where there is carrion, their eyesight must be exceedingly good or their sense of smell extremely acute, perhaps both, of which I have had some rather curious proofs. They say with truth, that the inferior birds do not attempt to attack a carcass should the king of the vultures be near, until he has gorged himself, whilst they sit on the neighbouring trees with watering beaks, witnessing His Majesty's epicurism as he helps himself to the tit bits.

I recollect an anecdote or two connected with these birds which as I have never seen in print I will relate although a digression. An officer in a regiment quartered at Trinadad, reduced to the weakest possible state by fever, and who was not expected to survive many hours was left by his nurse for a few moments alone in his chamber, extended on the broad of his back on his bed; he was perfectly sensible but without the power of moving a limb. Judge his sensations when one of these hideous birds flew in at the window, and perched upon his breast; he tried to move his hand, it would not obey the impulse of his mind, and he lay for some moments in the agonized expectation of having his eyes plucked from their sockets by the beak of this voracious bird. The return of his servant caused the retreat of the Corbeau, and the officer recovered to relate the anecdote. One of these birds was kept as a pet by the 65th Reg't. it was taken when very young at Demerara and when the Regiment embarked for another station Jack took up his quarters on board ship and went with it making lofty flights during the day wheeling in circles far above the white canvas of the ship. At one time there were several punishments in the Reg't. at which Jack attended and the bloody cat being laid down he endeavoured to pick the blood from it, and even made an attempt to jump on the mans back. After which he was always obliged to be imprisoned when anything of this sort went on. Jack was a constant attendant at the slaughter house, and paid several visits to the church alighting on the pulpit in the middle of the sermon eyeing the parson in the most knowing way, as much as to question the orthodoxy of his discourse.

I have witnessed an emigration of the large red ant called by the Spaniards "Hormigas guerrero"[6] and in some of the West India Islands the "Parasol Ant"; they had made regular paths through the woods about four inches broad, well troden. I tracked it for a mile in one direction but did not arrive at their abode. They were hard at work, each carrying a small round leaf having very much the appearance of a Parasol. We procured quantities of shell fish on which we fed, they were very good. We tried to catch a species of fish, but were unsuccessful probably from not knowing the bait the inhabitants of these streams were partial to. Saw no game. We found our Interpreter, Nod, who had been hired to make himself generally useful, as well as to interpret what we said to the natives a most lazy person— never was the proverb of "great talkers are little doers" more forcibly exemplified, than in this fellows conduct. He would never put his hand to anything requiring exertion and would stand with his hands

---

[6] "Warrior ants," or army ants, but what Caddy observed was a community of leaf-cutting ants, a very different and less feared form.

in his pockets, watching the fire, a 2nd fatboy Joe—almost falling asleep á pied.

Dec. 12—We started as early as possible, passing over some rocky ground and towards noon were greeted by the barking of dogs and the hallooing of people in the forest; we hailed them with the usual whoop of the Indians, and soon after several half breeds—Mestitzos —made their appearance with about a dozen meagre looking animals of the canine species. The men proved to be part of a look out band, who had been quartered at the huts which we occupied last night, but were removed—they were very civil and immediately assisted our people who were pretty well worn out to carry the loads. About three o'clock we emerged from the forest and entered on a magnificient undulating plain—as far as the eye could reach over uninterrupted open pasture with here and there clumps of trees. I shall never forget the joyous sensation I experienced, and indeed it was felt by all and our half famished animals pricked up their ears with delight, and it was with difficulty we urged them on, so greedy were they after the luxuriant herbage which they were treading under foot, only snatching a hasty mouthful as they journeyed on. We came to an encampment where a number of Indians were posted by the Commandante of Peten to prevent the return of his predecessor who had fled to Belize. Here we were informed that we could not proceed to Peten until the "Teniente"[7] in charge of the party sent off a dispatch to inform the commandante of our arrival. We procured some dried Tortillas from the Indians, the first bread kind we had had for sometime. They call it "Bastamente" when dried in this manner, and is the principal food of the natives when travelling, who make it into a sort of porrage by boiling, seasoning it with Chile and salt. However we eat it hard and crisp, being tolerably well starved, and altho' it had no more taste than so much dry chips, we crunched away until our very jaws ached.

After resting about half an hour allowing our unfortunate beasts to browse upon the rich pasture close around the Indian camp, we proceeded a few miles to the Hacienda of Santa Rosa, which consisted

[7] "Lieutenant."

66

of some cottages, the residence of cattle keepers. We got possession of a deserted and dilapidated building, formerly the temporary abode of the owner when visiting the Hacienda for the purpose of counting and marking the stock. It was in a filthy state, and the mud plastered sticks forming the walls were broken away rendering it anything but weather proof (it was with the greatest trouble we kept the dogs and pigs out of our abode; as they had free entrance into those of the natives they endeavoured to be on the same familiar footing with us) however we were obliged to make the best of it; and after having the ground—for floor it had none—well swept and spreading our tarpaulins as a carpet, placing our luggage to form seats, with our hammocks swung from the rafters, we should have enjoyed a degree of luxury, for rovers of the wilds, were it not for the increased illness of my poor servant Carnick for whom I now had most serious apprehensions. The fever had left him in a state of extreme weakness, and dissentary had ensued, most likely from drinking the very bad water along our route and although I had frequently cautioned him, and had given express commands to the men in charge of the poor fellow not to allow him to have it, yet his craving was so great from excessive thirst that they could not withstand the pitiful appeals he made to their commiseration and I can easily believe that this frequent recourse to the unwholesome water caused the complaint which he now suffered under. We made him as comfortable as our means permitted, and paid him all the attention that was in our power, after he had been in bed some time he appeared easier and during the night slept tolerably well, but his constant cry, when awake was water,water,water, which was denied him, tea or some small quantity of other liquid supplied, which he seemed to loathe. The following morning he appeared better.

We were obliged to remain, not only in consequence of Carnick's illness but also that we might receive an answer to a communication which we dispatched to the commandante of Peten. I got one of the Muchachos of the hamlet to go with me in order to point out where I might kill Quail or anything else that might come in my way in the shape of game, but we traversed a good portion of ground without

67

seeing anything, it was certainly in the middle of the day when the birds, like the Spaniards, indulge in their siesta—in this hot country. The ground over which we passed was thickly strewed with pieces of limestone, and was of an undulating nature in some parts rising into roundish hills, some about one hundred feet above the plain. One of these I went to the summit of, and was delighted with the appearance of the country. The only want in the scene was water. To the eastward were the Primeval woods the scene of our peregrinations, with little more apparent elevation than the ground on which I stood—to the northward the plain was lost in the extreme distance in a low belt of trees with scarcely any elevation of the land visible. To the west an undulating plain bounded by mountains of no very great height covered to their limits with trees, and running towards the south and S.W. gradually becoming lower until they were identified with the distant forest. Here and there I could observe a sort of ridge amongst the trees, where perhaps a river ran or a lagoon rejoicing in its calm loneliness, a paradise of aligators—unknown even to the wild Indian. I returned to my hut, unsuccessful in sport, half roasted from the scorching heat of the Savana, but pleased with the appearance of the country. The people of the Hacienda supplied us with some pork and sausages and hot tortillas, and as our drinkables were all expended we sent some distance for a supply of aguardiente—which proved a villainous compound. Our negro soldiers could not make out what it was, and we gave each his glass, and as they put it to their huge lips made their several remarks upon its properties. "Hi! Ingin make gin" says one, when he saw it poured out in a wine glass. "Cha, how you know he gin, afore you tase em?" replied another; "Must be gin; you no see he wite?" "Wha dat! Rum no wite, for dey put da dam tuf like a molasses in he for make him like he tan" Potts declared "it burn him like fire tick," as it went down "he troat"—Jocko refused it having made a vow to refrain from spiritous liquor for a certain time, however there was not much fear of his becoming a teatotaller as a decoction of that herb was not easily obtained, and I rather imagine was almost unknown in the country through which we are now travelling. Robinson Crusoe who must have been a disciple of the celebrated fire eater, Chaubert, declared it was "berry good, and no too trong."

We had a visit from a half cast named Torribio, who had formerly lived in Belize or its neighbourhood, and had made an unfortunate mistake in not knowing other peoples cattle from his own, in consequence of which he had been banished from the settlement. He came to offer his services to us and very kindly undertook to have Carnick carried to his own house, where his wife who could speak English should nurse him. As it was impossible he could proceed we gladly availed ourselves of the offer. Accordingly on the morning of our departure from the Hacienda having hired a man to carry him, a Silla or chair was constructed into which he was placed and the Carrier mounted his cargo on his back, in the same manner that the Indians carry their loads. As it was impossible to procure medical advice we were of the opinion that a good nurse was the next best aid he could have, and as some of these people, indeed most of them, have their little nostrums for the different complaints of the country, he would be better attended to at Señora Torribios than in the wretched place which we were now leaving—even were we to remain to take care of him. We were also visited by some creole Spaniards from Dolores, a village a few miles to Southward of Peten

Having obtained permission to proceed to Hunchichilob a Hacienda about 40 miles further on towards Peten—Horses were taken up from the Savanah, rather miserable looking creatures for a long journey, and we were en route once more having Torribio as our guide. The first two hours of the journey was over the Savanah which was gaily enameled with flowers, many of which resembled those of Europe. Several species of Lupin, yellow and purple—a single Hollyhock of a Pinkish colour, and a Thistle resembling the Scotch. We also disturbed several hives of Quail which was the only game we saw. Several of the cardinal bird flew past us, and a small flycatcher with bright scarlet breast and grey back and wings. We again entered the forest and proceeded along a path which could not have been much frequented, as we had in many places to halt whilst a passage was cleared by cutting away the bushes. There was another route to Peten which we were told lay through a swamp and in consequence of the late heavy rains was impassible. It was singular that although we left Belize in the height of the rainy season we scarcely had a shower until we got to Duck Run, where it rained for three or four days almost incessantly—and since we left that we had not had any.

As we were jogging on our way at as quick a trot as we could well get out of our beasts, considering the numerous impediments which lay in our path, our guide stopped short, beckoning to us to do the same, making signs to be silent—he dismounting and coming back to us as stealthily as possible, pronounced the word "Tigre" telling me to be ready with my gun, which was rather a needless caution as I took care always to have it well prepared for any emergency, and a brace of Pistols also. Presently we heard a mewing like that of a cat, and a more sonorous response from a greater distance in the bush; Torribio immediately espied a young tiger sitting in the fork of a small tree which he pointed out to us and as immediately set to work cutting down a long sapling to the end of which he fastened a thin cord with a noose and passed the latter over the head of the little animal which kept up a continued mewing and spitting like an angry kitten. It was dragged from the tree and shoved head long into a bag in spite of an angry growl that seemed to come from no great distance. I dismounted and entering the bush from whence the sound came beat about for a short time, and although I heard the crackling of the dry underwood as the animal retreated, I was disappointed in getting a peep at it. So was obliged to mount again and proceed. We heard the old animal several times as we went along, and the young one kept up its mewing, however Torribio carried it at his saddlebow with apparent contempt for "a tigress deprived of her young." We halted in the wood about two o'clock and our guide produced from his grass saddle bags or Alforgas a couple of cold roast fowls, tortillas, and chilis, which he placed on a clean white cloth on the ground, and with the hospitable expression of "Come Señors" invited us to partake of his good fare, to which we did ample justice, washing it down with a "Poquito Aguardiente." We arrived at the Hacienda of Hunchichi-lob a little after dusk, having had nearly as hard a day's journey as any since we left Duck Run. We were here received into the house of an old lady—a relative of the Ex Commandante of Peten Don Julien Segaurra to whom I was introduced at Belize prior to my departure from that place—who had three daughters, one married, and a son-in-law living with her; they were exceedingly polite, and endeavoured to make us comfortable, cooking us a very tolerable repast. After which we were glad enough to return into our hammocks early, being much fatigued.

On the following morning I strolled out before breakfast with my gun and killed a brace of Teal (Three or four of the men who followed me to the pond were much surprised at my killing them on the wing as they had never seen it attempted before. They would not risk the loss of a charge) and three or four Snipe at a pond close to the house. Salu killed a bird of the Gallinule tribe, its bill was 2 inches long, straight, and of a bright pink, Iris of the eye red—top of the head, back, and wings, greenish black—throat and breast white—tail short, square and a pink grey legs long and pink—I do not recollect ever having seen one of the same kind. After breakfast I procured a nag and with a couple of the "Mozos"[8] went to some ponds at a distance, where I got both duck and Teal and several snipe. Returning we were enticed into a patch of trees by the cries of the Curacoa, however I did not get a shot at one—but had several at a large black monkey—which I wounded severely, and knocked him off the branch the first shot, but could not get him down, although after waiting some time I saw he was evidently giving up the ghost, but he sat with his body along the branch, his tail encircling it, and his almost human face looking down upon us with a melancholy expression of countenance; I tried to get one of the "Mozos" to climb the tree and give the poor brute the "Coup de grace" with his machete but could not persuade either to do so. There were numbers of Cattle and horses grazing in the Savannah. The former although of a small breed were well proportioned, and in very fine condition as were also the horses, but they were cat hammed generally speaking. I was struck with what appeared to me curious that a great number of the horses were lop

[8] "Servants."

eared, but on enquiry I found that it was not natural, but produced from the destruction of the nerve of the ear by the Warri tick to which I could scarcely give credence however after having examined a good many I found it to be the case; I saw some horses whose ears actually laid flat upon their heads giving them a most frightful appearance. Their ears are sometimes so full of these tormenting insects that one would scarcely deem it possible that one more could squeeze itself in. The Tigers or Jaguars are exceedingly destructive to young cattle and sheep, but seldom attack a full grown beast.

On my return to the Casa I found one or two visitors one an old white gentleman who had a Hacienda on the same Savannah, at a short distance from us; he had a very scotch name—Ballantine—he seemed a jolly old fellow, and sent us a present of some cheese and fresh butter. The former was very like the small dutch cheese in flavour, exceedingly salt in order to make it keep. We had a good dinner having procured a sheep for which our kind hostess refused payment; we endeavoured to persuade them to partake of our dinner but could not get them to do so. We were served by her daughter who made our Tortillas and brought relays of them smoking hot. The mutton was delicious and our appetites must have surprised our fair friends, as we had not quite recovered from our great starvation in the bush. A dish of stewed beans Frijoles was something new to us, and exceedingly savoury; onions, chilis and garlic being the condiments which added to the flavour. We were entertained in the evening with music, the son-in-law played the Marimba, and guitar and the young ladies danced a sort of Fandango. Two of our men with part of our baggage were absent, and we were afraid they had decamped; however they made their appearance before nightfall.

We heard during the afternoon that the Commandante was on his road out to meet us. However about ten o'clock, not thinking he would arrive that night, we turned into our hammocks, and having exposed myself a good deal to the sun during the day, and being rather fatigued, I slept most soundly and it was only after my hammock had been well shaken by one of the Señoras, who kept bawling

"Señor! Señor! el Commandante, El Commandante que viene"[9] that I awoke—I wished the Commandante at the devil in very plain English which my awakener did not understand—so I turned out forthwith being half dressed; I am not certain that the Señora was quite so much. We presently heard the Tramp of Steeds, and expected, as there was a Revolution in the country, to witness some of the "Pomp and Circumstance of glorious war." The door was opened by Torribio, and in walked Ozeta, Commandante of the district of Peten, followed by the most motly group of fellows I ever saw—as his staff—dressed in any way most suitable to themselves. Ozeta had a very good address and was not a bad looking person, dark sharpish face, with a quick black eye and long curly black hair. He wore a broad brimmed Guatemala hat covered with black oilskin, with a white handkerchief round it as a band, the two ends flying out. An orange striped jacket and vest with grey jean trousers, and boots with a massive pair of silver spurs having rowels the size of a dollar. From a little above the knees hung a pair of loose tanned leather leggings, curiously stamped and pierced at the sides and round the foot. A sword of British regulation pattern was girded round the waist by a Patent leather belt of British manufacture. Our Interpreter introduced us, as our knowledge of the language was rather limited. We explained the motives of our journey, that we were travelling through the country for the purpose of gaining information, and with a view of promoting the intercourse, which existed to a small extent between the inhabitants of the District of Peten and Belize; and that we intended to proceed from Peten to the Ruins of Palenque in Chiapa, at which he expressed himself ready to assist us as much as lay in his power and a variety of exclamations began to proceed from his suite "Las Ruinas, Carambo! so muy lejos de aqui" "Que ruinas?" asked another "no sabe"[10] announced a third, so that we were not likely to gain much information from these folks with regard to their

[9] "Sir! Sir! The Commandant is coming!"
[10] "The Ruins, Carramba! They're very far from here." "What Ruins?" "He doesn't know."

locale. In the midst of our "Talky Talky" as one of our black soldiers called it, the gigantic Potts, of pitpan notoriety, stalked across the apartment passing through the midst of Ozeta's body guard, and taking his pistol from the wall, walked quietly back and stood at the other door. He had heard of the arrivals of the Commandante and merely made a "demonstration" to show that he was prepared to defend himself in case of an attack; however to prove that we had every confidence in the persons to whom we were talking, I made him replace it.

The Commandante informed us that he understood we had in our party a "mucho malo muchacho"[11] named Manuel Moralez who had given him some considerable annoyance, being connected with Segourra's party and requested we would give him up, however we begged that, as we had hired this lad, and had induced him to come back with us under a promise of interceeding with his Excellency—a compliment of this sort goes a great way sometimes—for his pardon, setting forth in the most favourable light the great service he had been to us, and after a little persuasion and a few compliments to his clemency—of which we knew a great deal of course—he consented to pardon Manuel on a promise of good behaviour for the future. Soon after this he told us that everything he possessed was at our service, and shaking hands with us wished us "Buenas noches" after making an appointment to take us into Peten with him in the morning. We went through the ceremony of shaking hands with each particular member of his interesting looking followers and on closing the door on them the "mucho malo muchacho" Manuel emerged from a pile of saddles, bridles, blankets &c &c that were piled in the corner of the room, and where he had been a witness to all that passed. We had a whole household, in exceeding dishabit, chatting away for an hour afterwards, and I believe I was fast asleep again long before they left the apartment.

We were up betimes the following morning and made the old Lady and her daughters a present of some Spanish books which we had brought with us, consisting of Bible and Testament, Prayer Book,

[11] "Very bad fellow."

The Pilgrims Progress and one or two others, at which they appeared much pleased and breaking our fasts on some new milk, sugar and aguardiente we bid them "adios" hoping to meet in Peten and joined the Cavalcade of the Commandante who had just made his appearance. He was mounted on the best horse I had yet seen, a dun of powerful make, handsome spanish saddle of red morocco, studded with brass nails—he sat his horse well, and greeted us with great urbanity of manner. We were about 20 in number altogether. Our route lay over undulating Savannahs for the greater part of the way to Santa Anna where we were to remain for the night and going at a pretty brisk pace we arrived there early—Taking up our residence at the Alcaldia[12] where dinner was served to the whole party from a neighbouring casa. After which we lit our cigars and strolled about, calling at one or two houses with the Commandante, where we were introduced to the fair of the place, who were few in number. They made us Segaritos, small cigars made with the husk of the Indian corn, rubbed smooth with a pebble or shell and cut into oblongs, a small quantity of Tobacco well dried and cut very small is placed along one side and rolled up, pinching with the nail at each end to prevent its coming out. These were lit by the ladies who after taking a whiff or two, handed them to us in a most winning manner with the expression of "Tome Señor"[13] always presenting the unlit end. At one house we heard a young lady whom they said was from Campeachy, sing and accompany herself on the guitar she sang with a dreadful nasal twang, a love ditty of a melancholy nature, a case of breach of promise or something to that effect, the burden of which was "No hai remedio, yo soy infeliz."[14] We returned to the Alcaldia, where the Commandante busied himself swinging our hammocks into which we turned having about half a dozen besides Ozeta in the same hut for it amounted to nothing more and only consisted of one room.

The next morning after taking a cup of what they called chocolate, but which was a mixture of that and parched corn—we proceeded on

[12] Mayor's residence.
[13] "Take it, Sir."
[14] "It can't be helped, I'm unhappy."

our journey to Peten. The road was exceedingly bad and was partly over the amphitheatre of hills which surround the lake of Itza. We emerged from the woods about three o'clock and came suddenly upon the Village of San Bonito on the borders of a magnificent sheet of water which sparkled in glorious sunshine, bearing the Island town of Flores, with some smaller fairy looking Islets, on its calm bosom. We dismounted on a green sward close to the shore, where canoes were soon in readiness to transport us to the Island. These canoes although large were exceedingly ill constructed, being little more than long troughs, without seats or any convenience for passengers, they were propelled by two paddlers standing up one at each end, using long handled paddles. The Island is about a mile from San Bonito. A house was procured for us by Ozeta who expressed regret that his own had not accomodation for our party and we were ushered into our abode—which was thatched cottage, having stone walls plastered and whitewashed, and consisted of two rooms—with a floor of composition of mud, lime & wood ashes, it was hard and even—there was a small kitchen in the yard. We soon had our baggage arranged with the assistance of a couple of tables, a seat or two, and hammocks swung was about the best furnished house in the town.

Soon after our arrival the Commandante sent us a dinner cooked at his own house, and a present of "Puro's," cigars, made by the hands of Señora Ozeta with some Aguardiente of superior quality. After which we strolled out, and ascended to the Plaza which commands an extensive view of the lake—a flat platform of about 200 yards square on the eastern side of which stand the Church of "Our Lady of Sorrows" in a half delapidated state—part of the roof had fallen in being thatched. On the northern side were the ruins of a convent, and Barracks, the latter might have contained from 200 to 300 men. Opposite to which on the southern side was the Ruin of the Commandancia, the residence of the former Commandantes. To the westward was the debris of a wall in which could be traced embrasures. The Island is about one mile and a quarter in length and not more than three quarters of a mile in breadth in any part. The houses are but mean thatched cottages, few of them having more than two

76

rooms, the roof being made of Poles strongly lashed together with "Tie Tie." The walls are mostly of stone plastered and white washed. There is not a pane of glass in any window in the town.

The furniture is equally mean: a few chairs of very primitive manufacture, generally covered with the tiger skin; a rude bench or settle with back and arms; a coarsely made table; with as many hammocks as will conveniently swing, forms the tout ensemble of what is called "La Sala." The bedroom furniture consists of a bedstead or two of rude workmanship, having hides stretched over them. A few boxes to contain a scanty supply of apparel, and occasionally a clothes press. The population of the town is about 500 souls—but many live most of their time at their Haciendas on the Plains and only pay Peten an occasional visit. The view from the Plaza is very beautiful and as we now beheld it, under the influence of a gorgeous sunset reflected in the calm mirror of the transparent lake, with its broken shore and densely wooded mountains surrounding it completely; the village of San Bonito in the middle distance on a carpet of bright green verdure, the smaller islands and the more distant villages of San Andres and San Jose, placed on rising ground their white cottages and surrounding hills vividly reflected in the water of the lake. The greatest length of the lake is from east to west and is about 16 miles, its greatest breadth is 7 miles. There is a long strip of high land which runs out from the eastern end, its extreme point being directly to the northward of the island town, at about one mile and a half distance. The size of the town has been greatly exagerated. Juarros states that the late is 26 leagues in circumference, and that Peten or Great Island, is about two leagues from the shore, by which he must mean from the northern shore, as it was most likely from that part, that the Spaniards who came from Campeachy embarked for Peten. He continues, "it is steep and lofty and on the summit there is a plain nearly a quarter of a league in diameter." The highest part of the island is not 100 feet above the beach of the lake—and the whole island is not larger than I have before stated. The smaller islands are insignificant, not one half a mile in length and uninhabited.

Juarros History of Guatemala[15]—This District was the strong hold of Canek a rebellious cacique of Yucatan who headed a revolt in the province of Chichen Itza, distant about 20 leagues from the village of Tihoó which is at present called Merida—and not thinking himself sufficiently secure in that situation, retired with all his party to the most concealed and impenetrable parts of the mountains: he also took possession of the Islands in the lake of Itza and fixed his residence in Peten or the great Island. In this new territory the Partizans of Canek increased in number in a most extraordinary degree: for when Peten was conquered he had under his authority 4 governments and 10 provinces, each containing many villages; in each of the five Islands in the Lake there were 22 divisions and according to the computation of the missionaries who went thither there were in these Islands alone from 24 to 25,000 inhabitants; whilst the Indians who dwelt on the borders of the Lake, and in the clusters of huts dispersed among the mountains, were, by the same persons said to be almost innumerable. (This must be a great exageration. The Islands never could have contained any such number unless they were much larger than they are now, which might have been the case as the lake is said to have no outlet.)

The conversion of the Itzaes was repeatedly attempted by the Franciscans of the Province of San Jose of Yucatan; and one of them Diego Delgado, lost his life in the enterprise, or, in the language of his order gained the crown of martyrdom. In 1692 Don Martin de Ursua y Arismendi Governor of Yucatan, submitted a proposal to the King to make a road at his own cost, from Yucatan to Guatemala a distance of 6½ Degrees of Latitude; under an idea, that the intercourse which would thereby be opened between the Province and the Capital, could not fail to facilitate the conversion of the natives, by rendering those who were situated contiguous to the line of communication more domestic, and accustomed to the manners and habits of the Spaniards. The proposal of Arismendi was extremely well re-

[15] Evidently abstracted by Caddy from the 1823 translation by J. Baily of *Compendio de la Historia de la Ciudad de Guatemala*, by Domingo Juarros, published in Guatemala in 1808.

ceived by the Council of the Indies, and readily accepted; orders were immediately transmitted to the Viceroy of Mexico, to the President of Guatemala, and to the Bishop of Yucatan, enjoining each to afford Arismendi every assistance that he might require: however these orders were not acted upon until 1695 when Ursua entered upon the duties of Governor of Yucatan—the road was commenced and carried a distance of 86 leagues but in consequence of some difficulties experienced by Ursua he was obliged to discontinue his operations until 1697—In this interval, several embassies were interchanged between the Governor of Guatemala and the King of Itza, and received at the respective courts with extraordinary solemnity; but either from a want of sincerity in Canek or from the extraordinary annoyance of his subjects, they were not attended with any favorable results.

On the 24th Jany. 1697, Arismendi set out from Campeachy; he sent a small force under Pedro de Lubiaur in advance, with orders to halt near the lake, and cut wood for constructing a galliot of 45 feet keel, and a Piragua of smaller dimensions. In the month of March the whole force reached the borders of the lake, where they encamped, and threw up an entrenchment for security against surprise; here they remained until the vessels were completed. While they were thus preparing for further operations, an Indian, a relation of Canek's, and the same person who had been sent ambassador to Merida paid a visit to the General; he was desirous of becoming a Christian, and was christened receiving the name of Martin Can. Ursua received him with pleasure, and shewed him much attention: many enquiries were made on various subjects, to which he readily gave answers, and among other things related, that when he was on his return from Merida, the Indians of Alarri had informed him that the people of Chatá and Puc, contrary to the orders of Canek, had killed on the very spot where the camp then was, the persons who came from Yucatan, and in the Savannah, those from Guatemala, whom they had surprised while asleep.

A few days afterwards the Cacique of Alarri, Chamarzulic, with several other principal persons arrived at the Camp: there was also perceived a squadron of canoes approaching; that of the Chief bearing a white flag: in these boats came the chief Priest Quincanek, first cousin of King Canek, accompanied by Kitcan, Chief of another party; they were all welcomed with great ceremony, received presents and were feasted in the best manner that circumstances would permit. Although they all came as messengers of peace, declared that they ardently desired the friendship of the Spaniards, and wished to be made Christians, yet the preparations observed among those of the Lake, as well as those on shore, demonstrated their intentions to be warlike; the military officers readily perceiving that all these external signs of peace and amity were nothing more than treacherous attempts to deceive, judged it expedient to declare war against them, and enter their territories with fire and sword to punish their deceit, and to avenge the death they had inflicted on the Spaniards. But the General, Ursua, firm in his determination to preserve peace as long as possible, issued an order, prohibiting on pain of death, either officer or soldier to commit any act of aggression against the Indians.

As soon as the vessels were equipped, Martin de Ursua, with 108 Spanish soldiers, and Juan Pacheco, the ecclesiastical vicar, with his deputy embarked; leaving the camp defended by 127 soldiers, and many auxiliary Indians, with two pieces of artillery, 2 wall pieces and 8 falconets under the command of Juan Francisco Cortes. At dawn of day the Galliot was under sail for the Island of Peten; and now it became most unequivocally apparent, that all the proposals for peace were deception; the lake was almost covered with Canoes all directing their course towards the vessels, and as soon as they came within reach a most furious discharge of arrows took place; the Island was now perceived to be covered with armed people. The Indians kept up so continual discharge of arrows, that it was alleged to be a miracle wrought in favour of the Spaniards, that none of them were killed; only two were wounded, one of whom being exasperated by the pain forgot the generals order and fired his musket; this example was followed by all the others, in spite of every interposition of the officers to prevent such retaliation. The vessel touched the Island, the soldiers jumped ashore and kept up a continued discharge of musketry; the noise of which so terrified the enemy, that they sought

Plate 9. *Caddy's map of the Yucatán Peninsula, showing the route taken by the expedition.*

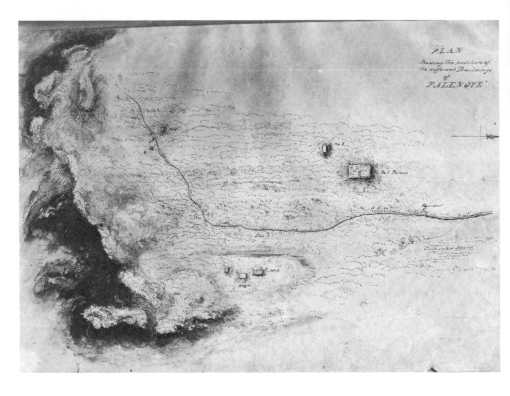

Plate 10. *Caddy's plan, showing the position of the different buildings of Palenque.*

safety in a precipitate flight; those of the Island as well as those from the Canoes, leaped into the water in such numbers, that from Peten to the main land there was nothing to be seen but the heads of Indians, endeavouring to save themselves by swimming—

The Spaniards entered the great town of the island called Tayasal, which they found deserted; The Spanish colors were hoisted on the most elevated point in Peten: the troops celebrated their victory by a thanksgiving for their escape from a danger so imminent, and the name of Nuestra Señora de los Remedios y San Pablo was given to the Island. This success was gained on the 13th March 1697; on the following day the territory was taken possession of in the name of the King of Spain, and the charge of it delivered to Juan de Pacheco, whom the bishop had appointed ecclesiastical vicar: in token of possession, the Pagan place of worship was dedicated as a Christian Church; water was consecrated, and afterwards mass was celebrated, at which the general and all his Troops assisted. So great was the number of Idols found in 21 places of worship that there were in the Island as well as in private houses, that the general, officers, and soldiers were unremittingly employed from 9 o'clock in the morning until 5 in the afternoon in destroying them. (There are not in the whole district of Peten any remains of the ancient Temples of the Indians—At least to all our inquiries we gained no information with regard to any.)

Three or four days after this conquest, some of the Indians began to return to the Island, and among them came 17 from Alarri, one of the smaller Islands: these Ursua employed in continuing the road that had been opened from Yucatan, until it joined that from Verapas, which service they cheerfully performed. The General endeavoured by all possible means to attract the Indians to the Islands, and those who came voluntarily he received and treated with the utmost kindness. In this demonstration of good will Ursua was greatly assisted by his godson, the newly converted Martin Can; he brought many families to Peten and among others Camarzulic the Cacique of Alarri; this chief in his turn persuaded the king, Canek, and the chief priest Quincanek, to come to Peten: the report of the kind reception given by the Spaniards to those who had taken courage to return, soon brought many others to submit to the Authority of the King of Spain. The other Islands in the Lake very soon submitted, without employing force against them. Arismendi sent a message to Cobox, the Cacique of the Coboxes, who inhabited 12 villages on the borders of the Lake, expressing his wish for an interview: the Indian Chief replied that he would be happy to receive his excellency at his own residence, as he and all his subjects were very desirous of having the honour of his visit. Ursua embarked with 40 men on board the Galliot, and proceeded to the territories of the Coboxes. These Indians approached without arms to meet him, manifesting the greatest satisfaction at his arrival; the cacique himself entertained them with kindness, and offered submission in the name of his subjects, and also for himself.

The Spaniards returned to their vessel, and coasting along the shores of the lake, visited the other villages of the Coboxes, at all of which they were received as friends. When Ursua saw himself completely master of Itza, he sent two officers, Alonzo Garcia de Paredes, Jose de Risalda Ongay and an escort of 10 soldiers, to Guatemala, with dispatches for the president and the royal audencia, giving a detail of the successful termination of his expedition, a description of the Island, and the advantages that might be derived from it; adding that in order to preserve the conquest just achieved, it would be requisite to maintain there a garrison of 50 men; but, that much as he wished to support this force, at his own cost, by the great expense he had incurred in opening the road, and in subjecting Peten, his finances were now so much exhausted as not to permit his taking that additional charge upon himself; and, for this reason alone, he now appealed to the royal audencia for assistance. The court, in reply to these dispatches, gave Ursua many thanks, in the name of the King, for the important services he had rendered to the crown of Spain, ordered him to select the necessary number of men for the Garrison from those under his command, and to appoint the proper officer, at the same time sending him money for their maintenance. The commander immediately set about building a redoubt on one of the most elevated situations in Peten; he appointed captain José de Estenoz Governor, placing under his orders, together with the fort its artillery and provisions, the galliot with its captain, crew, and 25 soldiers: the king Canek, Quincanek the priest, and another relation of the King against whom some crimes had been clearly proved, he left as prisoners, under charge of Estenoz. The island of Peten was by this time sufficiently well peopled by the return of its former inhabitants: the three islands were all reduced to obedience: 18 villages had also submitted: the work on the road was proceeding and as the period of the rainy season was near at hand, Ursua determined to return with the troops to Campeachey.

In the early part of 1698 Ursua received letters from the vicar of Itza, which gave an account of Canek, Quincanek, and many others, having become converts, and received the sacrament of baptism. About the same time, Alonzo Garcia de Paredes arrived at Campeachy, on his return from Guatemala, and informed him the road that had been made from the lake to Verapaz was considerably too long and that the president wished another to be opened which should, if possible, be shorter and more direct; in compliance with this request, Ursua employed Pedro de Lubiaur, and the Pilot Antonio de Carabajal, with troops for their protection, to survey and mark out a nearer road to Verapaz; this they performed, making the distance from the lake to St. Augustin, one of the villages of Verapaz no more than 35 leagues.

About the same period, the Itzaes, in one night without any previous intimation of such design, suddenly abandoned the island leaving behind them only the 3 prisoners and 12 women. A few days afterward they came back again, but only the women consented to remain in it, most of whom became converts. On the 24th January this Year (1698), orders were again received from Spain by the Viceroy of Mexico, the Governor of Guatemala and the governor of Yucatan, for continuing all possible efforts to effect the conversion of the natives; and that they were to endeavour to settle some of them, by families, along the line of new road, in order to ensure, at convenient distances, sufficient accomodation for travellers. The King also communicated to Ursua his particular thanks for the zeal and application he had shewn in his arduous undertaking, and appointed him governor and captain-general over all the territory that might be acquired by opening the new road; he was to be subordinate to the Viceroy of New Spain, but independant of the governor of Yucatán which appointment was made public in the town of Campeachy in November the same year. Animated by these marks of royal favour, Ursua left Campeachy for Peten in January 1699 and there on the 11th Feby., he was received at the garrison by the troops and other persons with every demonstration of joy. In the beginning of January 4 officers and 200 soldiers set out from Guatemala; one division, under the command of Esteben de Medrano, marched for the village of Dolores; and another, under the commander in chief, took the route of Verapaz, for the Isla of Los Remedios. For this isle the governor sent also 8 missionaries, several armourers, blacksmiths, carpenters, bricklayers, caulkers, and other artisans; many Indian labourers, 25 families to be settled on such land as might be convenient, and also upwards of 1200 head of cattle and horses for the purpose of breeding. On the 14th of March, Martin de Ursua, with the governor and officers of the Garrison left the island, and advanced about a league on the main land to meet the two commanders; Medrano and Mencos; after an interchange of civilities, the whole party embarked on board the Galliot, and passed over to their island.

Here a contest of courtesy took place between the two generals, Ursua and Mencos, each wishing to serve under the order of the other, which was finally terminated by agreeing that they should issue the necessary orders conjointly.

A council of war was then held, in which it was resolved, that the town his Majesty had ordered to be built should be founded on the margin of the Lake; that a reinforcement of 30 men should be attached to the garrison, because there still remained 15 nations of Indians, to the eastward of Peten to be brought under subjection; that the new road marked out by Lubiaur should be completed and huts, bridges, and canoes, built; that 50 Indians should be retained to cultivate milpas, or corn lands, for the public service, until 40 families of domesticated Indians could be sent from Guatemala to be employed in raising Maize and pulse to supply the island.

After this council broke up, the two generals sent the Captain Juan Gonzalez, with a party of 12 soldiers, to look after the division that had marched for Dolores, and which ought to have joined the other party before this time; they did not arrive at Peten until the 1st of April, having lost their way, and wandered at random for 12 days.

Captain Cristobal de Mendia with 30 men was sent to the deserted isle of Alarri; Captain Marcelo Flores with his company to the territory of the Coboxes; Captain Marcos de Albos had previously been sent out with a foraging party to collect maize, as had the Alferer Juan Guerrero with 40 soldiers for Tochemacal. All these officers received orders to use every endeavour to bring in the Indians who had retired to the mountains, or to persuade them if possible, to return to their villages, and in fact great numbers were by their diligence and industry prevailed upon to resume their former habitations. After these operations it was resolved, as the health of the troops began to be impaired, to retire from the territory for the present; another council was held to appoint a commander of the fort, the Soldiers that were to remain in garrison, and for the arrangement of other affairs. The different companies then commenced their march for Guatemala, taking the same routes by which they had arrived; general Mencos followed them with the company of Marcos de Avalos, to whom were also delivered the prisoners Canek, now called after his conversion Don José Pablo Canek, his son, and his cousin, who had, as it was presumed, instigated the Indians to their recent flight. After these departures, general Ursua and his troops set out on their return to Yucatan.

At Peten there remained Juan Francisco Cortés, as governor, judge of the province, and commandant of the garrison; Bernardo Guerrero, captain of the galliot; a surgeon, armorer, carpenter, and other mechanics; the ecclesiastical vicar, Pedro de Morales; Diego

Rivas and four ecclesiastics; 14 families of Spaniards, some Indian servants, and the Indian labourers employed in cultivating the milpas.

Soon after the arrival of Ursua at Campeachy, Don Roque Sobranis, the governor, died; and he succeeded him as captain-general and governor of Yucatán; to which he also united the government of Itza. Melchor Mencos arrived safely at Guatemala with his prisoners, who excited much interest among the inhabitants of that city, and were lodged at the residence of Mencos; how they were finally disposed of is unknown, as the history of Villagutierre terminates with their arrival. There is no doubt but that the reduction of the Itzas was completed, as, in the year 1759 there were in the district of Peten 7 villages, besides the chief place, which was served by 5 curates.

The villages now in existence, besides the town of Peten are San Bonito, San Andres and San Jose situated on the margin of the lake— Dolores, San Toribio, Chichachan, Santa Anna, Sacluc, and one or two smaller. The whole population does not amount to 7,000. On the opposite side of the hills which rise above San Andres, the river San Pedro takes its rise, and flows into the Utsumasinta. A short time before we arrived in Peten a gentleman who had brought a quantity of goods from Belize to sell to the natives, proceeded by this river to the Utsumasinta. Colonel Galindo formerly Commandante of the district in a letter to Mr. Evans of Belize says that he descended the Rio San Pedro to the Utsumasinta.

The Rio de la Passion also passes through a part of the Peten district, at no great distance from the lake, and according to Juarros, is navigable, as the Lacandon Indians who dwell upon its margin, formerly carried on a trade with Guatemala by this river. The road to Guatemala from Peten crosses this river where it is 50 or 60 yards broad and having a depth of 10 feet.

The morning after our arrival, I was up with the sun, having had a night's rest without even hearing the hum of a mosquito, a luxury we had not known since we left Belize—in fact for a much longer period as the latter place is the very hotbed of flies. The night was

86

quite cool enough to make me feel the necessity of a blanket; and the morning was chilly although the sun was rising over the mountains in all the splendour with which it only graces a tropical landscape. I observed the early risers moving about in their chimonas, their dress requires something over it of a cold morning, for it only consists of a pair of cotton drawers made very loose, and fastened round the waist with a drawing string, and a shirt of the same material worn outside the drawers. This is the every day attire with few exceptions of both high and low. We commenced marketting for our people, as well as ourselves, and found provisions exceedingly cheap. The beef and pork was cut completely from the bone, into long ribbons, this they rub over with salt—when required for keeping—and hang it in the sun to dry. In this state they call it Tasajo. We bought about three pounds of fresh beef or pork for one Rial—sixpence halfpenny sterling. A turkey of goodly size for 3 Rials, fowls one and two rials. Rice of the country, very good, was one rial for a measure which contained nearly three half pints. Vegetables such as plantains, maize, chilis &c were very cheap. Salt was the most expensive auxiliary to the culinary department, in consequence of the distance from which it is brought to Peten, either from Campeachy or Belize, but seldom from the latter. A small measure scarcely more than sufficient for one day's consumption for two or three people cost a Medio or half a rial—so that if you were to use the epithet of "you are not worth your salt" to a Petenero, at least to many of them, it might be taken as complimentary, and make them believe themselves of greater value than they actually are.

We were visited by all the principal inhabitants during the day—and were asked to a dance which the Commandante gave in order to introduce us to the fair Denizens of Flores.

Not to be too great a tax upon the hospitality of Ozeta we had prepared a dinner for ourselves, but about the middle of the day, we had a message requesting to know what hour we dined; and at the appointed hour an excellent meal consisting of a variety of savoury dishes was sent down from the Commandante, who also paid us the compliment of sending his two sons, boys of 12 and 14 to wait on us.

Soon after dark we prepared for the "gay and festive scene," which was to take place in the Alcaldia; and having stumbled over the loose stones of the neglected streets, which were once paved, but at present in sad state of disrepair, we came to the place of entertainment, an apartment that in the same morning had been anything but a place of entertainment to the unfortunates who had been brought up for political delinquencies, and were now listening to the noise of mirth and sound of music at the bars of the windows of the Carcel.[16] The ceremony of introduction was soon over, the person who acted as master of the ceremonies was a very facetious fellow by name Mendoza Mendez who held the office of Secretario del Gobierno[17] and Collector of the Revenue and appeared the best informed person we had as yet met with.

The dress of the Ladies was exceedingly simple, "half naked, natural" but not quite. It consisted of a chemizette of nearly transparent Cambric or fine lawn, with short sleeves, low in front, the whole being in narrow pleats. It was embroidered round the top, and at the bottom of the sleeves, and was the only covering to the body as far as the waist, from whence extended a gaudy coloured petticoat of printed calico, or embroidered muslin, white cotton stockings—silk ones are almost unknown—and shoes made from some gay coloured silk. The hair was drawn back from the forehead and hung in one long plait down the back, the end being tied with a bow of gay ribbon—a tortoise shell comb with a gold, or gilt band, embracing the whole of the back part of the head from ear to ear, and having large losenge shaped imitations of precious stones set in it. The young Ladies of Peten generally carry their dowries round their necks, in the shape of a necklace of coral intermixed with small gold coins from one to four dollar pieces—so that in a Tete a Tete one may make a tolerably nice calculation of the amount likely to be derived from under going the ceremony of having your hands joined together at the Hymnical altar by the Padre, who will take precious good care to exact as many of the gold pieces from the necklace as he possibly

[16] Jail.
[17] Secretary of Government.

88

can. There was not much beauty present, although there were some fine girls. They have generally speaking good figures, exceedingly well formed busts and arms, which from the simple nature of the dress admits of no deception. The music consisted of a marimba, a violin, and a drum. The dances were principally Fandangos and what they call "Arrabis" a sort of jig danced with a shuffling step. They also went through a sort of romping dance called "El Toro"—a lady and gentleman stand up, the latter holding a handkerchief by two corners which he whisks about as a sort of provocation as he advances in bravado stile, and retreats again dragging one end of the handkerchief on the ground before his partner in an enticing manner, in order to make her advance, which she does slowly at first, until at last it becomes a sort of race, the lady endeavouring to stop her partner with a backward movement, not exceedingly delicate, and very far from graceful. If she succeeds, another partner tries his agility, and so on until every one is satisfied that the young lady is perfect in her retrograde movements and fully qualified for the "Toro."

We tried a waltz. (It appeared odd that they knew nothing of the Waltz as they were all of Spanish descent), and several of the young ladies took to the step immediately, and having whistled one or two simple waltzes to the Marimba player he very soon played them without missing a note. About 11 o'clock refreshments were spread consisting of cold fowls, meat pies, fish, tarts and dulces.[18] The drinkables were different liqueurs the foundation of which was aguardiente having different names. I was asked to partake of some "Sangre de Virgen"[19] which was not bad. About 2 o'clock the company retired to their respective homes. When we left the scene of the night's amusement we were not a little surprised to find part of the ragged army patrolling the streets, and afterwards learned that, they were placed by Ozeta to prevent a rising of the opposite party which he understood was to take place during the time when the others were engaged tripping on the light fantastic and consequently would be least prepared for this outbreak and also that we were to have joined the

[18] Sweets, or desserts.
[19] "Blood of the Virgin."

insurgents with our auxiliary forces consisting of two officers, one N.C. officer in the person of our Interpreter, and four rank and file. What an opportunity for an aspirant to military renown! Carambo!! Falstaffe's ragged army was a force to this, Bombastes Furioso[20] never appeared upon the stage more appropriately attended than he might have been by these Petenero Soldados. Fancy a lot of meager looking Mestizados and Indians in cotton drawers, and shirt over them, straw Sombreros of a variety of shapes and sizes, black or tanned leather cross belts, muskets many without locks, and the barrels tied into their stocks with string. There were about two or three hundred of these fellows gathered together in consequence of the late revolution in Guatemala under Carrera, who had superseded Segourra, and placed Ozeta in command of the Peten district. It was a bloodless change, the former starting for Belize with a few followers, leaving his children to care for their grandmother, and sending his wife to Campeachy. Ozeta scarcely feels himself secure, and was suspicious of our movements and intentions for a few days—but in that time became quite satisfied that the reports he had heard that the ex-Commandante was returning from Belize with assistance from the Superintendent, were false. (Heard of the death of Carnick.)

The Commandante having business to perform at one of the Pueblo's on the margin of the lake requested we would accompany him; accordingly a tolerably large party, all males, started in the before mentioned ill constructed and incommodious canoes, having chairs placed in them for our accomodation, our canoe proceeded in advance with the Marimba and drummer beating away as if for life and death. After about an hour and a half's exceeding slow work we disembarked at the village of San Andre, picturesquely situated on the margin of the Lake on rocky ground composed of very fine lime-stone. The houses were on an equality with those of Peten, with the exception of one which was decidedly the best looking and largest we had seen. We found it was a holiday dedicated to the Patron Saint of one of the Towns people, and were requested to attend the procession,

---

[20] Chief character in a satirical play of the same name by William Barnes Rhodes, first produced in England in 1810.

so we accompanied the Commandante to the house of the individual, where we saw a figure of the Virgin dressed up in a ludicrous mode, placed on a temporary altar having for its background a printed Calico, stuck over with scraps of tinsel and miserable woodcuts of sacred subjects. This figure was carried on the small table by two men through the street preceded by the marimba and drum and followed by all the rag tag and Bobtail of the town to the Church which stood on an eminence at the other extremity of the town. The Virgin was placed on the altar where a few dip candles threw a dubious light "a dim religious light" would be malapropos—around a place resembling a shocking bad barn, and having some awfully grotesque figures of clay variously clad, meant to represent saints. A figure bearing a cross intended for our Saviour was a shocking burlesque. After prayers performed by the padre, a jolly looking fat mulatto and a chant accompanied by the marimba, maroons[21] were fired at the door of the church, and the saint was reconducted to the house under her peculiar care. The prayers were no sooner ended than the Cura took a Puro from his ample pocket and lighting it by one of the candles of the altar proceeded to puff away as if it had been part of the ceremony—we were introduced to him but did not find him very intelligent.

We were invited to return to the Casa, whose Patron Saint had been thus glorified, to partake of a feast prepared for the occasion and which was ready on our arrival, it consisted of a variety of edibles. Fish dressed in two or three ways, fowls stewed with vegetables containing a quantity of garlic, a sort of soup which they called "caldo" placed in basins round the table—everyone taking a sup as they pleased. The never failing frijoles and a variety of other dishes. We had silver forks served to us and an enormous "cucharro"[22] which would have graced the hand of the nerviest pig sticker in the country. Our friends held the forks in thorough contempt, making use of the Tortillas to scoop their victuals into their mouths, which they did in a

[21] Fireworks.

[22] Probably *cuchillo* (knife) is meant, since it would suit a pig sticker far better than a *cuchara* (spoon).

most dextrous manner. The drinkables were compounds having Aguardiente as a groundwork; we partook of a cooling drink made of ground maize mixed in water sweetened with an addition of an essence distilled either from orange flowers or something very similar in flavour—it was an exceedingly pleasant tipple.

Home made Puros and Segaritos were handed round, the tobacco from which they were made was very fine-flavoured but being new was rather strong. We visited during the afternoon several of the families living at San Andre, one the brother-in-law of Ozeta, whom he had made Alcalde, I believe contrary to the wishes of the greater part of the inhabitants who had the right of an election. We also visited the Croesis of the village a man who had actually grown rich by his own industry and was in consequence a sort of phenomenon among these "far niente"[23] folks; he was the owner of the Casa Grande which we took notice of on our first entrance to the town and also the father of a very fine girl who sat in Indian style on a mat on the floor with two or three companions one of which was the prettiest girl we had yet seen. Her features were classically beautiful and she might have personified Lalla Rookh, large gaselle like eyes, shaded by the longest and most jetty black lashes, with very white teeth and although her long black hair was drawn back from the forehead and hung down her back in one plait, a most trying mode of dressing it, as it requires decided beauty to set it off—it was very becoming to her—her figure was light and graceful with most aristocratic proportioned hands and feet. Indian blood evidently flowed in her veins. She was the only female we had seen who at all put us in mind of the description of the Mexican women given by the first conquerors of the country. She was married to the son of Croesis who was absent at the Trapechy or sugar works—may she live for a thousand years. The owner of the house was a white man, a Creole, his mother an ancient dame, was a Spaniard, she was dressed rather fantastically and had the remains of beauty; we were told she was a great gambler and exceedingly fortunate. The young ladies sang, accompanied on the guitar by one of our party.

[23] "Little nothing" (Italian).

92

It appears this visit on the part of Ozeta was one of Policy, as Croesis was of opposite party, and a great friend of Segaurras. We heard the latter spoken of as anything but honest in his dealings and a ruse of his to obtain dollars or an equivalent was rather good—if true—Finding his exchequer rather attenuated, and becoming more meagre every day, he hit upon the following expedient—calling upon a few friends who were not rich, he let them into his council telling them that the only means he had to draw the "Burzas" from those who held them, was to call a meeting of all the principal people and tell them that the state required a certain sum of money which must be made up in some way or other, as the exchequer was empty; and that after some considerable argument to prove their poverty and incapability to give much, they were to make an offer of so many head of cattle, of course naming considerably more than they could give, but that these would not be taken from them, but their offers would act as an inducement to the rich—who are generally proud and ostentatious—to name more than had been tendered by their poorer neighbours. This succeeded admirably and a considerable sum made its way into the hands of the Receiver General, whether it was ever applied for the purposes of the state was a matter of opinion.

After lounging about from one house to another, lolling in hammocks and accepting cigaritos from the lips of the Señoritas we adjourned to the Alcaldia where a dance was got up but which proved rather a failure—however a supper was prepared by the donor of the mornings feast, of which we all partook drinking the memory of his Patron Saint in "Silencia Solemna" as our facetious friend Mendoza Mendes called it—who begged he might be allowed to propose the health of the Queen of England which was responded to by a volly of "Vivas" that rather astonished the natives. After an hours conviviality, hammocks were swung in the room we had danced in & in two adjoining ones, to the number of about 20 and we lay down as we were, with the exception that each had a sigar in his mouth and a sort of independent sleep was kept up, first one and then another giving sonorous nasal evidence of his having successfully wooed the somnolent deity—nevertheless a constant chatter was going on during the whole night, as one awoke and happened to find another with his sigar nearly out and on the point of throwing the end from him he would ask for a light, which ended in a long conversation much to the edification of those who were not quite so wide awake.

The next morning we returned to Peten where preparations were making for Christmas; we went round several times with the processions and entered the houses where altars were dressed up to receive the figure of the Virgin Mary dressed in white muslin & pink ribbons, which was carried through the streets and into those houses; being placed on the altar and a chant enacted, and so on, to every house so decorated for her reception. Some of these altars were very tastefully arranged, being formed of evergreens, flowers, fruits and even vegetables—the only incongruity was the introduction of a number of trumpery little figures of clay and wax, a few daubs of gold leaf amongst natures choicest flowers, and some execrable prints. I pointed this out to our friend Mendez, how exceedingly out of keeping these articles were with the natural beauty of the flowers and fruits, which he was aware of, but as he said, Las Pinturas were considered by the natives as rare productions of the arts.

The church of "Our Lady of Sorrows" was rather out of repair, a part of the roof having fallen in, and the poverty of the people pleaded as an excuse for its having remained so for a considerable time. In a Catholic community if the church is neglected, the inhabitants must be poor indeed, for the zealous padres have the task of securing the wherewithal for contingencies from the pockets of their Parishioners. Somehow or other they always have the female portion of the community as their most strenuous supporters. For the Christmas festivities their edifice was decorated with a profusion of flowers &c but the burlesque figures again interfered to mar natures choice gifts—and an addition of some dozen skulls ranged on a shelf in a recess grinning through the rich foliage gave a savageness to the scene.

We did not attend on Christmas night but were invited to witness a rehearsal of the ceremonies, with the exception of mass, in a private house which was that of the ex-Commandante but I fear I cannot

94

convey a most distant idea of the Travestie of a sacred subject. The actors in the Piece, "The birth of Christ and the adoration of the Shepherds" were boys and girls from eight to fourteen years of age. The Virgin was seated on a raised chair, in an interesting condition and retired behind a sort of Procinium, soon returning with a huge wax doll in her arms, and reseated herself, when a number of boys and girls dressed out as shepherds and shepherdesses came from the rear of each side of the Procinium in two rows proceeding down the room—each pair joining hands at the bottom dancing up to the Virgin, each making a short harang presenting at the same time their offerings. A Buffoon came last in the procession, and after going through some antics, expressed his regret that his poverty prevented his making any suitable offering, but begged her acceptance of some Tobacco to make Puros from. It lasted some time as there was a good deal of chanting, and skirmishing in and out from behind the Procinium. After the ceremony was over, Fandangos, waltzes &c occupied the remainder of the night, with the exception of a short interlude of Liqueurs and dulces.

A few days after our arrival in Peten a party of Blacks who had taken part in the late Revolution—as they termed it—were captured in the woods by some of the Soldados who were sent in search of them by Ozeta, one man being killed and another old fellow having a buck shot lodged in his throat just beneath the skin and as I had been practicing upon the natives who took me for a medico from the circumstance of my having a small medicine chest from which I had administered a few doses of Quinine and simple medicine to several. I offered to cut the shot out for him, which might have been done with exceeding small surgical knowledge or dexterity, however the old gentleman declined and he went about for some days with it hanging in a sort of bag which its weight had formed from his loose and wrinkled skin.

We saw several of the blacks have their fetters rivetted on them in the street opposite the Alcaldia, after undergoing an examination—one of them was a most forbidding looking fellow who stood about 6 feet 4 inches in height, a runaway from Belize after committing some crime and breaking out of jail—he re-christened himself by the name of Marcelino and headed a rising of the Blacks of San Bonito before this last revolution & they were actually in possession of Peten. San Bonito is inhabited almost entirely by a Black population of run-away negroes from Belize, who made their escape during the time slavery was the Law of the land, all of them having committed mis-demeanors and some even having committed murder. There were also one or two deserters from the West India Reg't. however they kept aloof, and we saw nothing of them being afraid we might have them apprehended. Most of these Blacks are married to half casts or Indian women of pure blood.

My honorary post of Medico, which was thrust upon me by the persons I had administered to, occasionally caused me a degree of amusement, as I was consulted upon some delicate cases for which I was obliged to decline prescribing—particularly in the case of the young lady whom we met at the Hacienda—whose Father an elderly person was my first patient. I found him suffering from a severe aguish cold, which the inhabitants term "Frio" and I gave him a brace of No. 1 Pills, ordered him to bed, & to be well drenched with gruel made from ground Indian corn—the next day when I saw him he was much better, and was laying under a pile of Chimarros[24] with the perspiration oozing from every pore; on the following day he was up, and I was obliged to undergo the ceremony of being hugged first by himself, then by the old lady and by half a dozen daughters in succession—the latter I did not mind—but I have an abomination to a male hug.

I was requested to visit a young man who was too ill to come to me, I went accompanied by our interpreter and found an emaciated creature lolling in a hammock evidently in the last stage of decline— he had the brightest eyes I ever saw, there was a wild glare in them, an uneasy restlessness that made me feel uncomfortable every time they turned toward me—and his voice was almost inaudible from a huskiness that appeared most distressing. He was suffering moreover

[24] Poncho-like garments, usually quite thick, which served as protection from the elements, bed coverings, and, in this case, as an aid in sweating out colds.

Plate 11. *A pen-and-ink sketch by Caddy of the expedition's camp in the Palace at Palenque. Compare with Caddy's finished drawing of the same room (Plate 14).*

Plate 12. *View of Palenque.*

from an incurable issue in his cheek. I was sorry I could do nothing for him. His unfortunate mother, whose only child he was, stood with her arms folded listening with melancholy anxiety to the questions which were put to him, sometimes answering for him. She seemed conscious that human aid was now unavailing, and that a few days of suffering was all he had to look forward to on this side of the grave. I left the house of sorrow regretting his untimely fate; when my Interpreter informed me, that this young man not a year since had been one of the handsomest of the Petenero youth and had been desperately in love with a Señorita of the place, who had played him false. Jealousy took possession of his mind, and watching an opportunity sheathed his knife in the heart of his rival—since which he had gradually sunk under disease and become the object he now was. If remorse for his crime was the cause of his sad state, he was more severly punished than if the laws of the country had been acted upon and had made him a just sacrifice to their violation. But in Peten the murderer stalks abroad, the greatest crimes go unpunished while more petty delinquencies fill the court with Prisoners. Its present fullness was caused by Political offences. If a man was, or even supposed to be inimical to the dominant party "remache"[25] was the word and he was placed in durance vile. However I must do Ozeta the justice to say, that I think he was exceedingly mild in his treatment of his captives. He asked us what punishment he should award to Marcelino who had led the blacks and had been the cause of the death of one of his party. We told him that in England he would have been hanged, and that it might do good to make an example of such a wretch as he was. He contented himself however by having him well secured and kept in prison.

We had rather a laughable scene brought about by the fears of one Don Miguel Gueves, who was a great partizan of Segourra's and who came to our abode tolerably early one morning, and remained there all day, giving evident signs of uneasiness—asking many questions on the subject of imprisonment, one whether it was not the law of nations that when a person placed himself under the protection of a

[25] "Clap him in irons."

consul, he was not liable to apprehension from his own government—evidently fancying we were delegates of some sort or other, particularly when he saw our Passport which was drawn out on Parchement with a large seal attached. He kept fidgeting about, looking out every now and then from the door, not at all at his ease. We discovered afterwards that a letter of his to Segourra had been intercepted by the Commandante which was not couched in words that the latter could mistake as complimentary to himself—he was not imprisoned while we remained in Peten. He made a present of a pair of wild turkeys, to be sent to Belize for Colonel MacDonald. The male bird was a superb creature, with the most brilliant plumage. These and the young tiger which had become so tame that we could handle and play with it without any danger of a bite or a claw were to be left until we returned.

The ordinance department of Peten was a very small establishment. It consisted of four small brass Field Pieces 4 pdrs. of Spanish make, mounted on carriages made by some Petenero carpenters and were of novel construction half Garrison and half field carriages. They fired a salute on Christmas day, and at every discharge the guns hopped out of the Trunnion holes, having no cap-squares, to the distance of four or five feet, and were again lifted into their places by main force for the next round. I was obliged to satisfy the Commandante's curiosity by putting muskets in the hands of our four men and making them go through the manual & Platoon exercise in order to show our mode, with which he was much pleased as it was essentially different to theirs and was not quite so independent of unison of movement.

The habits of the Peteneros are decidedly idle—to a degree that is nearly incredible—and the country favours this natural disposition as with little trouble the teeming earth yields abundantly every tropical vegetable. Maize or Indian corn, which is their principal support, grows luxuriantly yielding two crops in the year—from this they make their Tortillas. The corn is par boiled in lime water in order to denude it of its skin, and is then ground into a paste & made into thin flat cakes and baked, very partially on an iron plate. The mode of grinding is most primative and the same used by the Mexicans before the conquest without the slightest difference.

A stone of about 18 inches long by a foot broad with legs to it, made so as to have a slope of about an inch in the length, with another stone like a rolling pin is the whole of the apparatus—a handfull of the steeped corn is placed on this, and is rolled or rather ground into a pulp, adding a little water if required to give it the necessary consistency. This work is generally performed by the young women, who have almost invariably finely shaped arms, whether in consequence of this healthful excercise I cannot say. They are to be eat as hot as one can swallow them, or they lose their lightness. Plantains, Bananas, Yams, Sweet Potatoe, Cassada or Manihot, rice several descriptions of beans and many other vegetables grow spontaneously, but with the Tortilla & Friholes or Black bean the leguminous desires of the Peteneros are quite satisfied, and they take little trouble to raise any other. The fruits are numerous and good, pine apples, oranges, shaddock and forbidden fruit with a variety of plum, the guava and in fact nearly all tropical fruits are abundant without culture.

There are many valuable natural productions that might be gathered to advantage were it not for the distance they would have to be transported to a market, and are therefore useless except for the wants of the inhabitants. Several gums & balsams, copal, capiricio, and amber, and it is stated that the gumarabic is also to be met with— besides sarsparilla, vanilla, cochineal, achiote or armetto, indigo, brasil wood, logwood, cocoa, coffee, & cotton, tobacco—most of these are scarcely cultivated at all.

The great drawback to this fine country is the want of good roads or navigable rivers which would enable the inhabitants to take their produce to market, and I have not a doubt that if these could be made available a stimulant would be given that would arouse the natives from the apparent lethargy which now hangs over them; and by a more frequent communication with Belize, they would find that with a little energy and industry they could add materially to their household comforts, which at present are in the lowest possible scale.

The mechanical arts are limited in the extreme. There is a blacksmith who also does work as silversmith and jeweller mending the ladies earrings and ornaments in a very blacksmithlike manner. A carpenter who manufactures his boards by splitting a tree with wedges and then with an axe fines them down to any thickness he may require. The great trade in Peten is that of Zapatero, shoe or mocassin maker—all the principal townspeople are Zapateros, it seems the fashionable business. Ozeta himself was one, and they say handled his awl and last with much ability. But he had aspirations of a higher nature, and considered the Patron Saint of his calling, the doughty St. Crispen, as too low a cast for him, the consequence was he gave up the business connected with leather and Prunella and took to Politics, paying a visit to head Quarters, Guatemala, and got appointed Commandante of the district by Carrera, whose opinions of liberty he very much admired. I have given a description of one primitive aparatus in the shape of a mill—there is another by means of which all the Aguardiente of the country is made—the only description of Stil in use. It consists of a large earthenware jar of native manufacture having a large mouth supported so as to allow of a fire being made beneath it—this is rather more than half filled with the fermented liquor. A vessel or pan as large as can be admitted into the jar is then suspended with strings above the liquor and a cover is put on and closed in with clay. The spirit falls into this pan which when nearly full is emptied, and so on until the whole has evaporated.

We were detained in Peten some time longer than we intended, from one circumstance or another—but on the 4th of January we were enabled to start hiring mules from an arriero who brought some cargos of salt to Peten from Rios as they call all the towns high up the Utsumasinta. We met with Bartlet, an Englishman—or as he styled himself an English Irishman, being born at Liverpool of Irish parents—domiciled in this place, having taken to himself a bucksome looking Meztitzo, whom he had married, and had neat cottage with a small garden attached on the Island and on the margin of the Lake. He was anxious to go with us to Rios where he had been before, in order to get work as he had been living in Peten for some time and had got very considerably into the idle habits of the Peteneros. We asked him if he intended to take his better half with him, he answered not, that he had only married her because he wanted somebody to keep house for him and that he never intended to take her across the lake. This was rather affectionate certainly—however we promised he should accompany us as Deputy Assistant Interpreter.

⋪{In Belize, nothing had been heard of the explorers since the arrival of the pitpans in late November. The *Belize Advertiser* of January 4 expressed The Settlement's concern: "Since notifying the return of the Pit-pans, in which those two enterprising gentlemen embarked for a visit to Palenque, with spirits, ambitious for scientific research and well worthy of enlightened minds, we have received no intelligence of their progress; a circumstance that might be brought about by the season of the year or the state of roads seldom traversed," following this with a lengthy and ponderous discussion of theories propounded by visitors to Maya sites concerning the peopling of the New World. Had the people of Belize known of the expedition's sojourn in Flores, their fears might well have been more for the depletion of funds and less for the safety of the intrepid explorers.}⋪

Our preparations being made and a few presents of combs & books distributed among those who had been civil to us, we embarked for San Bonito accompanied by Ozeta & all the Principal Inhabitants of Peten, where after sending on our luggage to Sacluc we took a most affectionate leave of them having to undergo a hug from each—and mounting our mules we were once more en route retracing our road to Chichachan on which we met one of our female friends of the Hacienda at that place returning to Peten—and as the part of the road where we met was ankle deep in mud, we embraced "a cheval" and parted. We took up our old quarters in the Casa real for the night and next morning made a detour on the Savannahs to visit some extensive cattle estates. At one of which "Espague" we remained to pass the day with the family, some of whom we had met in Peten. This was almost the only place where we saw an attempt at ornamental gardening and poor as it was, it gave the place a more comfortable appearance, and several large rose bushes in full blow in front of the house gave me great pleasure to behold. Their name was Pinello—they were white creoles and were one of the first families in the district—and dated their origin as far back as the early Spanish settlers of the country. There were several brothers and some more distant ramifications of the family tree located on the Hacienda or in its immediate neighbourhood. They had at one time possessed very considerable property in cattle, but complained of having been robbed by Segourra to a great extent. We were received very kindly and were made as comfortable as their mode of living permitted. A very good dinner was provided and we were surprised that the females did not join us at our meal as although this has hitherto been the case, we expected that in an old family house it would have been different, however, they attended to our wants and kept up a relay of snow white hot Tortillas, which from habit we now relished. We were obliged to lounge about and do nothing but smoke segars, speak exceedingly bad Spanish to the Señoritas, or hold a "talky, talky" through our Interpreters with the Dons. Throughout this country where the people are completely removed from what is termed civilized life, it is astonishing what natural good breeding exists—you seldom meet a vulgar person.

The next morning we started for Sacluc, our road being over Savanah the whole distance. Here we found our baggage which we had forwarded from Peten. We put up in a House belonging to the Padre and used by him on his periodical visits. We went to a dance in the evening got up for us; there was a very small muster of females and those not very attractive. We attended an evening service in the Church, a small thatched building, having two bells hung in an arch in one of the gables, to which the bellman ascended by a ladder, and kept up such a din that we were roused out of our hammocks. The congregation were all females, and the service was chanted by the aforesaid Bellman, who was a pluralist of the first water, holding also the offices of Sacristan and Sexton. The altar was dressed out with flowers &c and most of the lights were lamps made of egg shells stuck in clay to make them steady and filled with grease with a bit of raw cotton drawn through a piece of light wood as a float. The next morning we were aroused by a drummer going round the square of the village, beating away at a great rate—and on enquiry we found that a plot against Ozeta's life had been discovered, and an order had come to the Alcaldi to send as many people into Peten as he could muster—however the drum had caused a contrary effect to what was intended—the Indians decamping to the woods directly they heard it. We saw one detachment march off, they were nearly all drunk and were armed mostly with bows and arrows, the heads of the latter being made of obsidian. A few had fowling pieces. One fellow, a mulatto from Belize, was exceedingly pot valiant, and swore by "Gorramity" he "kill dem all hiseff." After their departure no others appearing, the Alcaldi sent invitations round to say that he was going to have a dance, in consequence of which many repaired to the Casa real where they were to their astonishment shut up and sentries placed over them to prevent their escaping. The Alcaldi himself was drunk as a lord. I made an agreement with a person living here, to collect me as much Indian Rubber—or as they call it Tounou and Oolee which he said could be procured for about a Rial a pound—as he could get together, and also specimens of the different Gums.

We were detained another day in consequence of rain, having remained one, under a pretense made by our arriero that the provisions were not ready. However we found that there was a Lady in the case & master Jose Maria, was something like the sailor who had a wife in every Port. It was as much as we could do to get him away on the third day after our arrival. 11th January, 1840 left Sacluc. Our Provisions were at last pronounced in a state to keep for our journey and consisted of Bastamente Tortillas dried in the sun—about a hundred yards of dried beef, Tasajo—some Pork and sausages—thus provided we started on the morning of the 11th. The first part of our journey was over a splendid Savannah, rich in beautiful wild flowers, and clumps of trees interspersed over the plain, as if they had been placed to give a Picturesque effect. The hills on these plains are irregular & present a curious geological feature, one would almost imagine them the work of art instead of being a freak of Dame Nature. They are conical hills of loose limestone jutting out abruptly from the level Savannah, and covered from base to summit with beautiful trees—and are like an encampment when you come among them; although at a distance they have all the appearance of combination; but each cone is separate & stands alone and except at these spots you will not meet with a stone for miles.[26]

At the entrance of the mountain pass we came upon an encampment of Ozeta's volunteers guarding against an approach by this path. After holding a confab with them for a short time we again plunged into the depths of the Forest—its cool shade was most refreshing after the burning heat of the plain. We overtook a party of negroes hired by Jose to cut logwood who had started the day before and had been obliged to halt in consequence of the illness of one of the party.

We encamped at night, building our huts in the same manner we had done in the Belize path, and started as early as possible in the morning. At about 10 miles distance from Sacluc, we came to the borders of an extensive lake. We descended a high bank and discussed over breakfast, or rather lunch on its margin, slaking our thirst from its waters which were not of the most limpid kind, but sweet & with the addition of a small quantity of Aguardiente made a very passable beverage. It appeared about 7 or 8 miles broad.

The country thro' which we passed for ten successive days, was primeaval forest alternate hill and valley, some of the hills steep and rocky—the bottoms rich black mould into which our horses sunk above their knees—which made it most fatiguing: added to this the path was much obstructed by fallen trees some of them of large dimensions. It is surprising how they manage to fall at all, supported as they are by the strong vines which are twisted and knotted round their trunks and among their branches from tree to tree, occasionally descending to the earth and taking root, acting as stays to a huge mast—however they do frequently fall without any apparent cause their roots tearing up the earth for yards.

---

[26] From this description, it sounds very much as though Walker and Caddy had come upon a Maya ceremonial center in ruins. With a picture of buildings fixed firmly in their minds, the two might well have mistaken the remains of a temple for a "conical hill."

We saw abundance of the Vanilla (Epidendrum Vanilla) vine which grows in wild luxuriance in these wilds; it is easily cultivated, as a short slip planted at the foot of a tree takes root and requires little care except to prevent its being choked up by other creepers until it has attained some height, when it will bear after the third year and continue to do so for 30 or 40 years.

There were also many gum trees called by the natives "naked Indian" from the colour of the smooth shining bark resembling the skin of an Indian. They say it is the Copal and certainly has the appearance of that gum. It is not soluble in water but partially so in Aguardiente—the strongest alcohol we had to try it with—& burns with a strong resinous smell. It oozes from the tree slowly in drops, very transparent at first, but becomes of a dull yellowish white after being exposed to the influence of the atmosphere for a few hours.

Our arriero Jose Maria had several dogs with him, one an enormous fellow whose "head was hung" "With ears that swept away the morning dew"; "Crook-knee'd, and dew lapp'd, like Thessalian bulls" whose deep base voice roused us from our soundest slumbers on several occasions—Jose declared he never barked unless he snift Tigers, and whenever this was the case, the whole of the "Perros" came barking and cringing among the people in the hut we were told that it frequently occurs that the Tiger will watch his opportunity—when sleep has overtaken the weary traveller and he swings in his hammock suspended between two trees, wrapped in his Chimarro with his faithful dog crouching under him—and seize his prey in an instant. They have even gone into the tucker huts and carried them away where several people have been sleeping. It is stated that seven men travelling in company were destroyed in this pass some few years since by these animals, which although sworn to most lustily by Jose and his people, I took the liberty of doubting—a single person, or perhaps two, might have gone down—but seven! We found Jose a most active fellow, and his culinary proficiency was great, his mode of dressing a Curacoa, or Qualm, was rather apician—Mrs. Glass[27] would say "Take your Bird"—sooner said than done, as we found

[27] Author of a famous eighteenth-century cookbook.

frequently much to the annoyance of our craving maws. However having killed one of the aforesaid Gallinaceous bipeds, and denuded it of its feathery apparel &c and by an anatomical process extracted all osseous particles, its interior was well stuffed with the savoury sausages redolent of garlic, and it then went through the process called "Pique au Lard" in the Gastronome Francais—put into a stew pan and cooked—this taken cold for breakfast was anything but unpalatable. The noise of the large black baboon at night is awful, you would fancy a herd of wild cattle were in full combat so loud is the roaring they make. They passed over our encampment one night and their noise was deafening—I fired several shots at these creatures but did not succeed in getting one down.

According to my usual custom, I always went as far ahead of our party as I could with the guide, and Jocko, in order to be as much out of the noise of the constant hooting of the arrieros "Macho! Macho! Mula! Carajo!"—with other less acceptable expressions which were sufficient to keep all the birds and beasts in the forest at a respectable distance—on one occasion my guide came to a dead halt and immediate retreat, pointing to the pathway and crying out "Serpiente, Serpiente." I dismounted and going forward a few yards I saw a most disgusting looking serpent about six feet long stretched in a gleam of sunshine directly in the path with his head towards us. I fired and killed the beast, cutting off his head—which I think was the ugliest I ever saw—leaving his body in the path. I disected it—the two fangs in use at the time were nearly an inch long, curved backwards, hollow with a slit about the 10th of an inch from the point upwards. Along the jaw on each side were six fangs in successive stages of perfection, the one next to that in use being almost as hard and perfect and the rest became softer as they were more distant—the roots entered a bag attached to the upper gum which on being opened contained a brownish matter—which passed thro' the tooth into the wound made by its bite—the head was very flat and broad and the body instead of tapering off gradually from the middle to the end of the tail had an abrupt decrease at about 8 inches from the extremity—

the back was very dark coloured streaked with black, belly a dirty lead colour with a yellowish tinge. [see Plate 8.]

My powder had become exceedingly damp, although I took every precaution, drying my guns well over the fire before loading, but it was next to impossible to prevent moisture getting to the nipples, brushing along through the wet bushes; the consequence was that I was often disappointed of a good shot from my gun missing fire and I was very nearly deprived of the satisfaction of killing the only wild turkcy, Pavo del Monte! I fell in with—as I snapped at it three times & was obliged to take a good deal of trouble to prick the nipples, insert fresh powder & crimp new caps, expecting every moment to lose sight of my bird, which was running along at a deuce of a pace & I after it, priming as I went along & exceedingly nervous, pricking my fingers, and nearly tumbling on my nose half a dozen times—at last I coaxed one of my barrels to go off taking a long shot with bristol blue, which made the fellow take wing, one of his legs hanging down, broken—he perched with his one leg on a tree from which I dislodged him with a second shot, and a crash through the underwood told well for qualities as an addition to our stock—his Plumage was magnificent and dressed, a la mode Jose Maria, was as gratifying to our gastro-nomic organs as the resplendent colouring of his feathers was to our organs of vision. We met with some Partridge but I did not get a shot at one, they are so very wild—They are nearly as large as a guinea fowl and resemble them a good deal. The rain fell in Torrents one night during our journey through this pass, and made us exceed-ingly uncomfortable, added to which the Warri ticks had so con-foundedly preyed upon me that my legs from the knee down were raw, causing great pain & constant irritation.

Poor Antonio was attacked with a violent pain in his back and made sad lamentations—he walked almost double—so we made an agree-ment that he should ride, one of our party giving up his horse for a day each—he had mine the first day and I walked but on the second he was likely to go without as there was no volunteer for padnagging but after a good deal of humbug and palaver one of the cargo horses was lightened and Antonio was placed on the top of the remaining baggage, how he escaped the fate of Absalom I can hardly comprehend, however the poor fellow in spite of dodging under bows from sundry hard jerks from the haulback, he was hauled off once or twice—and his general expression on making our resting place was "Oh Capin no use dis—I go dead for true"—poor fellow was regularly done up—Jose was obliged to perform an operation on him by opening a tumor in his thigh which gave him relief.

Our provisions were exhausted two days before we arrived at Tenosique & we had to eat broiled Curacoa without any bread or other substitute—Jose left us the night before our arrival & pushed on in order to get provisions and the next morning made his appearance on a fresh horse with well stuffed saddle bags to which we paid our respects. A few miles from Tenosique we passed a fine Lagoon, about 10 miles broad which appeared shallow—and a short distance from this we crossed the bed of a river that takes its rise in the Lagoon and flows into the Utsumasinta. Passing this river we fell in with five or six Indians quite naked—they had been hunting and had two or three Warri. We arrived at Tenosique about two o'clock and were saluted by the barking of some fifty curs, which caused the people to turn out of their huts to witness our entry into the village, and as Jose had given information that "dos Cabaleros Englis"[28] with retinue &c were travelling that way, they were at least anxious to pay us the compliment of staring at us—We proceeded to Jose's house where we were received by his wife, a dapper little half Indian who had evidently got herself up for the occasion by putting on her best toggery— We very soon made ourselves quite at home & after changing and performing our ablutions we visited the Alcaldi, armed with our Passport and found him measuring out liquor to some half drunk Indians—he kept a sort of shop if a counter could be called so, one end of which was occupied by sundry jars, bottles and measures, and the other with a few pieces of coarse cotton white & coloured, soap candles and a few &c. We found he was not inclined to be particularly civil, indeed his phiz was considerably against our being received in

[28] "Two English gentlemen."

a very cordial manner, and I must do him the credit to say that he did not even pay us a Spanish compliment and made some demur at our proceeding any farther—We wished him a good evening and returned to Jose's where we were soon delighted by preparations for a meal, whose savorship we augured well of from the odour which ever and anon was wafted by the gentle breeze from the cocinera to our olfactory nerves—It was soon on the table olla podrida—stewed fowls—Frijoles in such abundance that it put one in mind of Jack & the bean stalk and this washed down or rather kept down with a good glass of cherry brandy veritable Copenhagen—the best liquor we had tasted since the last of bottle of our Madeira was addressed to the health of the maids of the clear and rapid brook at Los Enquentros. Whilst reclining in our hammocks smoking native segars—not so bad either—we talked over the subject of the Alcaldi's non complaisant manner, and the steps to be taken should he refuse to let us proceed. We came to the determination to see him again in the morning and if he persisted in his determination, we should make an endeavour to go without his sanction—and so wishing him at old nick we composed ourselves to slumber.

Early in the morning I turned out to reconoitre and strolling through the village which is situated on a high bank overlooking the Utsumacinta, I came to the waters edge and looking up the river a beautiful scene presents itself. The river was still swollen by the recent rains and the water much discoloured, you could trace the river for many miles meandering thro' country overgrown with primeaval forest, except here and there where Ranchos were created and a patch cultivated. In the distance at about 50 miles—a range of mountains shut in the view to the southard—looking down the river to the northward you lose sight of it at a very short distance. The country appeared quite level, the banks were about 30 or 40 feet high—and thickly wooded. The village contains about 70 houses and a church, the latter a barnlike thatched building—the best of the houses were about the same as those of Peten. There are about 500 inhabitants. I startled a bevy of females, little indebted to manufactures for their costume. If "nature when unadorned is adorned the most," these nymphs were perfection. They gave a shout of "El Strangero" and turned their backs on me, as they could not get up the bank except by the path at the head of which I was brought up for a moment, but relieved them from their dilemma by proceeding in a different direction.

We visited the Alcaldi in the course of the day, and found a free and easy sort of fellow lounging in a hammock, to whom we were introduced as the Padre; entering into conversation with him on our intended proceeding to Palenque & mentioning that the Alcaldi had some scruples in permitting us to do so, at which he exclaimed "Como non, Carambo"[29] with a questioning look at the Alcaldi, who began a long story about orders from the Cabasera[30] &c so the Padre cut him very short, and settled we were to proceed to the Cabasera next morning, where he lived & would be very glad to see us. In consequence of which we hired small canoes, not being able to procure a large one, and started on the following morning—squeezing ourselves under a temporary awning made of hoops of bamboo thatched so low that we could scarcely sit up right although we were squatted on the bottom of the canoes. We launched into the noble stream which is here about ½ a mile broad and at the rate of about five miles an hour dropped down to the Cabasera where we found a civil Alcaldi, a very young man, and also a Prefecto—we went to the house of a don somebody or other, who unluckily for us was away from home, or we were given to understand we should have been entertained "en Primer." A house was procured for us by the Alcaldi next to his own, which consisted of but one apartment with a kitchen attached. Our friend the Padre came to us directly he heard we had arrived, and a merrier fellow I never met, and we were in a short time on as good terms as if we had been acquainted for years, He asked us if we were fond of dancing, singing, music, &c &c &c—told the Alcaldi he must get up a dance forthwith, send for "Todas las Muchachas muy Bonitas"[31]—asked us to supper and said he would call for us—and

[29] "Great Scott, of course!"
[30] Headquarters or principal town in a district.
[31] "All the very pretty girls."

ended by asking "Como se llama este negre cocinero"[32]—meaning
Antonio whom he saw preparing our dinner, on being told his name
he bawled out "Antonio! como me Juro[33]—you d-d—— &c." making
use of some awful expressions, at which Antonio opened his eyes and
stood aghast, at last he turned to me, who was as much surprised as
he was to hear the Padre deliver this oration which would have
shamed Billingsgate: and said "Capin! what sort Parson dis, eh?
My Goramity I neber ear parson swear like dis—Parson Newport
hissef no do lika dat"—at which with a hearty laugh he retired to
his avocations exclaiming every now and then "Well! Well! so
parson tan in dis country hi——?" The fact was the Padre had been
curate of a place at the arm of the Tobasco river where many English
vessels load with logwood and had picked up some words of very
immoral import without knowing their meaning.

In the Evening just after dark, our ears were assailed by the sound
of music in which the violin, guitar & flute mingled their sounds—&
on going to the door we found this was the Padre with about a dozen
friends coming to escort us to his domicile, the Padre playing the
violin, the Alcaldi the guitar and some other official the flute. After
a chat of a few moments we joined them and proceeded through the
Town to the Padre's house, where we found a table set out, ready for
the Viands which were soon set before us in the shape of a variety of
stewed fish, meat and fowls, & a salad of cooked vegetables of different kinds—& fruit. Our fare was arranged on the table by rather a fine
looking girl—whom the Padre called his "Mita"[34]—I thought I
detected a wink of the Padre's eye and a protuberance on his off cheek,
very much as if he had pushed it out with his tongue as he said so.
When these were removed, we brewed some punch of which they
had no idea but relished it much when it was concocted—a good deal
of music and singing succeeded, and some noisy mirth after which it
was proposed we should sally out and make calls at different places—
so away we went music and all, serenading the usually peaceable

[32] "What's the name of this Negro cook?"
[33] "Antonio, how I swear, etc."
[34] "Indian girl" (i.e., female companion).

town—going from one house to the other and after a few moments conversation and partaking of sigars—nothing is done without that—they present you with a "Calumet of peace" (like the North American Indian)—and a Poquito Aguardiente, after which you are at liberty to progress. We were escorted home by the Party who stayed some time at our Quarters.

The next morning we endeavoured to procure canoes, but in consequence of its being the season of logwood shipping all the large ones were engaged & it was with some difficulty we procured a middling sized one to take us to Balancan. I think the Padre was much inclined to visit Palenque in our company & would have done so, had he not been in daily expectation of being relieved from the duties of his present curacy, and expected to go to head quarters at Merida, and promised if he possibly could he would take a run to Palenque on his way down.

The day before we arrived at Cabasera the murderers of a poor fellow of the name of Baynham had been sent off to Tobasco to be tried—he was an Irishman of an enterprising character and had gone up the Utsumacinta carrying on a small trade with the wild Indians who were very partial to him. He built himself a house & lived among them, and had commenced a small plantation. Having some articles with him that caused the supposition in the minds of one or two evil disposed persons from Balancan that he must have money, they entered into an agreement with his servant to murder him which was carried into effect by splitting his head open with an axe as he lay asleep in his hammock. They then plundered his house and spread a report that he had been murdered by the Indians, which incensed them so much that they withdrew from the place, and gave such information to the Alcaldi of the Cabasera as to lead to the detection of the murderers and the recovery of the effects of the deceased—which we examined, and found a letter from his Brother from which we got the address intending to forward an account of his death to his friends.

The Alcaldi and Prefecto, we were told, had behaved with great energy on the occasion and it was owing to their exertions that the murderers were discovered, & they spoke of the transaction, as a disgrace to human nature. One of the delinquents was of respectable family at Balancan. We bade adieu to our friends at Cabasera and embarked on board a tolerable sized canoe for Balancan. The river was falling & the current ran at the rate of about 3 miles an hour. Flocks of Parrots & Paroquets, kept constantly flying across the river and we saw several pairs of scarlet maccaw passing over us like a flame of fire—they fly so close together that at a little distance you fancy it is one bird, and it is only when they are directly over you that you can distinguish two, they make little noise giving a croak resembling a raven at intervals. The banks are generally speaking low, every part higher than the rest being selected for a Rancho. The river overflows its banks nearly every year. We slept, that is we tried to sleep, in the Canoe but the mosquitos were an effectual check to our slumbers, and the heat beneath the awning was dreadful. I do not know that during our travels I had passed a more disagreeable night and I was delighted to find we had arrived at Balancan at a little before daylight. We had a letter from the Prefecto at Cabasera for Don Manuel Obria, whose house at the time we arrived was that of mourning in consequence of the death of his mother and we found Don Francisco his brother who had come up from the Palisades to attend her remains to their final resting place, on the point of starting homewards. We were obliged to hire another canoe to take us to Monte Christe as the one we came in from the Cabasera was obliged to return. We had the Padre's house lent to us, it was a mere hut, in which he swung his hammock when visiting this Portion of his charge. We waited on the Alcaldi, whom we found in the agreeable occupation of doing school master to about a dozen young Mestitzos. We found him civil and he made no silly objections to our proceeding. A person of this place brought a jug to show us which he declared had been dug up in the ruins of Palenque—it was of classic shape but appeared rather too new to appertain to ancient Palenque—it was made of clay burnt. The Indians make the same description of jug at the present day.

The Brother of a Person of some notoriety who had fled to Belize in consequence of having shot a Person, came to ask if we had met him—we had, and he gave us some information as to the situation of the Ruins. We had the whole story told us by both parties. It appeared the Padre was travelling in company with this person in a canoe or bungo and some dispute arose between them when the former snapped a pistol twice at his adversary, and was preparing to try it a third time when the other thinking he had stood target quite long enough levelled his gun and brought down the churchman—and knowing he had no chance of his life if captured made the best of his way to Belize—any other life would not have been considered but the sacreligious act of taking the life of a Padre, even in self defence, never could be tolerated. His friends who were respectable people of Balancan had pushed their interest to procure his pardon, without effect, but were in hopes of doing so in time—that is when the church were satisfied with the sums paid for the masses in behoof of the deceased's soul—and the extra charge for granting absolution to the assassin. Our slumbers were disturbed by the bellowing of an unfortunate ox doomed to death for the supply of the market, and which was tethered on the Plaza in front of our dwelling place. It was cut into ribbons, of which we purchased a few yards. The breed of horses about this neighbourhood is of a better description than any I had yet seen in the country.

Balancan is situated on the banks of the Utsumasinta about 60 feet above the usual surface of the water; however, in very wet seasons it frequently overflows its banks; there are about 150 houses and it contains a population of nearly 600 souls. At the back of the town or village is an extensive swamp, which must make it unhealthy—in fact almost all the inhabitants have the appearance of ill health, whether they are so or not. I shot some Teal and snipe within 100 yards of the houses. Many of the inhabitants use the oolee or Tounou for their shoes—first making the shoes of coarse linen or cotton and then giving them as many coats of the fresh liquid Indian rubber as they may require.

We embarked for Monte Christe in a good sized, but inconvenient Canoe having a similar Bamboo awning to that in which we came to

Balancan under which we were obliged to creep on our hands and knees, and then could but just sit upright. The heat was most oppressive; "not a breath the wave to curl." We descended the current of the River very slowly being mainly dependant upon it for our progressive movement; for our two rowers were the laziest fellows I ever met with, and did not seem to be at all in a hurry—so we set to work to count the alligators on each side as we passed along. There was not a sandy bank on the margin of the water that had not its occupants, in some places two or three together. Horrid looking monsters some 15 feet in length; they have the most malicious eye of any animal I know, and it was with the utmost pleasure I put a bullet into many of them. We counted about 27 each in the course of half an hour. We observed for some time, two old Black Monkeys, perched on the outspreading branch of a large tree that overhung the river, teaching their progeny to climb, and it was too ridiculously human to see the manner in which they lifted them in order that they might reach a higher branch and swing down again by their long tails. The Parent taking them in their arms and fondling them in the most endearing manner. I wished very much to get one to skin, but I could not bring myself to fire at these, although it was the best chance I had had. The remarks of our Negros when we fell in with Baboons or monkeys was rather amusing—they were particularly struck with the antics of this family group. Jocko could not bear to look at them, whether he had been struck when viewing his countenance in a glass, with the strong resemblance they have to himself I cannot say. If the question had been put to him "Pray sir do you know what are some mens antipathies" as it was to Ollapod, he would have answered "Baboon." He was of the same opinion which many negroes have expressed "That they saby too much, and they no peak cause Buckra[35] go make dem 'worky, worky.' "

On each Bank of the river, for the greater part of the distance from Tenosique down, and within a few hundred yards of its margin where the large growth of wood stops, the interior is swamp or savanah,

[35] White Man. The term, also used in the southern United States, supposedly is derived from "back raw," referring to the effect of tropical sun on light skins.

the former abounding in logwood which the natives use for the strong posts of their houses, although the general growth of this tree is so tortuous as to make it difficult to procure a straight piece of sufficient length. The current ran at the rate of about 2½ or 3 miles an hour— and we reached the Indian Pueblo of Monte Christe at about 3 o'clock. The head Alcaldi was absent, however the "Alcaldi de los Indios"[36] gave us up the Casa Real, which consisted of two apartments in one of which was a strong set of stocks for the benefit of the refractory and a verandah in front.

The village was a struggling dirty place, with scarcely a decent cottage in it & the natives appeared to be all drunk. The Alcaldi visited us about 7 o'clock and we submitted our passport to him, it was written in English and backed by the different Alcaldis as we came along, however it might as well have been in Greek or Hebrew as the only part of it he seemed to look at was the large red seal attached which he pronounced to be "muy bonito." He abused the "Alcaldi de los Indios" in great stile and at the end of every sentence addressed him as "Hombre" which word I think he must have made use of some 50 times during his peroration. We heard that the new Padre of Cabasera had arrived, so we determined to wait on him and see whether he was as merry a fellow as his predesessor. We found him an old man of kindly address and liberal in his opinions; after conversing with him for half an hour we returned to our dwelling for the night, and on the following morning witnessed the summary justice of our friend the Alcaldi, who was examining several cases in his magisterial capacity. One was that of a person who kept a sort of grog shop, who was brought up for harbouring a militiaman who had been called upon to repair to a place of rendezvous, but whose military ardour was not of the strongest nature thinking with Falstaffe that "discretion is the better part of valour." He had endeavoured to escape enrollment amongst the defenders of his country's liberty. The Alcaldi fined the defendant 100 dollars which after a good deal of trouble was collected and sent in. Several others were

[36] "Mayor of the Indians," as distinguished from the *alcalde*, whose primary concern was the non-native population.

116

fined from two to twenty dollars—fines seemed the order of the day—
and his worship must have made a good thing of it. The money is
supposed to go to the government deducting a small percentage to
the Alcaldi; however, report says that the percentage for collecting
is generally the Lion's portion and that these worthies who almost
always commence office exceedingly poor, manage in their year's duty
to amass a few thousand dollars.

We accompanied this dispensor of "even handed justice" to his
hacienda a few miles from the village where he had promised to
supply us with a canoe for our further progress. It was situated on a
hill about one hundred & fifty feet above the river, and stood in an
open pasture of some extent, where numbers of cattle were grazing,
and in which were several small Lagoons swarming with wild fowl,
among which were the large snow white Egret, and Heron, both
white & blue Duck & Teal—of several varieties among them the
whistling duck which is a beautiful bird—light brown plumage with
pink bill and feet—we remained for some time while our canoe was
getting ready, and partook of a drink made with the Seville orange
& some other admixtion it was not particularly palatable—bidding
our friend goodby & paying him for the hire of his boat & two
ramoneros,[37] we proceeded. After going down the stream for about
8 miles, we entered a slow running sluggish creek, strong with the
disagreeable musky odour of the alligator, and we saw the monsters
drop into the water from their muddy bed, awakened from their
afternoon siesta by the splashing of our oars. This creek was fringed
with beautiful willows, whose graceful feathery foliage waved in the
gentle breeze, reminding me of many a spot at home where I had as
a lover of the gentle craft passed the noontide hours under their
refreshing shade. We arrived at the landing place of the Hacienda
Monte Christe where there is a small sugar plantation or Trapiche.
The greater part of the cane juice is made into Panella, sugar rather
overboiled and poured into moulds containing about four pounds
each. Of this they make their aguardiente.

26th January—We procured horses here and had a ride of about

[37] Men detailed to collect ramon leaves as fodder for the animals.

four miles through wood to the Hacienda, situated on the edge of an extensive savanah with a large swamp in front of the house and at a short distance from it. We found the major domo, a young man of agreable manner who appeared inclined to accomodate us as much as lay in his power. This is the property of the Obria family, the most wealthy of any in these parts. They have large herds of cattle, and a logwood cutting establishment. Soon after my arrival, I sallied down to the swamp to have a few shots at the innumerable Duck & Teal &c which I observed from the house, and had good sport, snipe were very plentiful besides the former. The place was full of Aligators, but I did not see one larger than six feet in length. On my return to the house I found a tolerable dinner prepared for us, after which we made an agreement for horses to take us to Palenque on the following morning. A letter was despatched from this place to Mr. Shields H.M. Vice Consul at Laguna Terminos requesting he would forward us information with regard to the possibility of procuring a craft to convey us to Belize by sea, as we were not much inclined to retrace our steps through the woods and swamps after the toils we had suffered, I had been suffering much from the torments caused by the bites of mosquitos and warri ticks, and my legs from the knee downwards were in a state of rawness anything but agreeable.

In the evening towards sunset, I was attracted to some high trees at a short distance from the house, where flocks of Parrots were assembling for their night's repose, and for half an hour I blazed away right and left as quick as I could load—I never heard such a clatter as they kicked up, particularly the wounded & Bartlett who was picking them up had his hands bit several times. They were the yellow headed bird, with a scarlet patch on the wing—we had some of them made into a stew, and excellent it was—the young ones are much like the wild Pigeon in flavour. There were also large flocks of the scarlet winged rice bird which are as delicate eating as the Ortolan.

The 27th was spent in making arrangements. The 2d (28th) morning, after our arrival betimes we were on the move, but it was some time before we got under weigh. The whole country at daylight was hid by the dense fog arising from the swamps, but the sun soon dissipated it, and before 8 o'clock one could scarcely suppose there had been any. The first few miles after we left Monte Christe Hacienda our road lay through an abominable swampy wood, our horses floundering about—every movement of mine gave me pain, and when we emerged from the swamp into the open savanah it was as much as I could bear to urge my steed into a good gallop—over such enticing ground. We saw many deer but did not come near enough to try our luck at a shot. We were obliged to put up about 5 o'clock at an unoccupied hut on the plain. From this place the Palenque mountains were visible in the west.

After resting a short time and perceiving some deer grazing about a mile off, I was determined bad as I was to have a trial at them—so taking the advice of an Indian who said they would allow anything of a red colour to approach them—I tied a handerchief of that colour round my head and put another in front of me hanging from my neck, and thus prepared I advanced cautiously taking advantage of every scrubby bush, and progressing slowly as much under their cover as I could, when I got about two hundred yards from the foremost fellow, who raised his head several times and gazed at me in a suspicious manner, shaking his ears, and receeding a few paces—I could see nothing to hide me from him in my further movements except the prostrate trunk of a tree, which was not more than 60 or 70 yards from him. I tried to advance stealthily, but his quick eye was upon me immediately when I stood stark still—at last I was determined to do snake, and creep through the long grass, so watching an opportunity down I went, and shoving my gun before me I gradually approached the fallen tree, and became exceedingly tired, and very nervous, and when I gained the object of my wishes I was so done up that I could scarcely move—and raising my head at last I saw the fellow had moved away a few paces and was gazing with all his might at my position, he turned away and was making off much faster than I liked so I took aim & fired and down he came upon his knees but recovered himself again and was into the wood in a short time altho wounded & having no dog I could not follow—so I had all my trouble

119

for nothing and I returned to the hut disheartened, and covered from head to foot with warri ticks, and my legs bleeding from the scrubbing I gave them creeping through the grass.

Another annoyance awaited me, after I had changed & rubbed & scrubbed off these confounded little insects, we found the hut so full of fleas that the men who were sweeping it out, came dancing from the place, and brushing them off by the hundreds—however with a good deal of manouvering we managed to stow ourselves into our hammocks, without their company—nevertheless I was in such torture from the irritation of my wounds that I scarcely got a wink of sleep, and I was delighted when morning came, at dawn I was taking the benefit of the fresh air of the savanah, and watching the approach of day from the first streak of sun light till the whole eastern sky was one blaze of refulgent light. We were soon en route and I never regretted any circumstance more than my present condition while riding slowly over the level pasture, deer bounding from every quarter, and I in such a state as totally to prevent my following them. I killed a few birds of large size of the Plover species, they stood about 18 inches in height, and ran very swiftly.

We arrived at San Domingo de Palenque about 3 o'clock, and went direct to the Alcaldi—whom we found a crabbed old fellow, of sickly hew, with his head through a striped chimarro—he was anything but civil, however we took him very cooly, and lolled in his hammocks trying to make ourselves agreeable by smoking & praising his Puros. We asked if he could get us a lodging of some sort but at first he thought it was quite out of the question accomodating our party which consisted of eleven—however a young man happened to come in just as the difficulty was started & we went out with him to stroll through the village—and on coming to his own house where he had a counter set out with a Dutch case of bottles containing aguardiente of various qualities & measures of various sizes—he offered to clean away his traps and give up his house for a consideration—however as we had a good many mouths to provide for we bought his stock in trade—and took up our quarters in the Casa which consisted of two apartments. We found no difficulty in procuring prey, as there were abundance of fowls to be procured, and we had Tortillas made for our party by a Señora who lived hard by. The Prefecto was absent at his Hacienda but we wrote him a letter stating our object in visiting that part of the Country, to which we received a very polite reply, saying that he was sorry he could not be with us in consequence of the severe illness of one of his family, and giving the necessary directions for our visiting the Ruins. There was an order that no stranger should visit the ruins without taking a guide or Practico as he was called, and we therefore looked out for a person who knew the locale and we obtained the only man in the place who was acquainted with the situation of the different buildings. The following morning I was quite unable to mount a horse and my companion started to make a reconnaisance accompanied by Don Juan —— a Captain of the Mexican service on half pay, i.e. nothing a day and find himself, out of which he was dressed in a sort of uniform with a pair of fringe epauletts and overalls of tanned leather with innumerable little buttons down the sides, and his horse was caparisoned in black leather trappings that gave it the appearance of a Rhinoceros.

⊸{The colorfully dressed Captain had acquired his knowledge of the ruins by serving as guide for Waldeck in 1832–33, and following his service with Caddy and Walker he was employed as *practico* by Stephens and Catherwood, thereby managing to serve all three of the major expeditions to Palenque in the early nineteenth century.}⊷

I laid myself up in my hammock making use of a decoction of a plant which the natives call Malbi, and which proved most efficacious in healing my wounds. My companion's report of the ruins excited my curiosity and determined me not to wait longer than we could make arrangements for taking up our quarters in the ruin, and on the third day after our arrival we started with the whole of our retinue & provisions for a few days. After a ride which was anything but agreable to me in spite of the beautifully varied scenery through which we passed—undulating savanah with picturesque clumps of trees and brilliant wild flowers the scene shut in by lofty mountains covered with forest for a great part of the distance, and then entering the wood, we crossed several streams, and the rapid little river Micol, sparkling over rocks—from which the road makes a considerable ascent, and becomes difficult, being much overgrown with bush and you come upon mounds of crumbling fragments of edifices now prostrate with the earth. After riding for a short time over this steep & broken road, we came to a level tract of ground—at the base of a chain of hills which here separate the state of Chiapa from that of Tobasco through which a small clear stream runs. We tied up our horses at the foot of an eminence and scrambled up over loose stones overgrown with trees to a height of 60 feet where we came upon the walls of a large building and entered what appeared an arch into the interior.

v. caddy's description of the ruins of palenque

THE REMAINS of the Ancient City of Palenque,[1] or as some believe it to be, Culhuacan, which were accidentally discovered in the middle of the last century, after being concealed for ages amidst the dense mountain forests of the district of Chiapa, gave rise to various conjectures as to their origin, and some even went so far as to give them an antediluvian existence.

From the extent of these remains, whose fallen structures cover a space of some miles—the massiveness of the buildings which are still standing, the elegance of the Basso relievos—both sculptured on stone and moulded in stucco—and the beauty of the internal, and external, ornature, stamp it as one of the most extraordinary and interesting monuments of the arts of the ancient people of this country—and proves that, at some far distant period it must have been inhabited by a race both populous and civilized.

These Ruins are situated in the Province of Ciudad Real de Chiapa, the most northern of the Guatemalan states, and close to the boundary between Guatemala and Mexico, within nine miles of the Indian Pueblo or village of San Domingo de Palenque.

After a ride of about eight miles from this Pueblo, through a fine country partly savanna and partly Forest, and crossing many small streams, and a beautiful little river, the Micol, the road commences an ascent most difficult to the equestrian, from its steepness and from

---

[1] This description of the ruins of Palenque was prepared by Caddy to accompany his portfolio of paintings, and may be the text of the scientific paper he presented in 1842. Since it was designed as a separate paper, it commences by repeating some of the material of the diary proper.

the closeness of the bush, as well as from the circumstance of its being over mounds of loose and crumbling fragments of edifices now prostrate with the earth.

Scrambling through more than a mile of this steep and broken path we came to a level tract of ground, at the base of a chain of hills which here separates the state of Chiapa from that of Tobasco. A small clear stream dances over a rocky bed, issuing partly from a subterraneous aqueduct, and partly over it. This aqueduct is stated to have communicated with the Palace, but it does not now extend for more than thirty or forty yards, where it is blocked up by the falling in of the roof and superincumbant earth, but from the appearance of the debris along the stream towards its source, it would seem that it had been entirely covered in. On a large stone near its entrance there is a rude representation of an aligators head and forearm.

At a few yards distance from this spot we came to the base of the mound on which stands what is termed the Palace, and after ascending to a height of about 60 feet over loose stones, we came to the massive walls of the principal building, and entering one of the door ways we stood in the hall of the ancient Palencanos, whoever they may have been.—the natives answer "quien sabe."[2]

In the first Plate [see Plate 12[3]] I have endeavoured to give an idea of the relative situation of some of the buildings now standing, taking the liberty of clearing away the Forest, which completely screens them from view. I have also given the front of two of the Temples, and the end of another in order to show their construction— with the entrance to the aqueduct & part of the Palace on the extreme right—However this is more a fancy sketch than otherwise.

The Palace stands on a pyramidal mound, and occupies a space of 250 feet by 100. (See Plan B [Plate 13]). The buildings A,C,D, E,F,G are still in a state of tolerable preservation. G is a square Tower—J a small square building having steps in it descending to the subterraneous apartments H. B,B, are courtyards.

The front of the building A, has six door ways which have the

[2] "Who knows?"

[3] Plate numbers in brackets refer to the plates in this book.

appearance of arches, but this is caused by the falling in of the lintel, and part of the wall above it; they were originally rectangular—9 feet wide & 10 high. [Plate 18] The Piers or portions of wall between each door way are six feet wide, and ten in height, and have been richly ornamented on the outside with figures and hieroglyphics in bass relief, formed of stucco of a very fine and hard description resembling Plaster of Paris. The principal figure on each of these Piers is placed in a standing position, grasping in one hand a decorated staff, having an oval shaped ornament on its shaft with a cross in it. The other hand holds a tassellated ornament. The head dress is very large in proportion to the figure, and seems to be composed principally of feathers, in the midst of which, in one of them, is represented the figure of a fish.

There has been a tippet over the shoulders of these standing figures; and from the waist to the middle of the thigh, a description of kilt, fringed at the bottom and otherwise ornamented. These figures are in profile.

In each lower corner of the pier is a figure sitting crosslegged, but they were so much mutilated that it was almost impossible to distinguish more than a small portion of their outline; they seem to have been naked with the exception of a girdle around the waist, and there is some appearance of their having had head dresses. Round the edges of the Pier there has been a moulding like a frame work, and three oval hieroglyphics above the whole.

There is a considerable projection of the masonry about a foot above the tops of the Piers, which seems to have run the whole length of the building, but is now broken where the lintels of the door ways have given way, and it is almost impossible to say what the original design of the upper portion of the building has been—however detached parts show that it has been elaborately ornamented with mouldings and figures in stucco.

One of the six Piers of the front is different from the rest, being divided into a number of squares, each containing a hieroglyphical character, which no doubt could they be deciphered would give some account of the structure.

Plate 2 [see Plate 18] gives two of these Piers, and the centre arch, looking through to the Court.

The interior of this building consists of two long corridors [Plate 14], which seem to have extended to M in the plan, as there is a ridge of debris in that direction; and also to have joined another corridor at N which ran along the north end, communicating with the ramps of building C,D—The length of what remains of these corridors is about 96 feet, the width of each 8 feet. The walls are 3 feet thick.

From the floor to the commencement of the slope of the roof is 10 feet, and to the top 10 feet more. The roof is of a pyramidal form, and is constructed of flat stones placed so that each successive layer may project a little beyond the lower, thus gradually decreasing in width towards the top, until the sides are within 20 inches of each other when it is covered with large flat stones, and made even with a thick coating of mortar. The arch in the centre wall, which is of Saracenic form, is constructed in a similar manner, and it does not appear that the builders were acquainted with the principles of an arch.

Along the centre wall, in the front corridor [see Plates 14 and 15] there is a row of medallions of a circular form, with a richly wrought border in stucco, each of which has contained a bust of the same material within the frame, as the shoulders and neck of one, having a necklace of round beads, may still be traced. The frame work or border is surrounded by hieroglyphical characters containing the human face, and hands holding something within them.

Beneath these are several apertures in the wall, some partially, others completely through it. They are in the form of a cross ⊹ or of a T ⊤ —for what purpose they have been used it would be difficult to say. In the wall on each side of the centre doorway and within a few inches of the edge, both at top and bottom, there are semicylindrical holes cut in the stone having a strong bar down the middle of them; they appear to have acted as parts of rude hinges. There are also circular holes at intervals along the slope of the roof, which may have held the ends of beams. On the slope of the roof above the medallions there are shallow niches of the same shape as the arch in the centre wall.

The back corridor is the same as the front but has no medallions; and the niches in the slope of the roof are much deeper than those in front, and appear to have held figures.

Passing through the centre arch to the back of the building there is a flight of seven steps of well hewn stone 18 feet long, 18 inches rise and 1 foot tread, which lead into a Court 80 feet by 70 [see Plates 16 and 17]. On each side of the steps are gigantic figures cut on large slabs of stone, and placed in a slanting position, the tops resting on the upper part of the basement of the edifice, and corresponding with the slope of the steps. The figures are grotesque, and are ornamented with head dresses, earrings, and necklaces, one of the latter having a circular pendant of round beads with a cross within it. One figure on each side of the steps has a narrow apron hanging from the waist, with hieroglyphics on it, and these two figures are the only ones whose faces are turned towards the steps, and seem to look at you as you enter the building, as much as to question your right of intruding into the abodes of a by gone and unknown nation, of whose remains they are the silent guardians.

There have been figures on the piers of all the buildings but most are completely defaced.

The Court is choked up with the fallen fragments of the edifices. On the south side of it, there is a building divided into five small apartments, (See Section on P.Q. [Plate 28]) three opening into the court and two into a narrow passage at the back, all of which have been highly ornamented with figures and devices in stucco [Plate 19]; and in some there are niches ⊓ with the remains of rich tracing round them, and holes with a bar through them; these were very small [Plate 20, figs. 1, 2, 3, 4]. Clambering to the top of this building I found at the eastern end of it, the remains of what appears to have been a seat, with a canopy above it, and the mutilated fragments of figures; also the head and part of the body of a serpent, and detached portions of mouldings.

The second range of buildings parallel to the first is of similar construction, at least nearly so—It has no arch in the longitudinal wall, but merely a rectangular door way, as a communication between the two apartments. There is a row of medallions [Plate 22] on the centre wall but differing from those already described; they have a very heraldic appearance. An excavation has been made in the floor beneath these medallions, for the purpose of ascertaining, I suppose, whether they denoted the place of burial of the ancient inhabitants of these structures; however from its appearance I should imagine nothing of the sort was intended.

There have been steps up to the centre door way of this building, and there are two large stones on which figures have been, but they are so much worn away that it was impossible to make them out. On the basement there are projecting upright stones, which have figures cut on them [Plate 21,] and between these are tablets of hieroglyphics. The Piers have had figures on them [Plate 23] which appear to have been those of youths, seated cross legged. The remains of a head dress of feathers can be traced, and a description of kilt with a pouch hanging from the waist belt. The youth is holding out his right arm the hand of which contains some ornament. There is an oval hieroglyphic beneath the figure in the border which is usually moulded round the sides of the pier.

The steps from this building into the 2nd Court yard, are not in the centre of it, but are placed at the 2nd doorway. There is a door way in the south end of this building which leads into a narrow passage, the lintel of which is quite perfect; it is a stone 9 feet long, 3 feet broad and 1 foot thick, and is the only perfect one in all the buildings. On the upper part of the south end there are three of a similar description of seat as that already described and remains of rich work in stucco.

The 2nd Court is 34 feet wide, across which there is a third range of buildings nearly similar to the second. In the slope of the roof there are niches, one of which has communicated with the top of the building, where from the quantity of loose stones which are still on it, I should suppose there had been some superstructure. Pls 14,15,16, & 17 [see Plates 24, 25, 26, and 27] are those on the piers of this structure.

From the south west corner of the 1st Court there is an entrance by

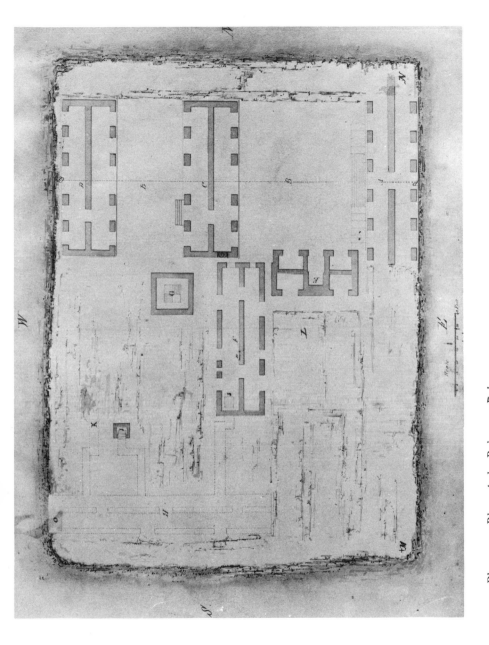

Plate 13. *Plan of the Palace at Palenque.*

Plate 14. *The interior of Building A.*

Plate 15. *Medallions from center wall of Building A.*

Plate 16. *Stairway, flanked by figures, leading into Court, Building A.*

Plate 17. *Group of figures at right side of the stairway shown in Plate 16 (Building A)*.

Plate 18. *Two of the piers of the façade of Building A.*

Plate 19. *Building at the south side of the Court, Building E.*

Plate 20. *Remains of tracing around niches in Building E, shown in Plate 19.*

a small doorway into the building F—similarly constructed to the others, with the exception that the door ways are irregularly placed; the corridors are 82 feet in length, having two door ways in the centre wall, near one of which there is an oval shaped stone built in at a . . . on which are figures in bass relief [Plate 30].

The principle figure appears to be intended for a female, she is seated on a couch representing an animal with two heads having necklaces of round beads to one of which is attached a human face. The heads of the animals are of a nondescript appearance. The head dress of the female is curiously formed—She has a necklace of round beads, with a pendant attached, also earrings and bracelets, and some portion of dress round the waist. Her right hand is pressed against her bosom while the left, rests upon her thigh. Her features are different from any of the others, and the forehead is higher.

The other figure is seated cross legged and holds out before her with both hands, an odd looking thing, which some have described as a human head, but I could trace no features upon it; and to me it appeared more like a rude representation of a Pine apple. The figure had a head dress, a tippet descending to the elbows, and a petticoat. There are seven hieroglyphics on the stone, three behind the principal figure and four above the other. This stone has had a border of stucco work round it, and a tablet beneath it, but both have been destroyed.

A manuscript work now in my possession gives a fanciful description of this stone. It is written by Don Ramon de Ordonnez y Aguiar a Priest of Ciudad Real de Chiapa in 1796—who sets forth in the Title Page, which is a very lengthy affair, that he has discovered the true origin of the inhabitants of Ancient Palenque, and states that they had a perfect knowledge of the Mythology of the Chaldeans and other nations of Antiquity. He connects these figures and some others with the fabulous story of Proserpine's descent into the infernal regions.

At the south end of the same apartment there is an opening in the floor at b, leading by some steps to the subterraneous apartment H, which appears to have been closed in by a slab of stone like a trap door. In the corresponding apartment on the other side of the central

129

wall, there is a large oblong slab placed upon four stone legs, which have some sculpture on them, but the slab has none, what it could have been meant for is difficult to say, but it has more the appearance of a tombstone than anything else, although it may have been a couch. There are some remains of mouldings, and a cornice and pendant in this building which show great taste in the arrangement and execution [see Plate 31].

The buildings at I were in such a state of delapidation that it was nearly impossible to describe them, but they appear to have been divided into small apartments similar to those in the building E— and most likely have been used as dormitories. The square Tower G in the Plan, and shown in the background of Pl. 7 [see Plate 19]—is 21 feet square and is about 40 feet high; it contains a curious rectangular staircase, the upper step of which comes immediately against the roof of the lower apartment, where further ascent is prevented. I climed to the top of this structure and into the upper apartment which is similar to the lower. I imagine from the appearance of the top of the Tower that it has been much higher than it is at present, but how the communication from one story to another took place I cannot say, as it could not be by the stair cases in their present state.

Descending into the subterraneous apartments by the steps at b, above the entrance the reclining figure Pl. 19 Fig. 2 [see Plate 29] is cut on stone in bass relief. The place was so dark that I was obliged to sketch by the light of a candle. This figure seems to be peering into the gloom of these dark passages, resting upon one hand, and having the other in advance and held up in a manner as if to demand silence. It has a description of Casque on the head, with a few leaves or feathers at the top, and an ornament hanging from the back part of it. The ornamental work on each side is tasteful.

These apartments are similarly constructed to all the others, and have nothing remarkable in them with the exception of several slabs mounted on stone legs, as before described.

There is another entrance to these apartments from a small square building J which seems to have been detached from the others, and appears to have been a lobby; there is a stone seat along one side of

130

it. I have no doubt there have been communications with these apartments from other portions of the buildings, as at K there is another short flight of steps over which the figures Pl. 19 Fig. 1 [see Plate 29] are sculptured on stone, they consist of two non descript animals, squatted at the upper corners of the entrance, looking towards each other, the one on the right is a half human looking animal, having an ornament on its head and some thing projecting from its mouth (See Section on the line P.Q. [Plate 28])—between them is some ornamental work—and beneath there is a human arm & hand on each side, and lower down an eye half closed surrounded by ornamental work.

Descending the pyramidal base of the Palace from the S.W. corner of it, and continuing in that direction for about 60 yards you come to the base of another structure and ascending about 100 yards up a very steep slope, you come to the walls of the building No. 2.

This building is about 75 feet in length (See plan and Elevation of No. 2 [Plate 33]) and 24 in depth—and is divided into apartments by the usual longitudinal wall down its centre, forming a long corridor in front, and having three apartments in the back; the centre one the largest, having a slab of Hieroglyphics let into the wall and a large pyramidal doorway communicating with the front corridor. The door ways into the other apartments are of similar form but much smaller—and the apartments are small and dungeon like, having no other aperture by which light or air could be admitted. There are two large tablets of Hieroglyphics let into the longitudinal wall in the front corridor. The piers are ornamented on the outside with figures, alternately male and female, each having an infant on the right arm, with the exception of those on the right and left corner of the building, which are divided into squares each containing a hieroglyphic.

On the top of this building there are remains of a superstructure, but so completely destroyed that it was impossible to make out its nature.

Ascending the stream from the front of the Palace for about 300 hundred yards I came upon a slab of stone, on which the cross and figure Pl. 20 [see Plate 32] is cut in bass relief, and which had been taken down from the wall of building No. 3 where it had formed the centre of an altarpiece. This portion of the group consisted of a richly ornamented cross, surmounted by a bird, evidently meant for the Quetzal, holding some ornament in its beak, and looking towards a figure on the right who appears in the act of making an offering. The whole of the work was exceedingly well executed.

Ascending to the eastward a slope of about 50 feet, we came upon a platform on which were pointed out to us the remains of a hut built by Mr. Waldeck in which we were informed he had lived for about nine months, making researches in the neighborhood. About 50 yards from the edge of this platform, we again ascended a slope from 30 to 40 yards high on the top of which was building No. 3. It is 50 feet in length and 30 feet depth, having three door ways, the piers contained figures & hieroglyphics but so much destroyed that it was impossible to delineate them. The interior is of similar formation to the other buildings, being divided by a longitudinal wall having a large door way in the centre and a small one on each side leading into three apartments, the centre one containing an oratory or tomb, nearly 12 feet long by six deep.—The top of which has been richly ornamented—[Plate No. 33]. The door to this oratory is 6 feet wide, and on each side of it there has been a tablet with figures, now removed to a house in the village. The back of the oratory contains the figures and hieroglyphics in Pl. 22 [see Plate 36] the open space having been occupied by the slab before described Pl. 20 [see Plate 32].

The top of the building has a turret running from end to end, consisting of two stories of a pyramidal form, with projecting stones by which you ascend from one story to another; (See plan and elevation of No. 3 [Plate 33]) it is pierced with numerous apertures, and has been decorated with human figures as large as life in stucco. We had some difficulty in mounting to the Turret, as there is no staircase or other means of ascent from the interior, and consequently we were obliged to clamber up, with the assistance of the trees and bushrope which almost covers the structure.

Close to this building is another of similar construction, but of different dimensions. It is 38 feet long and 28 feet deep. The corridors are nine feet wide, and the walls of the building 3½ feet in thickness. It has three door ways the centre one much larger than the others. The Piers have been ornamented with figures, the two end ones with Hieroglyphics. The inner corridor is divided into three apartments the centre one containing an oratory with the figures Pl. 22 [see Plate 36] on the back wall cut in stone, in bass relief, and is more perfect than any other in the whole of the buildings. The two figures making offerings are very similar to those on each side of the cross in Pl. 20 [see Plate 32].

There is another building, or rather the remains of one close to these but so much destroyed that I could make nothing of it—and indeed there were several masses of stone which appeared to indicate fallen structures—and descending from these structures, and following the stream upwards for about 300 yds. there is another building, whose base runs directly from the margin of the stream and is about 30 yards high. The building is 20 feet long and 18 in depth, and is in a very ruinous condition, the inner corridor being the only part standing, on the wall of which there are the remains of a figure sitting on a couch, having an animals head on each side, the legs being those also of an animal [see Plate 35]. The building differs from the others in as much as having two stories.

These are the whole of what now remains of the Ancient City of Palenque in a state at all describable; but the masses of masonry for some distance round indicate the spots where formerly stood many other buildings; and the natives state that ruins may be traced for several leagues.

VI. ON TO MÉRIDA

I REMAINED in the ruins for 14 days selecting the centre arch for our dwelling place, spreading leaves and fern on the pavement which was very wet and spreading the Tarpaulin over them hanging our Pavilions at night to protect us from the mosquitos; from this we made our excursions to the different buildings, climbing to their summits and procuring, from some, extensive glimpses of the open country.

Mr. La Groin's act. of descent of San Pedro River—Mr. La Groin, who had left Belize some time before us on a mercantile speculation in company with a Mr. Brown, an American who is married to a Creole lady and located at a short distance from Palenque—came to visit us, he had descended the Rio San Pedro from within a very short distance of Peten to the Utsumasinta, he described the river as flowing through a rich and beautiful country totally uninhabited. The river abounds in rapids which impede the navigation and he had the misfortune to upset several times thoroley damaging a great portion of his goods—however he attributed these accidents to the frail nature of the craft in which he descended which was small and ill-constructed.

We left St. Domingo de Palenque on the morning of the 18th Feby. and retraced our path through the savanah to Monte Christe where we found a letter from Mr. Shields and a present of some wine and et ceteras which were most acceptable. We also found that he had written to Don Francisco Obrea to request he would assist us and we found the major domo instructed to pay us every attention. The young man who was here on our first arrival had left, and an unfortunate looking person who had nearly lost the use of his limbs from paralasis had charge of the Hacienda and did everything he could to make us comfortable. We observed here a custom—which is that of all the well regulated Haciendas. The Indians, men & women, employed by the Proprietor assemble at daylight in the morning & at sunset in front of the house where there is a large wooden cross, and sing a hymn to the Virgin Mary.

{In mid-February, Superintendent MacDonald's despatch informing the Secretary of State of the organization of an expedition to Palenque arrived in England. On February 19, a reply was posted from Downing Street, bearing the signature of Lord John Russell:

> Sir:
>
> I have received your Despatch No. 21: of the 9: Nov. last reporting that you had authorised an Expedition to the Ruins of Polenki in the vicinity of Honduras & that you proposed to draw a sum of £200 from the Military Chest to meet the several expenses of the Expedition.
>
> The Deputy Asst. Commissary Genl. in Honduras has advised the Lords of the Treasury of this advance having been made & their Lordships have communicated to me their opinion, in which I concur, that you were not in any respect warranted in directing an issue from the Military Chest for objects of the description to which your despatch refers without the previous authority of Her Majesty's Government.
>
> Their Lordships further state that they would not be justified in giving their sanction for relieving you from responsibility on account of this advance, until the manner in which the money may have been disbursed has been distinctly specified, & such report of the Expedition has been made as may shew that the result of it has proved beneficial to the Public.

The thoughts of government in England were less turned to the preservation of English scientific prestige, and more directed to matters of fiscal responsibility, and MacDonald had got himself into a sticky bit of business. He had overstepped the bounds of his office, but the time was now long past for restoring himself to grace by recalling the expedition; in fact, MacDonald had no idea at all where Walker and Caddy were at the moment. By the time of the arrival of Lord Russell's dispatch in May, the expedition would have passed into history, and the solution to the problem would rest entirely upon the quality of Walker's report and Caddy's paintings of the ruins.}

We departed from Monte Christe Hacienda and embarked for the Hacienda Val Paraiso, where a large canoe was to be in readiness to take us to the Palisada—but when we arrived in the afternoon we found we should be obliged to remain a day before it would be ready. We here fell in with the new Padre of the Cabasera who was on a visit to the different villages in his care, and had been picking up considerable fees by Christenings, marriages, and deaths. He offered us any sum we needed—whether he meant it as a Spanish compliment (as they always say that everything they possess is "a la disposicion de usted"[1] which being translated into English means Don't you wish you may get it)—we had not an opportunity of judging as we did not put him to the test. He told us our old friend his predecessor had gone to Merida and that he had made him an offer of remaining to assist in the duties which were more than he as an old man could well attend to, making him a most liberal allowance, but having played first Fiddle so long he would not accept office on those terms—and he had proceeded to headquarters to endeavour to get an appointment to some other curacy. I strolled out with my gun, shot a few teal & some rice birds, the latter are jet black with a red patch on the but of the wing, they are most delicious eating. There was a brick and tile kiln at this place, and the house we were staying in was tiled, the first variation from the thatch we had seen since we left Belize.

The Indians were bringing in logwood from the swamp at no great distance from the riverside, it was transported on a sort of truck made of two long shafts with cross pieces about 4 ft. from the thickest ends, and uprights to support the logwood—this was drawn thro' the

[1] "At your disposal."

swamp by horse or oxen. From this place we sent our Interpreter Nod and all our Party with the exception of our four black soldiers back to Tenosique.

On the morning of the 21st we left the Hacienda Val Paraiso, and descended the river to the Cabasera calling at the villages of Moota and Pitu as also at another Hacienda where we slept. It belonged to the person whom we met at Monte Christe, and from whom the Alcaldi got the hundred dollar fine. I never saw a greater quantity of wild fowl than was contained in the swamp behind this house— and I had a couple of hours good sport and very nearly walked into an alligator's mouth, I was going along a truck road through the swamp which was up to my knees in mud & water and very intent upon a flock of duck that were sporting in some water in an open part of the swamp when Bartlet who was with me cautioned me to look out for the alligator, and looking ahead of me I saw the white jaws of a monster at about 20 yards distance; however I did not waste powder and shot on him as it was getting scarce, so I gave him a view halloo, which aroused him from his slumbers, and snapping his jaws together with a loud report he scuttled into the long reeds making them wave about, and showing his track for some distance, he did us a great service, for he made the duck take wing in my direction and I had both barrels into the whole flock, killing and wounding 8 or 9—six we got. The snipe were innumerable but my ammunition was almost exhausted so that I was obliged to limit myself to a few shots at them.

We arrived at the Palisadas on the afternoon of the 22nd and were kindly received by Don Francisco Obrea—who put us into capital quarters in a house which he had just quitted to occupy his present residence, lately erected at large cost. Don Francisco is the richest man in this part of the country & is worth 100,000 dollars—principally made by logwood. He also kept a store. The Palisadas is the Principal town on the Utsumasinta, and is the depot for the Logwood cut in this river. It contains about 600 inhabitants. The banks of this noble river are but thinly populated—and above Tenosique there is scarcely what may be termed a village altho' there are many clusters of huts occupied by the Indios Bravos or wild Indians, who get an easy and independent livelihood by hunting & fishing.

We heard there was an Englishman settled here and we went to pay him a visit, and found him suffering from fever—his name was Boyse and appeared an intelligent person and spoke highly of the capabilities of the country in an agricultural point of view. He was married to a Creole Spanish Lady, rather a fine woman by whom he had a family.

We also visited the Commandante of the forces now mustering reluctantly "Por La Libertad de su Patria"[2] & found him in his shop, measuring Calico & aguardiente to the natives. Having parted with our interpreter we had some difficulty in making ourselves understood, in consequence of which we got hold of a person, a native of New Orleans who spoke tolerable English, to accompany us about the Town.

We were obliged to remain here a few days until a Bungo the property of Don Francisco should proceed to Laguna with a cargo of logwood, and on the morning of the 24th we embarked having been supplied with all sorts of good things for our two days voyage by the kindness of Señora Obrea. We found a space had been left for our occupation at night and as a shelter in case of rain on the layers of logwood—on which we placed our Tarpaulins, Blankets and every article we could lay hold of to contribute to the softness of our couches, which after all were anything but agreable; and the mosquitos were dreadful. We were propelled by two oars, and with the assistance of the current got on at the rate of about four miles an hour. The Bungo was a large flat bottomed craft of about 30 tons burden with two masts.

At about 20 miles distance from the Lagoon of Terminos, the Tobasco branch of the river trends off to the N.W. and the branch which we entered trends to the N.E. and is considered more in the nature of a canal than a branch of the River. It would be difficult to say which is the main outlet of the river, and as we did not descend by the Tobasco branch I can give no decided opinion. The old Spanish

2 "For the liberty of their homeland."

maps I was told gave the main outlet into the Laguna Terminos. The banks along this portion are very low and you again fall in with the mangrove, the constant occupier of all the low coast of this country. On the 2nd morning after our embarkation, we opened the Laguna Terminos, and had a guard of honor of Aligators drawn up on each side of the mud banks through which we passed entering the Lagoon—enormous brutes some of them must have been 20 feet long. As soon as we cleared the mud banks at the debouchure of the river, we hoisted our sails and soon came in sight of the low Islands of Carmen & others which form the northern boundary of the Lagoon—and by degrees the shipping laying in front of the town & then the white houses of the Town itself became visible, which with the extensive strip of silvery beach dividing the dark green masses of foliage from the bright blue water had a most picturesque effect.

On our landing we were greeted by an Englishman gentleman in the employ of Mr. Shields, the British vice consul, who conducted us to the house of the latter Gentleman, where we were most hospitably received. We were put up by Mr. Shields in a house not very distant from his own as a sleeping tenement, but he insisted upon our taking our meals with him which we did the whole time we were at Carmen. We found a number of English vessels here loading with Logwood, as well as some American, one Hamburgh & one French—the Captains of which came to visit us. The Carnival and a Revolution were going on at the same time, and I think the latter was the most farcical of the two.

We were awakened one morning by the beating of drums, and other martial demonstrations, and when we got up we heard that the town had made its "pronuncimiento" and that the Fort was captured by the Patriots or Federalists. The manner in which this was effected was rather rich, and of course had all been arranged before hand. The Party being assembled outside the Fort, one fellow managed to get into it over the Parapet, when he was challenged by the Sentinel and answered "Viva La Federalism" when the Garrison returned a "Viva"—and the gates were opened and possession taken. The soldiers declaring themselves federalists forthwith.

The same day we accompanied a procession through the streets—it was headed by the Alcaldi accompanied by other dignitaries and the Proclamation read where a general "Viva" was given for federalism. One of our party thought as cheering was the order of the day, and being an Englishman and a loyal subject, proposed in honour of her majesty, "La Regna de Engleterra" which was immediately responded to with good will by all present. The Carnival was of course a humble imitation of the same festival in all Catholic countries. Processions of Characters in Masques, attended by music & dancing at different places in the street mostly—where temporary awnings were erected and decorated for the occasion with branches of cocoa nut, evergreens & festoons of flowers, and lit up with paper lamps. We perambulated the Town for some time amusing ourselves, with the different groups of performers in these revelries, and then returned to our abode to discuss an oyster supper, having found out that they were to be procured in abundance on a bank not far from the Town we engaged a fisherman to bring some for us. I was much surprised to find them of a different description from the mangrove oyster which is the only sort I have ever met with in the West Indies. They were larger and as delicate in flavour as the English native, our friend the fisherman had constant employment during our stay, in catering for our palates.

Our kind host Mr. Shields is a merchant and British vice consul, and has been long settled in the country having naturalized himself by marrying a bucksome Donna from Merida, the capital of Yucatan, where he formerly resided. In all the stores of this place, as a matter of course, there is a grog shop attached, and generally speaking, it is a portion of the store—being placed at one end of a long counter which runs the whole length of the room, and merely separated by some slight bars. It is a source of great gain to the owner.

British goods are burdened with an excessive duty which would be nearly tantamount to a prohibition, were it not that the Officers of the Revenue are quite open to bribery—From the Commandante to the lowest custom house officer—the consequence is that a system of smuggling is carried on to a very great extent.

Logwood is the staple of this country, numbers of vessels—English, American, French, and etc. load here with little else. A very small quantity of Cocoa, Tobacco and a few drugs are also exported, and a considerable number of hides—some Tortoise shell & wax.

The Town is situated on the Southwestern end of the Island, and consists of two long streets parallel to each other, with straggling buildings at each extremity. It contains few houses of any size—there are about 7,000 inhabitants. There is a well built Fort at about ½ mile distant from the town to the Westward which defends the entrance to the harbour—the latter is deep & commodious, but a sandbar across its mouth prevents vessels drawing more than 9 feet of water to pass over it—the consequence is that the ships are obliged to complete their loading outside, which is inconvenient and sometimes dangerous, particularly during a prevalence of the northerly gales which set in about November & continue for two or three months, but are not constant. The Lagoon is shallow, its average depth being about 7 feet, but there are many shoals in it on which the loaded bungos frequently ground. The Southern shore of the Lagoon is mostly mangrove swamp with sandy ridges of open country extending inland here and there—and cut up with innumerable creeks, forming a labarinth out of which it would be difficult to extricate oneself. These are the very hotbeds of alligators, where they multiply their disgusting species unmolested—and you may here see them of all sizes from those just emerged from the egg to the bloated monster of 20 feet in length. The Lagoon as a northern boundary has a range of low Islands of coral formation, of which the largest is the Island of Carmen and Port Royal. There is a channel for Bungos between the latter & the main land. During the period of loading the vessels there is considerable activity evinced by the whole community of the Town, and much exertion made to get the logwood down the river—which is generally slow work—and it frequently happens that vessels remain for a considerable time, at a heavy expense to the consignees for demurrage. There have been two steamers brought to the Utsumasinta by, or rather under the auspices of a person of the name of Brown, a Yankee who married a native Lady—however he did not appear to have been a favourite with the generality of the inhabitants & I was told that the loss of those vessels was not altogether accidental.

I should imagine that under proper management two or three small steamers would find ample compensation by towing the Bungos up and down the river, and prevent any unnecessary detention of the vessels, besides carrying freight of dry goods. However there is one thing to be considered, which is, that labour is difficult to be procured, and without it logwood is not easily got—as it is often some distance inland from the margin of the River—and although the Indians, I was informed, work steadily, yet a day's work is trifling in comparison to what labourers perform in other countries. Although these Indians are nominally free, I must say there is a species of slavery existing in the country—particularly up the Rivers where there is even less law carried into effect, than in the more settled part of the country. And the proprietors of Haciendas & Logwood establishments have their employed Indians in a state of subjection which would surprise a slave owner of former times. The manner in which this is effected is thus, at least as far as I could learn—a person possessed of sufficient capital to commence a logwood cutting establishment, takes up a certain portion of unoccupied land paying a fine to the Govt. upon each axe which he puts into it. He then hires as many Indians as he wishes, making them advances, seldom in cash, but in cottons, check or other articles, with a considerable addition of aguardiente, which is scored up to the unfortunate and generally unprovident individual at an enormous price, thus getting him into debt by degrees beyond any visible possibility of its liquidation—and until it is paid off he is virtually the bondsman of the Proprietor—altho' any person may pay the debt and take the Indian to work it out—but the amount against him is generally so large that a case of the sort seldom occurs.

The climate of Carmen is not unhealthy, and in the winter months is tolerably cool, the Thermometer is often as low as 54.

The best description of Tobacco exported from this place is grown in Tobasco and is considered of excellent quality, I purchased very good segars at the rate of six dollars a Thousand of a large size, not more than 80 to 90 in the pound. During our stay here, we lunched on board a Hamburg vessel, and I do not ever recollect being on board a more tidy vessel in the merchant service, and we had some most undeniable Champaign.

◄{While Caddy and Walker were savoring the pleasures of life in Carmen, Superintendent MacDonald was growing anxious about the fate of the Palenque expedition. Early in March he penned at least two letters to Frederick Chatfield, Her Majesty's consul at Guatemala, inquiring about the general state of political affairs, and asking if anything had been heard of the explorers. On March 26, Chatfield replied, "I have no intelligence of the Travellers. Stephens is flying about the Country to get materials for his Book, & if he escapes fevers & other mischiefs he may perhaps be here soon . . . ." In responding to a second inquiry, Chatfield offered little encouragement to those seeking the ruins of Palenque, writing on April 8:

> We have no news of Mr. Walker & Lt. Catty, & I am almost afraid that some disaster has happened to them. I never heard that there existed a road from Peten to Palenque, it might be through the Monte or bushwood, & hardly practicable. Mr. Stephens & the Yankified English artist who accompanies him, are gone to Quesaltenango, intending to get to Palenque across the Mexican frontier.
> They must traverse Tabasco to reach the Laguna de Terminos. Persons who desire to see Palenque should go by sea to Villa Hermosa at the mouth of the River Usumasinta, for to go by land is in my opinion foolhardy, especially as there is little or nothing to see when on the spot . . . .

Although Walker and Caddy by early March had emerged from the jungle into the version of civilization to be found at Carmen, communication was so paralyzingly slow that the return of the expedition to The Settlement preceded the posting of Chatfield's second letter by several days.}►

We remained at Carmen six days before we could procure a

conveyance to Campeachy where we hired a Bungo for 100 dollars to take our party to Belize touching at Campeachy & Sisal—and on the morning of the 3rd March we bade adieu to Mr. Shields and his amiable wife, to whose kindness we were indebted for much attention and hospitality.

Our Bungo was a boat of about 20 tons, flat bottomed, rigged with two masts and large sprit sails—quite open except that she had hatches which shipped from side to side over a portion of her stern sheets, under which we spread our blankets &c as couches. We ran down along the Cays inside the Lagoon to the eastern entrance, through which only small craft can gain admittance from the shallow and rocky state of the channel. The wind failing we landed in the afternoon on the main land of Yucatan, where there is a small port and a Hacienda, from whence a road leads to Campeachy to which place a carriage can drive, and a vehicle is kept for the purpose of conveying the mail & an occasional passenger. The person owning the place got us up a dinner & we strolled about on the beach, where we saw four or five enormous sharks in a state of decomposition, which had been washed on shore, having been killed by the fishermen.

The owner of the place like most people of this country was a gambler, and endeavoured to persuade us to play; however after sundry attempts & finding we were not inclined to risk much, he proposed a sort of lottery in which his wife, daughter &c joined, we played for a few Reals—the young lady was the successful party.

During the afternoon, a canoe put in from Carmen, bound to Campeachy with despatches, announcing the glorious achievement of the Federalists having gained possession of the Forts at Laguna after *considerable* opposition from the Central party—"Viva la Federalacion!"

In the evening, we again embarked in our Bungo, and coasted along the low shore of Yucatan, being favoured with a light but fair wind, which however died away soon after dark, when we were obliged to bring to, casting anchor within a few yards of the beach in very shallow water. We had given a passage to Campeachy to a Spaniard from the Palisades, who had been to Belize and also to New

Fig 2.

Plate 21. *Human figure on platform of Building C.*

Plate 22. *Medallions on center wall of Building C.*

Plate 23. *Figure from one of the piers, Building C.*

Plate 24. *Figures from one of the piers of Building D.*

Plate 25. *Figures from one of the piers of Building D.*

Plate 26. *Figures from one of the piers of Building D.*

Plate 27. *Figures from one of the piers of Building D.*

Plate 28. *Section on the line* PQ, *showing the elevation of Building E and Tower G.*

Orleans, at which places he had picked up a little English & French, so that in endeavouring to make himself agreable his conversation was a happy mixture of these languages with Spanish—the latter forming the largest ingredient. He was on his way to Campeachy to hire labourers for a Logwood establishment, and was taking a tolerably large sum in order to emancipate those he might hire from their bondage of debt to their former employers.

On awakening the next morning we found our Patron endeavouring to arouse his crew consisting of three men and a boy, from their heavy slumbers, which he succeeded in doing, with a good many carambos! & carajos! on his part & a tolerable share of grumbling yawns on theirs. However, at last they bestirred themselves, and we again got under weigh.

Our fireplace was a most primitive affair, consisting of a portion of a cask filled to within three or four inches of the top with sand, having four or five stones placed so as to support a pot or kettle, and in this the whole of our cooking was carried on. The Mozos continual employment was grinding the corn, previously steeped in lime water, for the purpose of supplying the crew with the everlasting Tortilla, which was their principal diet.

Two days coasting along a flat uninteresting looking country brought us in sight of Campeachy which is built on the seaside between two fortified emminences and has a very picturesque appearance as you approach it by sea.

March 5th. We landed on a stone pier which extended about 200 yards from high water mark, and were questioned by one or two officials, our fellow passenger making our bad Spanish intelligible. We were provided with a letter to Mr. McGregor the United States consul, from Mr. Shields our hospitable friend at Carmen, and were immediately conducted to his residence where we were most kindly received by his family, Mr. McGregor himself being ill in bed. This gentleman is an old resident of this place and is one of the most wealthy merchants in it, he married a lady of the country by whom he had a numerous family, the sons & one daughter were educated in New York and spoke English fluently.

We were on the point of sallying forth in search of lodgings, when we were introduced to the French consul, who on being told the purpose of our intended walk, most politely offered us beds at his residence, accordingly our Portmanteaus were forthwith dispatched to it, and we proceeded with Mons Farimond to see our apartments—and after lounging about the House, and a stroll through part of the Town, we returned to Mr. McGregor's to dinner, to which we were welcomed with every mark of kindness—and many apologies made for the absence of the host.

The evening is the time at which visiting takes place in this country—and there is no possibility of making use of those few occasionally convenient monosyllables "not at home"—as the houses are open to all who have the slightest acquaintance, and they walk in, make their bow, take their seats, and after the usual complimentary phrases are gone through, make their exit, with a "Buenas noches" to all. The lady of the House takes up a position on the sofa, from each end of which a row of chairs extends down the centre of the room for the accomodation of the visitors. We had some music, after which we retired to the French Consulate, where we enjoyed a good segar & agreable conversation until about eleven o'clock when we were right glad to turn into bed, as we had had most uncomfortable couches on board the Bungo.

Up early and strolled to the fish market which is held on the beach close to the Pier. It was plentifully supplied & I was much surprised to find the young shark eagerly sought after, and indeed preferred to any other fish—on enquiry I found it was considered the greatest delicacy by the Campecheanos, and few of them eat anything else for breakfast—in fact no breakfast table is complete without Cason.

The Vegetable & Poultry market is also well supplied with abundance of English vegetables in addition to those of the country at exceedingly moderate prices, indeed every article of food is to be purchased cheap.

On returning to breakfast, I found we had a dish of the Cason and very good it proved, rather a peculiar flavour perhaps, but not at all unpalatable. It was well stewed & seasoned with garlic herbs and chilis.

Campeche derives its name from two most disagreable companions as I found to my exceeding annoyance. Cam signifying, in the Maya language, Serpent—and peche that most troublesome little insect the warri tick, called by the Spaniards Garapata. The town is also called San Francisco Campeche—it is the principal Sea port and trading place of Yucatan and is stated by some to be situated at the mouth of a river San Francisco, however no river exists anywhere in its vicinity—and it is a curious fact that throughout this peninsula there is but one stream of fresh water—the Champoton River, nearly midway between Campeachy and Laguna Terminos. It must have been at this river where Terminos was surprised by the natives when taking in water for his vessels.

Campeache is a well fortified town, being completely surrounded by a wall and dry ditch and has eight bastions—one at each angle of an irregular octagon. They are well placed for the defence of the town, but overtaken the latter must fall also. It has four gates the one on the north opening to the Pier. It is also protected by a Fort on high ground both to the East & West and has two Batteries beneath the latter.

The town is well built containing some excellent houses (the houses are built of the stone quarried in the immediate neighbourhood, which is a calcarious limestone easily worked) in the old moorish and Spanish style—consisting of a block of buildings forming a hollow square having Piazzas on each side of the interior, from whence doors communicate to the different apartments—many are two stories. The square is often tastefully laid out with flowers and Plants and frequently contains a fountain.

The Harbour or Roadstead is very shallow, and consequently ships drawing any depth of water cannot approach the town. The vessels loading with logwood are obliged to anchor about 8 miles from the shore, and consequently are exposed at some seasons to heavy gales of wind particularly during the months of Novr, Decr, and Jany.

In former times the Town was frequently plundered by the French and English Buccaneers. In 1659 it was taken by the English under Sir Christopher Mims—In 1678 by the Buccaneers and in 1685 by the Pirates of St. Domingo, in the last named year they set fire to the town and Fortifications, and plundered the adjacent country to the distance of fifteen miles; they also burnt £50,000 worth of Logwood, because the Government would not ransom the place for an enormous sum which they demanded. When the Spaniards first took this place, it contained 3000 houses with many beautiful monuments of the Indian Arts, which were destroyed by the fanatisism of the Priesthood.

By the treaty of 1783 the British were allowed to cut Logwood in the province, but they had incessant quarrels with the Spaniards who constantly broke faith with them, and put them under restrictions which at length drove them from the vicinity.

The Cathedral is a handsome building, richly decorated in the interior with gilding & silver adornments. The principal altar is gorgeous in the extreme. There are a good many paintings but none of any great merit. There are fourteen churches in the Town & suburbs, many of them handsome structures—besides Convents & Hospitals.

The Alamada is outside the Town and is a cool and pleasant promenade after 5 o'clock in the evening & to it many resort to enjoy the fresh air after being cooped up in the hot town all day. You here see all the beauty of the place, unbonnetted and gaily dressed as for an evening party—dark locks tastefully adorned with flowers—or simply braided on the younger portion of the Señoritas—They all have very dark eyes and fine teeth—and when young, good figures—but as they advance in years, particularly those who have families, they become stout—very stout—in fact fat & punchy—and you often see a very pretty face on a mass of flesh without form.

The day after our arrival we were conducted by Mons. Faramond to visit the Governor Genl Rivas; we found him much harassed by existing affairs, expecting daily to be placed in a state of siege, as it was reported that an army of Federalists was on its march from Merida, vowing vengeance to the Central Party—he expressed his regret that under these circumstances he could not offer us much attention, but that it would otherwise have given him the greatest pleasure to have had us as his guests during our sojourn in the Town. We thanked him for his politeness, and left him surrounded by a number of those who were, or pretended to be, of the same opinions in Politics.

Numbers were arrested, and others made their escape to Merida to join the "Brave Army"—others had their cash and valuables packed and placed in safe keeping—in order that they might bolt at the shortest notice. There was a mustering of troops now & then, extra guards posted on the places most likely to be assailed first. Scouts arriving with and departing for intelligence of the enemy—and Sentries posted over the gates of the Barracks to prevent the Militia from joining the rebels, as they were called by one party, Patriots by themselves.

The Governor, officers, and soldiers composing the Garrison were Mexicans and Centralists, at least most of them were so, and I fancy had few of the same opinion amongst the inhabitants—who had been long disgusted with the tyranny & oppression exercised towards them by the Central Government—and the little interest it took in the welfare of this particular portion of the Mexican dominions, although they were taxed their quota towards the support of that Govt—consequently their dander was raised, and they had declared themselves independent of Mexico & had appointed a Governor and officials at Merida—the headquarters of the Federal party.

I was introduced to the Colonel of the Artillery, who spoke good French, and was about the best dressed man I have seen for some time, he appeared very intelligent, and was a thorough Centralist, and exceedingly bitter against the opposite party. He kindly gave me an order of admittance to the works of the Town.

Having called upon Segourra, the ex-Commandante of Peten, who had arrived here from Belize, where he received considerable attention from the inhabitants, we were invited to dine with him, as also our kind friend Mons. Faramond. He gave us a most sumptuous entertainment which was served on silver even to the cheese plates—

149

as I have always made a rule of never saying anything to the prejudice of a man who feeds me well, au contraire I would uphold him as a pattern to be followed, I beg to state that all the stories we heard in Peten with regards to Segourra having made use of various stratagems to elicit money out of the people over whom he was placed, must have been base calumnies—particularly as he had a nominal salary, expensive establishments, and retired, or rather retreated with a few doubloons and some trifling articles of plate.

We also dined with a French gentleman, a merchant, Mons. Fremont, who entertained us well, giving us some of the best claret & Champaigne I have tasted for a long time. After dinner he conducted us to see a house and garden in one of the Suburbs which belonged to the last Governor, the gardens were beautifully laid out & contained many choice plants, among them some varieties of cactus, and orchidian plants bearing very beautiful flowers. There was also a delicious looking bath, which had a most tempting appearance considering the heat of the climate, and I longed to plunge into it forthwith. The paths were flanked by a small canal; by which water was conveyed from a well, being pumped into a reservoir to all parts of the garden. Nearly all the wealthy inhabitants have gardens, with ornamental cottages attached, to which they occasionally resort for the sake of cool air & retirement.

The commerce of Campeache is principally carried on with Havana, although several American and English vessels trade with the place. Most of their goods are smuggled into the country for the duties are so high that otherwise they would not be worth landing. Cotton goods of a certain texture are prohibited, in order to cherish the rising manufactures of the country. However, at present nothing but the coarsest description of cotton cloths are manufactured. The exports consist of Logwood, sugar, hides, wax, salt, coarse bagging made from the Hanakin or aloe which are shipped to Havana for the purpose of packing sugar, coffee, &c. Tobacco is also grown to some extent.

We passed six days very agreeably at Campeache, and left it with regret, and I must say nothing could be kinder than the attention we met with from Mons. Faramond and the family of Mr. McGregor to whose house we generally adjourned of an evening when we were entertained with music, dancing and agreeable conversation. The Captain of the Port made some little difficulty about granting us a clearance—however, after a little altercation we got the necessary document.

The French consul had held the same appointment at Malta where he had been acquainted with several of our Officers—he parted with us as we got into our Bungo to proceed to Sisal—which we did on the morning of the 10th March. After leaving Campeche the coast becomes low and covered with stunted trees and scrub bush. We brought to at night, and set sail again at daylight the next morning. Landed in the afternoon at some salt ponds which supply Campeachy, Merida and most of the country of Yucatan with this necessary article—besides exporting some. The ponds were divided into shallow pans, and had all the appearance of being frozen, a thin incrustation of salt being then ready to collect.

We were three days getting to Sisal, and glad enough we were to leave the uncomfortable Bungo. We immediately waited on the Commandant with our Passport and found him up to his ears in business making ready for war—the whole place was in a bustle, and a schooner was fitting out for the protection of the harbour and town. We took up our abode for the night at an Inn, I believe the only one in the place, and sat down to a capital dinner at a Table d'Hote with a good many persons, all employed in some way in the cause of the Revolution, one long fellow with a maimed hand seemed to be the head man and gave numerous orders, while employing his game hand shovelling Frijoles and other dainties into his mouth. They were manning two or three vessels to Blockade Campeachy.

After dinner strolled through the Town which is of mean appearance, all the houses being only one story high, with the single exception of the Commandants, and thatched. There is a small Fort and Battery for the protection of the harbour, and a wooden Pier or wharf for the embarkation of merchandize &c but the depth of the water will only admit Bungos or small craft coming along side of it.

Our Inn was a sort of grog shop, and exceedingly noisy; we amused ourselves in the only tolerably quiet part of it which was the veranda where we dined. It looked into a court yard in the middle of which was a duck pond, constructed for the aquatic amusement of a variety of Pet wild fowl—among them were several of the whistling duck. We were accomodated with a couple of stretchers, on which we spread our own bed clothes. Just before I turned in I put a paper containing some 30 or 40 dollars into the corner of my Portmanteau which unfortunately I could not lock, and in the morning I found some kind person had appropriated my Pesos. I was uncharitable enough to suspect the Master of the house was the culprit from his manner, when the loss was mentioned & he having slept in a hammock directly over the Portmanteau. We provisioned our people and started them to proceed round Cape Catoche to Ascension Bay, where we were to meet them, and we hired a Caleche to take us to Merida the next morning. When we paid our bill the host made a show of not taking our money as we had been robbed in his house and *hinted* that he wished to repay our loss, but the attempt at restoration was so exceedingly slight that we paid our money and wished him adios. Our living only amounted to a dollar a day each, for which we had a cup of excellent chocolate and a biscuit the first thing in the morning, an excellent meat breakfast with Bordeaux at 10 o'clock, a good dinner at four, and chocolate again in the evening. To be sure the accomodation otherwise was very limited.

The vehicle called a Caleche, was a two wheeled affair, without springs—the body being half covered,—to which one horse was attached by long shafts, the driver riding the said nag & another being attached on the off side, as a reserve—our Portmanteaus were lashed on behind—and in this we started for Merida.

The country round Sisal is nearly level—the Town being placed on the highest ground in the neighbourhood, and no portion of that is more than 20 feet above the level of the sea, which at high water overflows the land at the back leaving shallow ponds of stagnant water, which must cause sickness. Over this portion the road is raised so as to form as good a road as one would wish to travel; it is about 20 yards wide. We trotted along at a tolerable pace in a comparatively comfortable style, after the fatiguing journeys we had had lately, through bush & swamp, and in canoe & Bungo—all most uncomfortable. We halted for a few minutes at the village of ———, where our Moso put in the led horse—and we again progressed on our way, which was monotonous in the extreme—straight level road, with stunted trees & scrub bush, growing from the fissures of broken rugged limestone.

As we approached Merida the country improved, we passed a few houses embedded in beautiful evergreen trees, the Ramoon, of large growth. We met many mules laden with sugar & other produce, and a quantity of corn or maize for the "Brave Army."

The numerous spires of the churches of Merida rising above the surrounding country gave notice of our near approach to the metropolis of Yucatan, and soon we were driving through a good street to the address of a Gentleman for whom we had a letter; and who was requested to put us in the way of getting lodgings &c. We found him at home and exceedingly civil, but very cautious, evidently having the Revolutionary excitement strongly upon him—and not quite at his ease. To be sure we made sad havock of her Majesty of Spains "Lingua Castillana"—however we made him understand that we wanted a place to put our heads under, and he directed us to a Posada and followed himself to see that we were all right.

The Posada was kept by two elderly ladies, and was more a boarding house than an Inn—we hired a room (the only spare one) and a bedroom in which were two stretchers, without mattresses & some other furniture of very fair description, and what we had not been used to in our travels, such as dressing Table & Glass, washhand stand &c.

The house consisted like most others of a hollow square—it was one storey having a corridor or Piaza along two sides of the square, with benches Chairs & Tables, it being used as the daily habitation & the rooms only for sleeping in. The yard was laid out with flowers & shrubs, and had a well in the centre. Our side of the square contained stable, coach house, &c. The entrance was by a strong folding gate, studded with huge iron nails, and had a wicket in it—and the windows which looked into the street were strongly barred with iron and were not glazed. The place could have stood a siege. We were too late for their dinner hour however they managed to get us up a very tolerable meal & with some light claret we fared well for travellers.

The first fact we were desirous of knowing was, whether there were any persons in the place who could speak English, and we were told there were several, our Hostess offering to send for a gentleman of her acquaintance who could do so. However in the evening we strolled to the house of the Gentleman to whom we brought a letter, and were introduced to his lady, whose occupation seemed to be attending to a retail business carried on in an apartment attached to the wholesale warehouse. She was a goodly looking dame of a "certain age" exceedingly stout, and good tempered. Her curiosity was excited hearing we had been at "Las Ruinas" de Palenque and as she could not perfectly understand our attempt at Spanish, sent for a friend who spoke English, and then we had no end of questions— which we satisfied to the best of our abilities, and returned to our Posada.

Yucatan was to us such a Terra Incognita that beyond a few villages, we did not expect to fall in with any greater progress in civilization and we were much surprised at finding Campeache so fine a Town; however, we were much more surprised at the extent and general appearance of Merida, a Town thirty six miles inland covering a space of nine miles in circumference, having good broad streets with elegant houses & shops, a splendid Cathedral, besides numbers of Churches, Convents, Hospitals, and a College for the education of the Clergy at the head of which was a Bishop, a handsome Theatre, extensive square or Plaza, an Alamada tastefully laid out and planted with trees and shrubs for the benefit of the inhabitants—In fact every necessary thing to form an opulent & well populated city. The square or plaza is about 200 yards wide, one side containing the Cathedral and Bishops Palace. The House of Assembly is also in this square, and that of the founder Don Francisco Montejo, which house is called the house of the Conquest [see Plate 5]. The Facade of it has much architectural beauty, although of curious design.

The Cathedral is a good building, and the interior is gorgeously decorated, the principal Altar being of massive silver with gold ornamental work. There were many paintings but none of any great merit, the best picture was done in crayons. We attended at mass once, all the congregation were females with very few exceptions, most of them Indian women all dressed alike with only the difference of some having the embroidered work round the edges of their dress of different colours & patterns; the dress was invariably white, and consisted of a chimise with short sleeves and low at the neck, and a sort of long jacket made tolerably full with long sleeves—many of them had muslin veils—or mantillas.

{With this brief description of Mérida, Caddy's diary inexplicably breaks off in mid-page. Whether Caddy ceased taking notes at this point, or simply failed to complete the expanded version of his account of the travels, we shall never know. The remainder of the journey, probably both unpleasant and rather dull at times, is described briefly in Walker's official report of the expedition, which follows. After traveling over one thousand miles by river, land, and finally by sea, the Palenque Expedition returned on April 4, 1841, to Belize, whence it had set out 144 days earlier. The journey was over at last, and the travelers must have been weary indeed.}

VII. the official version —walker's report

⊰{To read John Caddy's diary of the Palenque expedition is to see the land and the people, as well as the ruins, through the eyes of an artist and a romantic. Walker's official version of the journey stands in marked contrast to Caddy's lively account, for Walker, with the official's businesslike, perhaps overmeticulous approach to life, made enquiries and observations as he went along, recording data on soil, labor force, and the military-political situation. The difference between the two accounts is approximately the difference between a novel and a government statistical report. Nevertheless, Walker's version is not the less valuable but only the less readable of the two. Although Walker's words cover the same ground as Caddy's, one is complementary to the other, and for this reason it seems worthwhile to retrace the course of the expedition with Walker, and see what sometimes seems a different land altogether.

Walker's report contained many observations on the sentiments and actions of Mexican and Guatemalan subjects which the Colonial Office deemed unsuitable for inclusion in any published account; these passages were bracketed by the Colonial Office, and are similarly marked here. Otherwise the report appears as it was written. It was submitted to Superintendent MacDonald under the date April 6, 1840, which may be the day on which the writing was begun, but certainly is not the date the report was completed. After the usual prefatory remarks, Walker's account begins:}⊱

ALTHOUGH THE SEASON at which we started is seldom or ever chosen for river travelling and the great floods caused by the continuous

156

rains which had prevailed for some weeks previous had rendered navigation by Pitpans somewhat critical, we nevertheless managed with the flush of paddles supplied us by Your Excellency from the strength of the 2d. West India Regiment, and with the assistance of nine hired experienced Creole Boatmen to reach Tiger Run, a distance of 189 miles[1] up the Belize on the seventh day from our departure.

In accordance with Your Excellency's commands I made it my particular study on my way up the river to enquire into the nature of the soil as regarded it's adaptation for agricultural purposes, and likewise to ascertain as exactly as possible the working of the existing free labour system.

Excepting where clearances are made around the establishments of the Mahogany Cutters and those of a few other persons, the wood on each side of the River forms an almost impenetrable wall, but on the different banks at which we rested for the night I pushed my observations as far as I possibly could, and I have the satisfaction to state that the major part of the land, from the specimens of production exhibited to me, appeared to possess all the capabilities for cultivation which nature can well bestow and that I saw but very few places destitute of the elements of fertility.

The river abounds in a fluor-spar of a superior description which will become most useful to the Settlement as furnishing material for the preparation of the finest lime, and there is also an inexhaustible quantity of clay adapted for the manufacture of brick, an article which is now generally preferred to wood in constructing the houses and stores in Belize.

At present the purchase of brick from England is not found to be expensive as it is brought out, as ballast, in large quantities by the numerous ships which come out to Honduras in ballast alone—but by making the brick in this country it would enable such ships to bring their ballast in coal, which will be of primary necessity when steam machinery, as it soon must be, is in play here.

[1] This is an impressive figure, and it may indeed have seemed 189 miles running upriver at flood stage, but the actual distance is between 100 and 110 miles.

157

In Honduras, where, as in times past, as regarded treatment, the distinction between the slave and the free laborer existed more in sound than in substance, little scope is left for any comparison to be drawn between the present system of voluntary service and that which formerly obtained in the Settlement. I have never been able to discover that with their independence, the formerly apprenticed Africans have shown an unwillingness to labor for a fair remuneration. The sole point on which I think that they are justly reprehensible is in the disposition which they manifest to cavil at the ample supplies of provisions still furnished to them. Great quantities of the finest fish are taken at different times in the various Creeks and Lagoons, yet the people will not suffer their allowance of fat pork to be curtailed even when the Master imparts to them as much of this excellent fish as they are disposed to receive.

And altho' in the Mahogany Works there are always large droves of cattle they will not take a half or even a quarter of their allowance in wholesome fresh meat, but insist upon exacting to the increased expense of the Employer the full quantum of English mess pork, which often unable to use, they waste. The disposition of the negro, engendered by his nature and the circumstances under which destiny has placed him, it is impossible instantaneously to change—inhabiting a country where the overpowering nature of the atmosphere engenders a lassitude against which it is difficult to contend, and where nature's spontaneous and bountiful mess affords him with little exertion the complete gratification of his moderate wants, it is a circumstance not be wondered at that he is so supine. All that I have seen has shown me that his only look out is how to fend off hard work, and his sole study to consist in endeavouring to gain any sort of living in the easiest way. This is not difficult in a place which is justly styled "the poor man's country"—where fish and game in great variety are inconceivably abundant and easily taken, and where with the slightest trouble and the exercise of a little patience a good plantation can be easily cleared and cropped. Many of the negroes, however, wont exert themselves so much and even those who are the most vehement in their complaints. To cite a homely specimen of this class and from whom the character of too many may be learned is Joe Terrell an emancipated African at Society Hall on the Belize. Joe is a good workman when he can be kept from liquor, but an idle good-for-nothing dog while it lasts. In former times, he said his intention after emancipation was to make plantation or keep grog-shop and his constant cry used to be "Gor Amighty me wish dis free make haste and come," yet still he remains with his old master, and probably will as long as Mr. Usher will retain him in his service.

At Tiger Run we remained during the afternoon and night of our arrival and on the forenoon of the next day we proceeded up to Duck Run. At both of these banks I found considerable settlements, but no appearance of that insubordination which was reported to have existed in those places. The only marauders who infest this part of the Settlement are the wild Indians in the vicinity, who, during the night or in the absence of the proprietor, at various times emerge from the secret recesses of the Forest for the purpose of plundering any domestic animals or articles they can lay their hands upon. Some slight disturbances had taken place about three weeks previous to our arrival here but they had their origin and were entirely confined to a party of Spaniards, who, on account of the existing revolution in the Guatimalean Republic, had fled from Peten following the fortunes of the deposed Commandant Don Julian Seguro. These refugees, however, from above the number of a hundred, by betaking themselves to Belize and elsewhere had dwindled down to the insignificant number of three, and these consisted of two helpless women and an infirm man. The inhabitants of Tiger and Duck runs seemed to me to be comfortably situated and in good circumstances. They appeared to be industrious and well-behaved, and amongst the number I remarked two or three individuals of African descent who are in the habit of visiting Belize and who were previously known to me as of good character and habits. I found it therefore unnecessary to leave the detachment of the 2d. West India Regiment at either of these places, and according to Your Excellency's directions, with the exception of four men who proceeded on with us, I sent the soldiers back with the Pitpans to Belize.

At Duck Run we were detained eight days by the heavy and incessant rains which rendered it impossible for us to proceed. This period of our detention was employed in procuring horses, mules, and Indians for our journey, all of which, much contrary to our expectations and the assurances we had received, we had the greatest difficulty in obtaining.

Before leaving the Belize Main River I am compelled, though unwillingly, to report that from the "Great Falls" only seventy one miles from its mouth it is unfitted as a water communication for the transportation of the produce which may be cultivated on it's banks and in the vicinity. The numerous falls, shallows and runs above the part to which I have referred render it's navigation by a loaded boat even of the smallest size if not impracticable, entirely unsafe. What the application and operations of art might do to improve it by the blasting of rocks and deepening the channels it is not difficult to determine, but the circumstances of a young Colony or one situated like this Settlement would prevent the expenses necessary for such an undertaking from being realized for a longer time than it is pleasant to contemplate.

Having at length succeeded in furnishing ourselves with the most indifferent but only means of transport at command, we proceeded into the Pass which leads to Peten, and here in this wild and dangerous road for thirteen days, until we reached a place called La Cinquentra, we had to encounter difficulties of every description. The vast quantity of water which had lately fallen had swollen the numerous creeks over which we had to pass to an extent, that it was at much hazard, with extreme labor, and after very great delays, that we were enabled, even after unloading them, to get our horses and mules across the greater number of those serious obstructions to the traveller. The swamps again were so much inundated that for five consecutive days we hardly advanced a step without the horses being up to their girths in mud or water. Besides the path in some places was absolutely shut up and reduced us to the necessity of cutting a way with our machetes thro' the bush.

Under these circumstances Your Excellency will be able to judge how much our progress was retarded, and on a route where we had no covering from rain, sun, or the heavy evening dews, except that which, with our own hands, at the close of day and with the leaves of the forest we reared for our nightly security and shelter.

Throughout the whole of this road we fell in with an unbounded quantity of Cedar and Mahogany, of most gigantic dimensions, besides an immense number of Indian Rubber trees and many others of a valuable description.

La Cinquentra, before mentioned, where we arrived on the 11th of December, is a wild and romantic spot on the stream San Pedro which falls into a Branch of the Belize. This place was formerly by the Spaniards and is still by the Peteneros used as their lookout for an approaching enemy; but on the occasion of our arrival we found it unoccupied. Resting here for the night we proceeded onwards in the morning through a pass of a mountainous character but much superior to what we had been accustomed to, and at San Felipe a distance of about seventeen miles, where the Savannah is opened we encountered the first military guard, which consisted of a Sergeant armed with a tolerable fowling piece and twenty Indians with their bows and arrows. From this place after partaking of some refreshment we set out for the Hacienda of Sta. Rosa where we were to take up our quarters for the night. To this Hacienda we were attended by the Sergeant of the Guard, who had in the meantime dispatched an Indian to acquaint the officer in charge of the next station with our approach. The ride from San Felipe to Santa Rosa lies thro' a descending series of Savannahs disposed in platforms, amidst which the most beautiful panoramic views meet the eye on every side and form one of the finest sights in this most interesting district. Here we were on high ground—the grasses and wild plants were similar in species to those in Britain and the common wild Scotch thistle was in abundance all around.

In the evening the individual who was officer of the next post made his appearance in the person of a Mr. Torribio who was banished from the British limits about nine months ago for a cattle depredation and at whose trial I was one of the presiding Magistrates. Mr.

Torribio altho his ideas on Cow-stealing were known not to be over scrupulous appeared to be a person of some consideration in the neighbourhood—he volunteered to be our conductor through the remaining parts of the forest and Savannah which we had still to traverse before reaching Peten, and as he was known to be a capital Bushman we accepted his services.

At Santa Rosa we were obliged to remain a day and a half to procure fresh horses and Indians.

Of the horses and mules which we took with us from Duck Run two had sunk under the fatigue and died on the road. One Indian deserted from us and two others were rendered by sickness incapable of being of any service to us. I should be glad if those trivial casualties were all I had to record, but, I have with regret to state that Private I. Carnick of the Royal Artillery, who attended Lieut. Caddy in the capacity of servant, was taken ill with fever three days journey from Sta. Rosa—all along the road he was subjected to no privations which we did not share—he had his horse to carry him and partook of the same fare as Lieut. Caddy and myself. Finding him unable to go on, a litter was constructed and he was sent to a neighbouring village to be placed under the care of a woman and her daughter who all understood the English language. On this unfortunate point I may here anticipate a little and inform Your Excellency that in a few days after Carnick had been so disposed of, intelligence of his death reached Peten. From what I saw of this man on our journey he appeared to be a most respectable person and his officer told me that he was a good soldier. As he was a member of the Roman Catholic Church I sent a letter to the Cure of Peten enclosing a fee, requesting that prayers for the repose of his soul might be said in the Church there in accordance with the Romish ritual.

On the [*blank*] of December, having seen the remainder of our party prepared to continue on their march, Lieut. Caddy and myself escorted by Torribio set off by a shorter cut thro' the Forest and after a fatiguing ride of forty two miles thro' a path almost as bad as that from the Belize we reached late at night the first Pueblo to be met with in the district called Titchalic and where we stopped two days to enable our people to overtake us and to enjoy some needful rest. The Hacienda of the Ex-Commandant Seguro, now confiscated by the opposite party, is situated in the vicinity of this place. [there we met with some individuals who had experienced his kindness who displayed an unaffected regret for the misfortunes of their fallen chief—His successor Manuel Ozaeta seemed to be correspondingly odious in their eyes, his name never being sounded either here or in any of the parts we had as yet been in but as something fearful and to be dreaded.] To this officer I had thought it proper on entering the province, in consequence of the disturbed state of the country, to forward a letter informing him of our intention to pass through Peten on our way to Tabasco and intimating to him that my companion and myself would feel much pleasure in making his acquaintance. At Titchalic we were assured that the moment the Commandant received this letter he would come out and meet us. And this visit he favored us with at the extraordinary hour of Two o'clock in the morning attended by his staff and guards. After a few ordinary compliments had passed he informed me that the unusual hour he visited us at was to be attributed to his having been riding day and night through different and distant Pueblos. [I have no doubt however that his intention was to take us by surprise, foolishly imagining that we had come into the country with unfavourable intentions towards him. The appearance of Ozaeta and his party, whose garments and accoutrements would have done honor to Rag-Fair, was not over prepossessing. He demanded the surrender to him of a young man, whom I had hired at Duck Run as an attendant upon the mules, that he might throw him into chains as a follower of Seguro. After some slight altercation on this subject, during which I stated to the Commandant that I should consider his pressing this demand as a great breach of hospitality he consented to allow the lad to remain under my protection for the present.] He proposed that we should accompany him to Peten at eight oclock, and on our assenting to this proposal he took his departure for the purpose of reposing himself till that hour.

[From the character I had received of Ozaeta, from the demand he had made on us as before mentioned, and from the Brigand appearance of himself and his followers I was disposed to think that we had made rather an uncomfortable acquaintance: this feeling however gradually wore away as he opened up his mind and gave expression to sentiments of a liberal and humane description. Before we had gone half a league he granted a full pardon to the lad who was the subject of discussion on our first meeting.] We accompanied the Commandant to the Pueblo of Santa Anna where it was necessary for him to swear in the Alcaldes, and at his desire we deferred proceeding to Peten till next day in order that we might spend the remainder of this one at a property of his close to the Pueblo of Chacchaclun. Our travels this day were entirely confined to Savannahs of the richest description. Here and there lay clumps of forest and hills of various sizes covered with foliage which varied the prospect, alternately limiting and extending the view. To any one whom the heat of the sun does not affect a ride through these magnificent pastures is exciting and animating in the extreme, the gale frequently sweeping over them as fresh as the breeze from the ocean.

The road from Chacchaclun to Peten lies through a forest of a mountainous character, passing over a portion of the extensive amphitheatre of hills which binds in the lake of Itza. Emerging from the forest the traveller comes out on the village of San Benito which is prettily situated on the margin of the lake. Here a wide view of this interesting sheet of water offers itself to the beholder, and at the distance of about half a mile from the shore stands the island town of Peten, which presents a most picturesque appearance as it rises gradually from the water's edge to the Plazza on which are the larger buildings erected by the old Spaniards and all crowned by the Church of "Our Lady of Sorrows."

San Benito as far as regards the majority of it's inhabitants is quite an Anglo-African town—it's population is composed chiefly of runaway negroes from Belize, who at various times during the existence of the slave system, absconded from their owners not infrequently with great plunder and in a few instances after having perpetrated the murder of their master. At the time the Guatimaleans accomplished their independence they offered great inducements to the negroes within British limits to quit the Settlement and become free citizens of their Republic. But in the district of Peten they now see reason to repent of their anxiety to desire the ingress of the negroes, as they form quite a community by themselves, and during the revolutions to which this fine but unfortunate country is perpetually exposed they take sides as their feelings for a particular chief or their supposed interests prompt them and keep Peten in continual excitement.

Having crossed to the town in Canoes, the contrast between the splendid developments of creation and the works of man was not long in showing itself. The houses of the inhabitants are for the most part uncommonly mean, and, with the exception of a few grass hammocks and a rude table, totally unfurnished—they are formed of stone walls plastered over with lime which is whitewashed and the roofs are of thatch. The streets which used formerly to be well kept are now altogether broken up and in such disrepair that it is not only uncomfortable but difficult to perambulate them. The Plazza is of considerable size. On the western side stands the church which is of considerable size, retains some tolerable pictures and some grotesque figures of various saints, with a fair show of sacramental plate and the different staves and crosses used in the processions peculiar to the Roman Catholic Religion. On the top of the Church the Imperial Crown of Spain and the Indies is very well sculptured. This is the only one of the old buildings which is still used for its original purposes, but so great is the ignorance of every one here that the only information the Cure could give me was, that the church is erected on the site where in former times stood the principal temple of the Itzaens. The archives of the Church are not in existence. The baptismal Register alone remains which was made patent to me and from which I took an interesting extract and which purported to be a record of the baptism of King Canec the soverign of the country, a short time subsequent to his subjugation in 1697 by Don Martin de Ursua Governor of Yucatan. The old barracks form a line of buildings which stretch along one side of the Square and if in repair would be capable of containing six hundred soldiers. A convent, now in ruins, adjoins the Barracks. The Commandancy, from its outward appearance, walls, disposition of the Rooms and ample culinary appurtenances, exhibits the aspect of having been once capable of lodging an officer of rank and large family. The plazza possesses a strong battery and the town seems to have been completely surrounded by a defensive wall as fragments of it yet remain and the embrasures for the guns are still seen in various places. The peeps from the fine elevation of the Plazza on the different points of the lake are very delightful and form as pretty views as possibly can be imagined. The hills on every side, tho' not of any very great height, yet admit of a diversity of shades, and these again thrown on the water, when combined with a beautiful sky render it altogether a scene of peculiar sweetness and which rises to a calm magnificence at the setting of the sun.

We found the town in some little excitement from the place having been so lately the Theatre of a Revolution. Various troops of half clad soldiers armed with useless muskets were continually parading the streets—The Gaol was full of prisoners, but if report spoke true their captivity seemed only to be merited by the injuries which they had inflicted on the party now in the ascendant.

Left completely to themselves by the Supreme Government, and possessing no local legislature, for which indeed the district of Peten does not afford the elements, there appears to have been for some time back a continual struggle between two factions, and by whom political power seems to have been kept or lost as each showed the best front. When the one faction triumphed, the old hands were removed from confinement and new tenants for the gaol provided from the party last in power. There is no law, no sort of trial, no statement or condescendence of the particulars of an offence. The prisoner is taken, hurried before the Commandant when one single word is uttered "rematcher," which answers to our word "clinch him," and away the poor devil is hurried to a prison which must be his home till another "emente" takes place and makes him a Gaoler in his turn. There is not the slightest provision made for the support of captives of any kind, every one must be dependent on his own resources or on the

bounty of his friends for the means of existence. Political delinquencies, which mean opposition to the party that happens to be in
power, are visited with much more severity than the highest of human
crimes. Murders, especially arising from jealousy, are of frequent
occurrence. As you go along any one of the passes which communicate
with the different pueblos and Haciendas or Farms, a spot is pointed
out where a murder has been committed—the incidents of the case and
the atrocities of the appalling act powerfully and faithfully narrated,
and when you enquire how long the legend has been in existence,
you are told that it is an event which occurred seven or eight months
before. Murderers and thieves here stalk abroad in the open day and
not a soul seems to feel any disgrace in associating with them. Five
persons, each separately guilty of the crime of murder, were pointed
out to me during my short residence in Peten. There is one brute
occasionally to be seen in the streets of the town, who lives with
his own daughter in incestuous connection. The only punishment
awarded to this abominable offender is his not being permitted or the
infamous partner of his crime to reside within the town, but he may
come and go when he chooses for the purpose of negotiating his
affairs.

I am sorry to say that with no very great number of exceptions
the Peteneros in general are lax in principle and immoral in their
habits. The Belize Merchants, anxious to encourage, often give the
Peteneros credit—this liberality is too frequently badly requited—
they laughing in Peten at the simplicity of the Belizians and applaud-
ing themselves in having only performed a dexterous feat, piquing
themselves upon their skill in overreaching as a proof of their address
and considering the greater the swindle the better the joke. [It is
pitiable to witness a race so degraded, and it is melancholy to behold
a place once possessing a respectable establishment and in it's ruins
showing the traces of all the emblems of national strength dwindling
down so low;—but under the baneful influence of a weak and con-
temptible government every relic of civilisation and strength is so
fast disappearing, that it would seem as if in this district of the Guati-

malean Republic the Indians were doomed again to become independent and to possess in sole and undisputed right the Savannah and forests—the dominions of their ancestors.]

Under other circumstances and with a government based on principles less mutable in their nature, while the bad might improve, what is good and industrious in the Petenero Character would not be long in appearing. An open intercourse with the British at Belize would most quickly effect this consummation and be of material advantage to both. At present the people of this district indulge in a most lazy and inactive life which the richness of their Savannahs and their productive plantations enable them to do; but having created no facilities for the transportation and sale of their numerous live stock beyond their own territory, they are almost entirely without money and consequently are destitute of all the commodities and luxuries which abound in other fertile countries and even in the neighbouring provinces. This state of things would be easily remedied would they apply themselves in earnest to the construction of a good and direct road to the British limits to be met by one which Your Excellency commenced last spring. Knowing your views and anxiety on this matter I urged on the notice of the Commandant the advantages which would accrue to the State of Peten from the formation of this road—he pleaded want of funds and the unsettled state of the country, but he informed me that he had long desired the accomplishment of such a design, and promised that it would be the first thing he would pay attention to when he had got matters quiet, and that then he would communicate with Your Excellency on the subject. Once effected it could not fail of being a source of vast benefit to the people of Peten, as the Mexicans of Chiapas, Tabasco and different Pueblos on the Rivers which lie near or diverge from the Usumasinta, and who are now the principal purchasers of the little ventures which the Peteneros bring from Belize, would with avidity, so anxious are they for British goods, buy in large quantities, and render Peten quite an intermediate depot between Belize and those places. Before the era of African emancipation the Authorities of British Honduras, and with considerable justice, opposed themselves to a free communication with Peten on account of the facilities for escape which it would give to the slaves of the Settlement. This obstacle however has happily ceased to exist and for our own interests I hope soon to see the two places easy of access to one another, as it will create a vent for a large quantity of British goods, it will afford ample supplies of provisions for our increasing population, and at a short notice it could furnish what might be needful in this way, in case Belize from it's well protected and favourable position might at any time hereafter be used as a refitting station for our Navy. Besides these advantages a great many articles of high commercial importance are the natural & spontaneous production of this district— a great proportion of the land adjoining the Lake of Itza with eleven islets which stud the water are fertile in the extreme, yielding fre quently two harvests in the year, and producing maize, pepper, balsams, vanilla, cotton, indigo, cochineal, achiote, amber, copal, dragon's blood, mastic, and various valuable drugs—also Brazil wood and innumerable aromatic plants. The Lake is about thirty miles long and six miles broad making altogether a circumference of nearly Eighty miles. It is situated, as correctly as we could calculate with an imperfect set of instruments and those too injured from the accidents met with in the Belize Pass, in the 16th degree north latitude-Longitude 91° 16′ West.

Having visited the Indian Pueblos of San José and San Andreas on the western side of the Lake, as likewise some other places worthy of observation we were anxious to continue our journey, but owing to the unsettled state of the place we could procure neither horses nor mules, and the Indians were not willing at this particular time to leave the idleness and dissipation consequent on the prevailing feasts. The Commandant who during our stay had shown us considerable attention and kindness had promised to provide us; but foolish and untrue reports coming in every day of enemies advancing to Peten through the Passes, the animals were as often sent in pursuit of these phantom foes. We were therefore compelled to wait until the ridiculous fears of this officer had exploded. On Christmas night we returned his numerous civilities by giving him a ball for which we issued a general invitation. Notwithstanding our repeated assurances that we came to Peten unconnected with any party or in any way mixed up with the conflicting interests of the inhabitants, a lingering feeling to the contrary lurked on the Commandant's mind, as was evinced by his increasing on this evening the already numerous and unnecessary stations for guards and doubling the number of men at each. He could not be made to understand that we were merely passing through on our way to Palenque. Those ignorant and of course suspicious people could form no idea of the inducements for actuating any individual to travel such a distance, and to expend money merely to view a place which formed no object of curiosity to them. While we were thus doomed to wait the Commandant's pleasure and the decay of war's alarms, an individual in the habit of carrying from the Rios, a general term by which any place on the numerous rivers within Chiapas & Tabasco is denominated, to Peten cargoes of salt arrived with his mules, and with whom I lost no time in making an agreement. I was obliged however to allow him until the 3d. of January to dispose of his cargo and prepare for his return. The delays to which we were thus often subjected were exceedingly vexatious—but they were irremediable.

On the 5th, sending forward our people to Sacluc, a Pueblo about nine miles distant from the entrance of the pass thro' which we had to proceed into the Mexican territory, I made a round with Lieutenant Caddy in the Savannahs visiting one of two of the large cattle estates of the country. Arriving at Sacluc early on the morning of the 7th for the purpose of proceeding on our journey, the rain again came down in torrents, continuing six successive days, and necessitated us to remain for that time in the shelter of our quarters. On the morning of the 11th the weather clearing up we moved forward and on the 19th we arrived at Tinnosique, a large Indian village on the banks of the River Usumasinta. The road, or more properly speaking mulepass from Sacluc to Tinnosique lies partly round and partly over a chain of melancholy looking hills arranged together like pyramids. On approaching them each makes an appearance by itself but as we gradually left them behind when we could obtain a view of them through the dense foliage, they assumed all the majesty of combination and had a striking effect. The soil of those hills is rich and luxuriant in the extreme and if shorn of their superabundant and stupendous timber and appropriated to the more useful purposes of agriculture, no land would be more productive and no scenery would be finer. By ascending trees in elevated situations, we could sometimes trace, from analogous appearances, the course of the River San Pedro and other streams to the banks of which thro' this pathless forest no civilized individual has ever approached, and at which no one ever slaked his thirst but the prey of the Indian, and it's still wilder pursuer. It would be a work of supererogation and irrelevant to the subject matter of the present report, to mention the various natural productions to be met with thro' all this route, they are well known by the descriptions of Humbolt and others relative to various places of this continent which have been visited by them. Suffice it to say that mostly all the originals of their descriptions abound here, and that Mexico has not in all her fair domains a finer climate or more fertile soil than this. It is gazing on rich & fruitful lands like these that the omnipotent voice of nature seems, tho' inarticulately to murmur, that "the world shall not pass away like a scroll" till these desolate places shall have been made glad and till they shall have fulfilled their required ends by giving life and animation to thousands yet unborn. An assumption reasonable and tenable and which goes far to defeat the foolish absurdities of those who proceeding on a false philosophy pretend to determine the duration of the earth on which we live by twisting and turning the words of sacred writ to answer their vague and speculative prognostics.

The pass from Sacluc to Tinnosique resembles the one from the River Belize to Peten in being destitute of any habitation, but going over higher and consequently drier ground it is much easier to travel. About twenty miles from Sacluc we passed by an extensive and beautiful lake called San Diego and on approaching to within three miles of Tinnosique we encountered another large lake which bears the name of the Pueblo to which it is so closely situated.

Being unable to procure a boat at Tinnosique capable of conveying our party to its destination, we proceeded in small canoes down the noble river Usumasinta to the Cabasera or head Pueblo of the upper part of the River, for the purpose of procuring one; but it unluckily happened on our arrival that all the boats and large canoes were at that time employed in the conveyance of logwood, and three entire days were consumed before we were enabled to hire one to take us to Balancan. From this place we had again to make fresh agreements to be forwarded to Monte-Christi a small Indian Pueblo upwards of a hundred miles from Tinnosique, and at which place we were given to understand that horses could alone be procured to take us to Palenque.

As we arrived late on the evening at Monte Christi, the succeeding day, 27th Jany 1840, was spent in making the necessary arrangements about horses &c. These we obtained about four miles further down to the river and to this point we were again constrained to go by water and in a different set of boats.—From whence in two days easy travel through forty four miles of beautiful Savannah we at length reached the Pueblo of San Domingo de Palenque.

Upon our arrival I lost no time in waiting on the Alcalde, who very soon got a house hired for us and ordered horses to be in readiness in the vicinity, so that we might command them at a short notice, whenever we were disposed to proceed to the ruins—he also informed me that there were certain regulations to which strangers were required to conform, of the exact nature of which he was not quite aware, but that he would the same evening write to the Prefect who was then at his Log-wood works about fifteen miles distant informing him of our arrival and requesting instructions. To this Official I likewise wrote a short note enclosing a letter of introduction which I had received for him. In the afternoon of the following day I received a very polite letter from the Prefect stating that illness alone prevented him from attending us to the ruins in person, referring us for assistance to the Alcalde and his own nephew, both of whom he stated to me he had charged to show us every attention: he mentioned that it would be requisite for us to hire a person to act as Practico, his orders from the Mexican Government being that he was to allow no stranger to inspect the ruins without such an attendant, in order that what remained might not be defaced or destroyed. We had heard the discouraging intelligence at several places in our course down the Usumasinta that the Mexican Government had absolutely issued it's veto to strangers being permitted to view the place without an order from the Chief Secretary of State. Fearing that such narrow policy might attempt to thwart us in the object of our journey we were prepared in case of opposition to reach our destination, by the less frequented route up the River Chacamas, long before we could have drawn down observation on our harmless proceedings. The polite letter of the Prefect set things to rest, and the next morning, Mr. Caddy being indisposed, having suffered severely from flies, warrieticks and similar nuisances of the road, I set off with the Practico and two Indians for the far-famed memorials of a nation long passed away, more with the intention this day of choosing the best situation for our future quarters than of making a minute inspection. After a ride of about eight miles distance from the Pueblo through a fine country, partly Savannahs and partly forest, and after crossing innumerable small streams and the beautiful little river Michol twice, the road commences an ascent most difficult to the equestrian from it's steepness, the closeness of the Bush, and mounds of the loose and crumbling fragments of edifices now prostrate with the earth. A mile of this much obstructed path brings the visitor to a small tract of level ground at the base of a large chain of hills which here separates the State of Chiapas from that of Tabasco.[2] Here he leaves his horse and enters on the somewhat arduous task of exploring. The ruins which have best withstood the ravages of time are situated on the summits of mounts of considerable height, in gaining to top of which and in coming down again the traveller meets with considerable difficulty and no little danger from the quantities of stones which have fallen in heaps from the various buildings. One requires to tread with some circumspection and to feel his footing else a false step may entail some disastrous consequences on the frail anatomy of his person.

[2] A comparison of this description of the approach to Palenque with Caddy's suggests that Walker had either Caddy's notes or his assistance in preparing this part of the report.

Close to where I left my horse I climbed one of these mounds by a path almost perpendicular and about 60 feet in height, on reaching the top of which the wall of a building presented itself to my view, the sight of which at once repaid me for all the toils of my travels past. The peculiar structure of the edifice and its splendid exterior ornature stamped it at once with the impress of great antiquity and gave me sufficient and convincing proof that my anticipations of surveying something wonderful were not doomed to be disappointed. On further examination, "the cloud capped towers, the gorgeous palaces and the solemn temples" though shorn of their pristine proportions, were yet spared enough by time's defacing hand to indicate that here had once existed a people, great, powerful, and perfected in art, the grand test of advancement in civilization.

The denseness of the wood, the heaps of fallen buildings and the uncertainty of the direction to be taken in order to come at places worthy of observation, occupy the time of the uninitiated so completely, that before I had seen an iota of what I desired to do, the lengthening shadow warned me, however unwillingly, to return to the Pueblo.

All our little preparations for a residence in the ruins being made, unfavorable weather prevented us from locating ourselves till the 5th of February. On which day our whole party took up its quarters in the building which I have mentioned my attention was first directed to.

I will now proceed to give an account, as distinctly as I can, of the remnants of those curious edifices. The views taken by Lieut. Caddy will more than supply my deficiencies, but I may premise that there are not so many materials for description as I could have wished. The buildings as yet discovered, and most probably they are all that still exist showing vestiges of what they formerly were, are few in number compared with the endless hills of wrought stone—they can hardly be called ruins—which are strewed around in every direction; And when we consider the thickness and consistence of the walls, the massy and durable nature of the parts of the buildings which remain and the splendid quality of the mortar used in their erection, ample and indubitable proof, were it wanting, of their extreme old age is afforded.

Up to nearly the close of the Eighteenth century no mention is made of these ruins by writers on America while treating of events either previous or subsequent to the Conquest. Until that time, even to the all-searching Spaniard they appear to have remained unknown, buried in the gloom and obscurity of the mountain-wood. Since the above period the few travellers who have visited this remarkable place and reduced their observations to writing, as well as one or two individuals who have treated on the subject, though without personal inspection, have all severally attempted in the most visionary manner to fix the ancient and proper name of the city. They all appear to have proceeded on existing orthographical data. They have omitted consideration of the fact that there are a great many different Indian languages prevailing in America and even in the vicinity of this very place; and they seem never to have reflected that although the "Maya" tongue, the fount from whence they draw their inspirations, obtains for the most part at present, it may, and, in all human probability, must have succeeded to one more ancient and even that not coeval with the original habitation of the city. Upon as weak a foundation I might give a version equally plausible, but altho perhaps I might get credit for a little ingenuity I am sure I could not ensure conviction to the correctness of my theory, as it, like the rest, would not be able to stand against the sober tests of investigation and truth.

Though little skilled in the science of civil architecture my first but strong impression regarding these ruins was, that they were of Egypto-Indian origin[3]—and bearing in mind the conclusions of Hornius(?) and other learned individuals that America was originally colonised from Asia, this impression more mature observation has tended to confirm. Each building rigidly constructed according to one undeviating model marks the despotic character of Egyptian architecture, while the arch and many of the figures of warriors and idols are denotive of the East—both together forming a character sombre yet fantastic.

[3] It is curious that this idea of the origin of Palenque appears in Walker's report and not in Caddy's written description of the site, although Caddy is credited with the opinion in the Society of Antiquaries note. Perhaps the idea was adopted latterly by Caddy, after reading Walker's statements.

It would be presumptuous in me to assert that my ideas on the subject are correct, but I trust that future travellers more competent to judge of the origin of this wonderful place will ultimately be enabled to decide the question; and I am the more hopeful of this from the circumstance of many eminent men having attained to great knowledge in hieroglyphics which can form the only clue to elucidation. These glyphs abound in Palenque. Once a key is found to surmount the difficulty of deciphering them, as is the case with Egypt, the history, customs, manners and religious worship of Palenque may be correctly ascertained.

The building I have already alluded to as the first which presents itself and which we selected for our residence appears to have been and is styled "the Palace."

The extent of this building must have been originally very considerable altho' its remains only now comprise a Square containing two oblong Court Yards and the portion of a Tower, which stands however distinct by itself. The length of this square building is 82 feet and 86 feet in breadth. It's entire front consists of a double portico.[4] The Pillars of this portico are rectangular and form part of the outward wall—the faces of those pillars are decorated with figures in bas-relief of the most exquisite workmanship and intended no doubt to represent warriors and Kings. On the intersecting wall, a chain of medallions, portraying to all appearance Coats of Arms, runs along just beneath where the arch of the building begins to form, and in the arch are niches in which Lamps may have stood or on which statues or other ornaments may have been placed. Passing through the centre of this Portico you descend seven steep steps into the first Court Yard, which when entire must have been of a highly fanciful and elegant description. Crossing this Court Yard you ascend into the opposite Portico which is a single one; the Court Yard behind which is one

[4] Beginning at this point and continuing at intervals through his description of the buildings of Palenque, Walker inserted a series of numbers referring to a set of paintings prepared by Caddy to illustrate the report, and transmitted to England with Walker's manuscript. The paintings and a copy of the report were sent by Lord Russell to the Royal Geographic Society, but no record of them now exists. Useless without the drawings, these numbers have been removed.

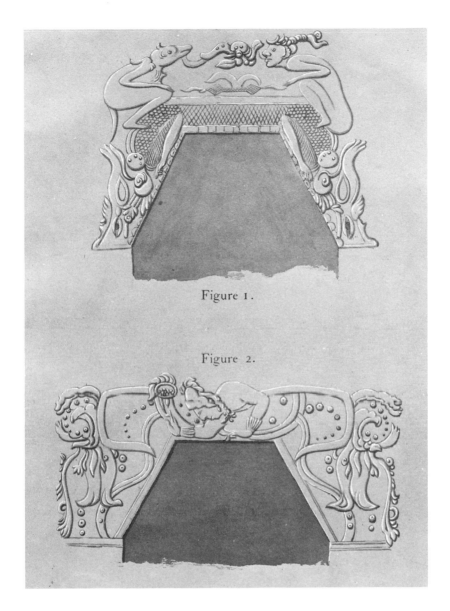

Figure 1.

Figure 2.

Plate 29. Figure 1: *Sculptured figures above steps at K, in the Palace.*
Figure 2: *Figure above the entrance to the subterraneous apartments at b, the Palace.*

Figure 1.

Figure 2.

Plate 30. Figure 1: *Figures in bas-relief on stone in center wall,
Building F.* Figure 2: *Portion of stucco molding, Building F.*

Plate 31. *Remains of moldings and cornice, Building F.*

Plate 32. *Cross and figure cut in bas-relief on slab about 300 yards from the Palace.*

Plate 33. *Plans and elevations of Buildings 2 and 3.*

Plate 34. *Figures from the piers of Building 2.*

Plate 35. *Remains of a figure on the wall of the inner corridor of* Building 5.

Plate 36. *Bas-relief figures from center apartment, Building 4.*

half narrower than the first one and opposed to it again is another similar single Portico. The extremes or sides of these oblong Court Yards consist of one centre room open to the Court and two which it gives an opening to on the right and left. Most of those rooms are adorned with bas reliefs or slabs of sculpture fastened into the wall— the only inlet for light that these side rooms possess are small openings about the width of an ordinary ancient porthole and shaped in the form of a T—Directly beneath this pile of buildings runs a continuous range of vaulted passages all communicating one with another. The entrances to these passages are sculptured or stuccoed in a highly grotesque manner and are admirably executed. From the roof of the building ran up an open pyramidical arch or tower of elaborate workmanship, which to the massy pile below must have given a light and handsome look.

There are seven more buildings in the vicinity of the Palace all situated on the summits of hills and in tolerable preservation excepting the turreted roof-work or superstructure. These edifices are divided into compartments such as I have represented the sides of the oblong squares in the Palace, and contain in the centre of the back wall of the Middle-room large slabs of sculpture and hieroglyphics, over which is placed a ponderous canopy of stone faced with rich and handsome stuccoe-work. These structures have all the appearance of mausoleums; And from the similar habit of the Egyptian race from whom I have partly ventured to deduce the origin of this place we may conclude that they answered the double purpose of habitations for the living and receptacles for the dead. It is not however from what now exist, important as these relics are, that we are enabled to conjecture the former importance and greatness of Palenque—The covered aquaducts, the great paved roads which wound round and were carried up the neighboring lofty hills, the solid walls, the massy bridges, and the piles of fallen buildings scattered over many leagues of the surrounding country best attest the fact—but the memory of those who once inhabited them has passed away like a sound, offering a marvellous check to proud ambition and shewing the short lived tenure of human glory.

The situation of Palenque is admirably adapted for the site of a large city—It's elevated situation, the extent and fruitful nature of the soil for agriculture and the immense Savannahs which lie in every direction afford for pasture the amplest scope. It is also irrigated by a thousand streams. The River Chacamas situated at about four miles from the parts I have been describing runs into the Usumasinta and thus affords a facility for communciation and transport necessary to bring the resources of a large expanse of country to one focus where the largest proportion of the inhabitants resided.

We passed fourteen days in the ruins for the purpose of exploring and taking sketches. At the expiry of this period, from the length of time we had been absent from Belize beyond what we had calculated on at our setting out, I judged it prudent to make the best of our way homewards. So short a residence amid ruins, of which it would require a year at least to gather anything like a sufficient knowledge, contracted our researches, depriving me of the power of collecting much information I was desirous to obtain, and Mr. Caddy from making a variety of drawings.

Excavations have been made, and the large and ponderous flooring stones of the houses broken up, for the purpose of discovering articles which might tend to throw light on the history of the city, but without effect. If any such exist they must have been deposited under the foundation-stone, and to procure them it would be necessary to raze the building completely. The founding of Palenque may give rise to many hypotheses—the one I am most prone to indulge in is that a large fleet had ploughed the Atlantic in search of undiscovered country; The adventurers having penetrated up the Usumasinta through the Laguna de Terminos arrived here, and dismayed by the dangers which they had undergone in their voyage across the seas or allured by the fertility of the soil they were unwilling to return and here fixed their abode. It might likewise have been one of the Colonies, of which many are known to have appertained to the Asiatics, and might in ancient times have had frequent communications with the mother-country, which revolutions, changes of dynasty, and other casualties to which we know the East was so frequently exposed, may have interrupted.

As the Empire of Mexico at its conquest by the Spaniards was inhabited by an unskilful and feeble race, incapable of great designs or the ability to execute any work of magnitude and art—ignorant also of the use of letters it's traditions for previous generations had been preserved by means of paintings of a peculiar description, we may infer from this circumstance and from the presence of regular letters and tablets in the ruins, the great space which must have intervened betwixt the time when a language expressed in written characters prevailed and that which obtained by means of figurative emblems. And until we obtain a knowledge of those characters, which are most decidedly Asiatic in the conformation, the legislators, Orators, Poets, Painters, and Architects of the once proud Palenque must share with the humblest peasant that ever trod its streets, one common fate in the gulph of oblivion, where lie entombed so many records which frail humanity sought to render perpetual.

On our first arrival at Monte Christi I had forwarded a letter to Mr. George Shields His Majesty's Vice Consul at Laguna de Terminos requesting him to be so obliging as to forward me information as to a conveyance being secured for the return of our party by sea to Belize. To this letter I received a communication from Mr. Shields saying that a small vessel could be obtained and that he would be glad to assist me in any arrangements I had to make. Upon this I determined to return in that way as it would give me an opportunity of seeing the Laguna which from its situation promises at no distant time to become a Port of great importance in the Mexican gulf. At Monte Christi we crossed the Usumasinta and proceeded to the Hacienda of Valparaiso where we remained a day to prepare for our further travels. I paid the Peteneros the wages due them and sent them back to their own country. I also sent the Interpreter back by Peten in order that he might take charge of and convey to Belize the natural curiosities and antiquities I had collected on the road. On our way down the river we had landed at the various towns on its banks

Cabasera, Balancan, Moolta and Pita all of which contain a mixed population of Creole Spaniards and Indians. The Palizada within two days sail of the Laguna is the principal town on the Usumasinta; its superior houses, the Chief proprietors residing there, and being the great Logwood depot of the river and its tributaries, renders it a place of some consideration—it contains about six thousand inhabitants. I found one English and three French families settled there, all thriving prosperously in their vocations, as any one possessed of the least industry cannot fail to do amongst a people so addicted to habits of lethargy. At this town we were most hospitably entertained by Don Francisco Obrea the principal person in the place. From this gentleman we learnt all the particulars of the Revolution which was at the time spreading itself over Yucatan and adjacent places against the Central government of Mexico.

[Throughout the spacious savannahs of the Commandant and priest-ridden Peten, as well as at every place on the banks of the magnificent Usumasinta the inhabitants expressed an ardent anxiety to be under such a Government as the English, when their persons and property would be safe and not subjected to the conscriptions and exactions which their present rulers unsparingly visit upon them while they boast of the freedom of a Republic. In large towns the misdemeanours of the subordinate officers of justice may be less frequent or perpetrated with more circumspection as to discovery, but in the smaller towns and villages if the Prefect or Alcalde forms an alliance with the Padre, there is no enormity they will not together commit and for which the poor object of their atrocity seldom obtains redress. Still while those abject wretches would be glad for their own security to see their country added to the Colonies of England they would feel exasperated and indignant if the stipulations of the transference were clogged with any humiliating concessions—such as the here loudly talked of abandonment of Yucatan to England in consideration of the loans which the former cannot find means to repay to the latter. At an alliance founded on such a basis they would revolt as they would consider themselves sold and the object of barter—but in any honorable way they would be glad to get rid of the galling fetters which priests and interested individuals calling themselves Statesmen have fastened upon them.] One of the greatest anomalies in the country is the boasted liberty of the Indian, that he is not a slave—but his bondage is far more hopeless than ever our Africans groaned under—he has freedom each day before his eyes and as he is made to believe within his grasp—each day, however, it is as distant from his possession and each day "hope deferred which maketh the heart sick" is his portion—The way this is brought about is as follows—An Indian hires to a Master at so much a month, thoughtless, improvident and debauched when he has the means at his command, he soon gets largely into his Master's debt for supplies furnished without hesitation. By the Law of the State, till this debt is repaid the servant must be subject to his Master and is bound to remain with him. It often happens that this sum is drawn out to an amount beyond what the Indian can ever in his lifetime hope to realize out of the savings of his wages. It is not an infrequent occurrence that he is a stake at play. When the Indian is unfettered he is not much inclined to task work; his untamed independence will not conform itself to regular labour. He prefers cultivating his plantation when it suits him and occasionally to kill game for the use of his family and to sell part of it that he may get sufficient money to pay his poll-tax to the Government and a trifle to procure salt & spirits. This renders labour very high in Rios and makes the Master keep a watchful eye over the dependant who is in debt to him—and woe betide the Indian who attempts to evade his obligations.

The River Usumasinta from six miles above Tinnosique down to within twenty miles of the Lagoon of Terminos is nearly half a mile broad. From this point where the Tabasco branch strikes off it gradually lessens in breadth—a child might direct the crafts that ply upon it as it's course is uninterrupted by Falls or any other impediment. The current runs to the sea at the rate of three miles an hour, so that the barges float down with the utmost facility exempting the people who man them from labor, which they only experience in ascending. The land adjoining is wonderfully rich and prolific—the climate is most healthy—there is not a medical person from the top of the River to the Lagoon and his absence is not felt as they rely upon the medicinal herbs which abound in this country and are an antidote for most of their ailings. Fever and ague is very prevalent but I attribute this to the thin clothing which the people wear and which they do not make any alteration in during their winter months. From the number of alligators in the Usumasinta it might not inappropriately be called "Alligator River"—we counted thirty seven within an hour lying sometimes alone and sometimes by twos and threes on the banks basking in the sun. This admirable river has quite an English look from it's sides being completely lined with the willow-tree.

The town of Carmen in Laguna is of some size, the buildings belonging to the principal Merchants and Logwood Cutters are large and spacious—there are about seven thousand inhabitants. On our arrival there were sixteen ships in the harbour—viz—one Belgian, one French, one American and thirteen British. This port is every day making forward strides. [The Vice Consul Mr. George Shields a Merchant of the place is a very intelligent person and appeared to exert himself in keeping matters straight between the Mexican Authorities and the Masters of the British Vessels—with whom misunderstandings occasionally occur, and wherein an undue exercise of power is frequently displayed by the Officer of the Port and others. The occasional presence of a British Man of War at Laguna & Campeche would effectually restrain all attempts to impose on the interests of British Commerce in that quarter of the world.]

Late in the evening of the day on which we arrived at Carmen the Federalists rose on the authorities of the town—and having deposed them they thereafter drove the Centralists out of the Fort and took possession of it—all this was accomplished in a very short space of time, and without the loss to any one of life or limb—a mode of warfare being adopted which is sometimes practised here of firing their guns for the purpose of frightening and not of killing the enemy. As the new Captain of the Port would not furnish us a clearance to Campeche, that town being then in possession of the Centralists we departed on the 3d of March in the craft which he had hired, taking our chance of being able to satisfy the Campechanos of our neutrality.

On our arrival off Campeche on the evening of the 5th, I was agreeably surprised to see a fine handsome town—completely fortified, with it's walls and towers as entire as the day on which they were built.

So deficient are we, even at Belize, in information regarding places at no great distance from us that I had always been led to think that Campeche was nothing more than a mere fishing town—whereas it contains many large and elegant Squares, Churches and Streets—with a population of 18,000 inhabitants. The stone pier is very handsome and extends a great way into the sea. Large ships cannot lie near the town from the shallowness of the water and are therefore obliged to anchor off in the roads at about three miles distance. Campeche owes its present state of preservation to the isolated situation of Yucatan, having on that account been less exposed to those intestine wars of which the rest of the Mexican dominions have been so frequently the scene. This exemption has also powerfully contributed to preserve more pure the moral principles of the inhabitants, who have not been so much debased by the dreadful effects which spring from the unlicensed acts of war. Intrigue is less known amongst them than in all the other parts of Spanish America and their manners have a reserve and shyness which altho not so suitable for the amusement of a stranger will yet be preferred by every well thinking individual to the levity of demeanor which characterises too considerable a proportion of the females of this country.

A visit to the Market of Campeche is an interesting and amusing sight. It is situated in an extremely large Square. It is every morning filled by female Indian venders of various articles, who are all regularly disposed in rows and they keep their places as scrupulously and as rigid to their bounds, as if they were divided by partitions as in Covent Garden. Fine cabbage, radishes, garden turnips, onions and many of the best European vegetables as well as plenty of tropical fruits and vegetables were in abundance. As the market is held every morning each person only purchases a sufficient supply for the day's consumption and consequently the articles are portioned out in small quantities. Here I first witnessed a novelty in the monetary system. The lowest coin in use is half a media which is the one portion of a media cut into two—when an individual does not feel inclined to purchase to the extent of half a media, the current coin below this amount is the bean of the cocoa nut. This conventional usage has grown into a legal tender. The Federalists having seized on a few small vessels and armed them had now invested Campeche by sea, while their troops were rapidly advancing from Merida to attack it by land—and it was now the only place in Yucatan which had not thrown off the Mexican yoke. In conversation with General Rivas the Governor he informed me that he had only about 100 regular Mexican troops upon whom he could depend and that unless he received reinforcements from Vera Cruz it would be impossible for him to hold the town as the Militia he had under arms could not be depended on—they were deserting every day & had to be guarded and confined like so many cattle.

On the 10th March we left Campeche for Sisal a considerable sea port on the coast—from thence dispatching our craft with the rest of the expedition round by Cape Catoche to meet us on the other side of the peninsula in Ascension Bay, Lieut. Caddy and myself set off for Merida the Capital of the Province where we remained four or five days—during which time we were greatly gratified beholding the beauty and splendor of a city about which, all but its existence, little is known in Europe. The building of this city was commenced under Don Francisco Montejo Lieutenant Governor of Yucatan in 1542. There were in Montejo's plan four hundred large stone houses, divided into wide and spacious streets—these all exist and now form the centre of the city which contains thirty six thousand inhabitants. The principal Square is 193 feet from side to side. In this Square stand the Cathedral, the Governor's Palace, the Bishop's Palace, the House of Assembly and Montejo's house, which is called the House of the Conquest. The front of this house is covered with sculpture of excellent workmanship & in which great art is displayed. The Cathedral is a most superb edifice. The length of the knave from East to

West is 231 feet and from North to South 110 feet—In this space 12 columns of doric order which form three knaves from North to South and seven from East to West—corresponding to these columns others are incorporated with the walls of the edifice forming a variety of domes very elegant with a crowning one of larger size in the centre and of beautiful structure. Attached to the Cathedral are four Chapels which are entered from the Cathedral. The Principal Altar is of silver inlaid with gold & magnificent silver Corinthian pillars of various sizes adorn it.

With Don Juan Cosagua the Governor I had various interviews, he having requested me to visit him every day. [He commissioned me to inform Your Excellency of his anxiety to settle in a harmonious manner all the difficulties which had existed on our boundary question and blamed the Mexican Government for not having turned its attention to the matter long before. He expressed his intention to dispose of the question immediately after the settlement of affairs with Mexico. The revolution he accounted for by the simple fact that the connection had ceased to be beneficial, that the citizens of Yucatan besides being strongly opposed to the centralization system, derived no visible or positive advantage from the union, nor in case of need did they perceive that they could experience any efficient protection from a distant, changing and irresponsible government to compensate them for the sacrifices they must sustain by a perpetuation of the league as under the present system.]

On the 22d March we left Merida, and travelling across the country we reached Ascencion Bay on the 30th where we embarked and had a tedious sail along the Coast till we reached Belize early on the morning of yesterday. I have made many notes on Yucatan which time will not permit me to submit to Your Excellency at present—but I hope soon to be enabled to put them in a form for publication illustrated by the drawings made by Mr. Caddy.

{Here ends Walker's official report, which presents a useful picture of the political climate and the agricultural and commercial potential of the areas visited, but fails to provide the scientific description of

Palenque which supposedly was the primary aim of the expedition. Little wonder that officials in England characterized the journey as a well-meant blunder, although had they been able to peruse Caddy's more detailed description of Palenque and see the full range of his drawings, they might have thought the £200 well spent indeed.}

VIII. aftermath

UPON THEIR RETURN to The Settlement, Walker and Caddy set out to produce an official account of the expedition, to be forwarded to the Colonial Secretary in England. To be sure, they had bested Stephens and Catherwood; when these two arrived at Palenque they found that they were expected, Walker having informed the prefect of San Domingo de Palenque of their impending arrival. This was pleasant news for Stephens, for it meant that Walker and Caddy had not been speared by Indians, a rumor which had reached Stephens' ears some time earlier. It meant, too, that the later arrivals would not be prevented from visiting the ruins, as Stephens had feared. Nonetheless, the race had gone to the swift, and the better-known explorers had to be content with retracing the steps of the earlier pair.

On entering the Palace at Palenque, Stephens and Catherwood found that their predecessors, following a time-honored tradition, had added their names to several others inscribed high on the walls of the building. Thus Walker and Caddy had left a seemingly permanent record of their expedition. Their more immediate concern, however, was the written and painted record which was required if the Treasury was to absolve Walker and MacDonald of responsibility for the expenditures incurred on the journey. The adventurers quickly set to their task, and just over a month from the date of the expedition's return Superintendent MacDonald was able to reply to Lord Russell's February dispatch:

13 MAY 1840

MY LORD,

I have the honour to acknowledge receipt of Yr. Lordship's despatch No. 14 of date of 19 Feby. last.

187

I am in possession of Mr. Walker's report of the expedition to Palenki and of his journey thro different states of central America and I only wait Lieut Caddys finishing some drawings illustrative of the expedition to forward Mr. Walkers account of it to Your Lordship.

I am quite sensible that previous to authorising any expedition of the kind I ought to have had the authority of H M Government but I trust that when I have submitted to Your Lordship my explanations on the subject that Your Lordship will free me from the imputation of having acted prematurely or without consideration in the matter.

With MacDonald breathing heavily at his back, Caddy, who in August was promoted to the rank of second captain, seems to have completed his part of the official report in near-record time, and at some time in the fall of 1840 the document was placed on shipboard for transmission to England. After considerable delay, the report was finally laid on Lord Russell's desk, and on February 2, 1841, Russell acknowledged its receipt in a dispatch to MacDonald:

I have received from Boulogne, where the vessel conveying them had been stranded, Mr. Walker's account of his Expedition to the ruins of Palenque, & the drawings of Lt. Caddy who accompanied him.

The drawings are very curious & interesting & I give Mr. Walker & Lt. Caddy great credit for the zeal & spirits of enterprise which they have evinced in undertaking this Expedition.

I have forwarded Mr. Walker's report & Lt. Caddy's drawings to the Geographical Society omitting from the former those passages in which Mr. Walker adverts to the conduct & political opinions of certain Mexican Subjects & Functionaries & those also in which he speaks of the desire of the People of Yutacan for the protection of such a Government as that of Great Britain.

As Mr. Walker contemplates publication I have to suggest to him as a Servant of the Crown that he should observe great caution as to such points in any account which he may publish.

No despatch from yourself accompanies the Report of Mr. Walker to you, & I apprehended therefore that there must be some accidental miscarriage of your despatch. On receiving the account in detail of the expenses incurred I will, provided it shall appear that the expenses were moderate & reasonable, recommend to the Lords of the Treasury to relieve you from the responsibility that I informed you in my despatch of the 19. Feb. 1840 would rest upon you for this Expedition.

Lord Russell's admonitions to Walker regarding publication of his report of the expedition soon proved unnecessary, for in 1841, John Lloyd Stephens, never one to let time drag on between an adventure and its reporting, got out his two-volume *Incidents of Travel in Central America, Chiapas, and Yucatán*, which with its descriptions of Palenque and many heretofore unknown ruins, was an immediate success, and also an effective damper to any dreams of fame and profit entertained by Walker or Caddy. However, John Caddy, perhaps recognizing that his drawings had artistic merit at least the equal of Catherwood's, for some years entertained the idea of publishing some of the Palenque scenes, perhaps as a small folio, rather like the West Indies work. He had, in fact, planned to use his own description of the ruins as an accompanying text. Unhappily, like the remainder of the West Indies series of portfolios, the Palenque volume was to remain unsought and unseen by the public.

Patrick Walker, probably spurred by the press of his multiple government obligations in The Settlement, seems to have abandoned all thought of putting the record of the Palenque expedition before the public. Yet there remained the matter of the accounting, and on April 21, 1841, MacDonald was finally able, or so he thought, to relieve himself of this burden. He wrote to Lord Russell:

> I have the honor to acknowledge the receipt of Your Lordship's Despatch No. 36 of 2d. February, informing me that Mr. Walker's account of his expedition to Palenque and the drawings of Lieut. Caddy had arrived in England.
>
> I have communicated to Mr. Walker the favorable opinion Your Lordship has been pleased to express of his zeal and spirit of enterprize, and I have likewise submitted to that gentleman Your Lordship's suggestion as to the caution which he ought to observe in political remarks in the event of his publishing his manuscript.

Captain Caddy having sometime since proceeded to England consequent on his promotion, it has therefore been out of my power to convey to him directly Your Lordship's sense of his merit.

I forward to Your Lordship letter from Mr. Walker covering the Account of Expenses[1] incurred by him in his expedition.

Appended to the dispatch is a short note dated July 10, 1841:

Mr. Walker took this despatch with its enclosures to Jamaica in expectation of meeting Captain Caddy there— Capt. C. having left — reference may now be made to him at the Royal Artillery Barracks, Woolwich.

With this additional delay, the account of expenses, dated April 16, 1841, was received in England on October 14 of that year, just over one and one-half years after the expedition's return to The Settlement. The accounting was accompanied by a letter from Walker to MacDonald:

I beg to place in your hands for the purpose of being forwarded to the Secretary of State Account in duplicate *of a portion* of the expenses of the expedition to Palenque.

In stating that I expended upwards of $600 from my own funds on the general expenses of the expedition, I do not mean to advance any claim for remuneration as I am perfectly satisfied with the approbation of the Secretary of State and his Lordship's recommendation I will not fail to keep in view in the event of my publishing an account of the tour. Captain Caddy being aware of every item of the general expenditure will be able to join me in attesting the accuracy of the account.

Portions of the account are rather difficult to fathom, as for example the indicated advance of $1,000 (£200), leaving a deficit of $418.50 by account, rather than "upwards of $600," unless government officials had begun at that early date to round off figures in the modern way. In general, the expenditures appear to meet Lord Russell's requirement that they be "moderate & reasonable," and Walker and MacDonald presumably submitted the account in the

[1] Appendix I.

190

firm belief that it would serve to relieve the Superintendent of responsibility for the advance, if not to repay Walker for his expenses out of pocket.

Unfortunately for MacDonald, the reception accorded Walker's account in the Treasury was a little less cordial than expected. In a series of comments written on the cover of MacDonald's dispatch, officials of the Treasury and the Colonial Office dissected not the account but the expedition, found it wanting in several respects, and, disregarding the question of whether or not the expenditures could be described as moderate and reasonable, took what they felt was appropriate action. The first comment, by an anonymous government figure, is dated October 14:

> As Mr. Walker makes no claim for reimbursement of these expences, I fear that it is quite certain that the Treasury will not pay them, especially since the expedition was undertaken without their sanction, and as it has really proved of no use at all. An American named Stephens made the same journey, & has published a full account of Palenque with drawings & c far more complete than any which were made by Captain Caddy and with a far more extensive range of general observation. I fear, therefore, that nothing can be done with this Despatch than to lay it aside.

On October 20, one G. Barson passed the dispatch on to J. Stephen, apparently a higher authority, with the request: "Will you look at the accompg letter from the Treasury on the subject of the expenses of the Polenki Expedition?" Stephen examined the letter and Walker's account, and on the following day appended his note, the final one, to the much-handled dispatch:

> I see from the letter to which Mr. Barson refers me that the Treasury have desired to know how the money issued to Mr. Walker was expended before they finally sanction that issue. Mr. Walker's present report will answer that enquiry, and should therefore be communicated to Their Lordships. But for the reason already mentioned it seems to me hopeless that they should indemnify Mr. Walker in full. Colonel Macdonald and Mr. Walker & Capt. Caddy exe-

cuted this scientific mission with no previous sanction from the
Treasury. The motive was merely that we might not be outstript in
this case in scientific zeal by the Americans. This was not very wise,
and the result is that we have been beaten by these new rivals in
scientific research, who will now boast over our inferiority instead of
having to boast only over our comparative inactivity. After all the
Drawings and Travels have not been published, and now it is hardly
to be supposed that any Bookseller would hazard the publication.
In short the whole affair has been a blunder, though a very well
meant one.

With the exception of the deprecatory comments about Caddy's
paintings, the remarks penned on MacDonald's dispatch were correct,
although unkind. The expedition had not brought fame to the British
government, any more than it had to the men who undertook it. Perhaps to avoid shedding more light on a potentially embarrassing incident, government followed the course suggested by the anonymous
official, that of laying the dispatch aside, which in this case seems to
have meant burying it at a sufficient depth in the files to make its exhu-
mation exceedingly unlikely. As far as the archives show, no further
action of any sort was taken in the matter, not even to the extent of
informing MacDonald that Treasury was unwilling to pay the expedition's expenses. Thus the British government added its bit to the
interment of an expedition causing so little stir that it might be said
already to have been forgotten, except by a few.

Following his return to England early in 1841, John Caddy, perhaps the only person still anxious to publicize the expedition, continued in his effort to make the results of the journey and his drawings
of the ruins known to at least a limited segment of the public. The
Geographical Society may for a time have possessed the original
report and drawings, as Lord Russell's dispatch indicates. If so, they
seem to have caused no great stir, for neither the documents themselves nor any record of them exists in the Society's files. Perhaps in
the hope of arousing some interest in publication, Caddy arranged a
presentation of his drawings before the Society of Antiquaries of
London in 1842. The Minute Book of the Society contains the follow-

ing entry under the date of the 13th of January of that year: "Captain Caddy exhibited to the Society by the hands of John Britton, Esq., a Series of interesting Drawings of ancient Sculpture, etc., from the Palace, Temple, or Pyramid at Palenque in Yucatan, in Central America.—Having the appearance of great accuracy, and varying as they do from others published by Lord Kingsbury and Mons. Waldeck, they are entitled to particular attention to the English Antiquary. Captain Caddy supposes these ruins to be of Egypto-Indian origin."

Thus Caddy's work, and perhaps also his supposition regarding the origin of the Maya civilization, not atypical of his time although strongly counter to Stephens' published opinion, gained the imprimatur of the recently formed society. Beyond this single paragraph, however, no further encouragement was forthcoming. It was to be some eighty years before Caddy's work would again attract scholarly attention, which even then had only the effect of recording the existence of the paintings and text, not of bringing them before the public. Less than two years from the time of its completion, the expedition had been stuffed into a dusty corner and forgotten by all but the two men whose brief adventure into archaeology it had been.

IX. the later years

WHILE THE YEAR 1842 marked the end of the Palenque affair, the careers of Walker and Caddy, both of whom were still young men, stretched on before them. With Captain Caddy's return to England in 1841, the two men were separated, never to meet again, and there is no evidence of correspondence between them. In fact, Caddy's few brief references to Walker in his diary impart the feeling that their association in the Palenque adventure did not make the two fast friends, and it is likely that neither gave much thought to the other in the ensuing years.

John Caddy returned to his home in Woolwich in February of 1841 for the rest and recreation he had earned by a taxing tour of duty in the rigors of tropical climate. In early 1842, the fifth in what was to be a family of eight children was born. In July of that year the Caddys embarked for another military post, Caddy having exchanged a posting to Malta for duty in the cool and pleasant setting of London, in southeastern Ontario, Canada, not a great distance from the place of his birth. This was a time of happiness for the Caddys, with the family together and comfortably settled for the first time since John and Georgiana had married. Serving as an engineer with the local Royal Artillery battery, Caddy found time once again to pursue his painting, and began to record the life and look of mid-nineteenth-century Canada.

The enjoyment of the Canadian post was disrupted in 1844 by the arrival of new orders, directing Caddy to yet another West Indian tour of duty, perhaps in the thought that his previous experience would serve him well in the Caribbean islands. Caddy thought otherwise, and his reluctance to leave home and family crystallized in his decision to retire from the army, an action he had contemplated as early as 1834, by which time his parents had returned from postings in England to settle in Canada. On May 28, 1844, Second Captain John Herbert Caddy was retired from the Royal Artillery on half-pay, to begin what is often termed a life of leisure, but what may well have seemed to Caddy a life of labor in contrast to his life in the West Indies.

Caddy commenced his civilian career by utilizing his army training, becoming the first city engineer of London, in the days before the city was incorporated. There is no official record of Caddy's position in London, but it is claimed that his engineering knowledge was employed in laying out plans for the city. It is known that Caddy owned a great deal of land in the London area, including two complete city blocks acquired in 1844. In a relatively short time, John Caddy made the transition from impecunious army officer to landed gentleman and respected member of a growing community.

The Caddy family continued to grow, with the last son arriving in 1849, and the Caddys seemed permanently rooted at last. However, John's eyes turned elsewhere in 1851, and, having disposed of his holdings in London, he transported his family the short distance to Hamilton, Ontario, which was the last of their many homes. Here Caddy for a time held a position in the engineering department of the Great Western Railway, for which his Royal Artillery training may somehow have qualified him.

After a brief period with the railway, Caddy changed occupations and for the first time succeeded in turning his artistic ability to a real profit. As a teacher of art, he instructed the youth of Hamilton and surrounding areas in the finer points of watercolor painting, with an occasional bit of work in oils thrown in, though this was never his favorite medium. For several years private teaching was coupled with the position of art instructor at Wesleyan Female College in Hamilton, a title and activity adding markedly to his growing local recognition.

Concurrent with his teaching, Caddy began to paint in earnest, roaming the Canadian countryside and recording the mid-century scene on canvas. For the first time, an eager market developed for his work, and he was soon known locally as an artist of considerable ability, a fame which later extended to the artistic world itself. In addition to his many paintings of Canadian landscapes, now highly prized for their historical accuracy, Caddy also produced scenes of Scotland, Ireland, and Wales, and redid a number of his West Indian works. These and his drawings of Palenque were widely famed in Canada, where his paintings still grace the walls of many homes and museums. John Herbert Caddy, Capt., Royal Artillery, Retired, died at his residence, No. 22 Main Street West, on March 19, 1883, near the end of his eighty-second year, eulogized as one of Hamilton's oldest and most respected citizens. He left behind him a large family, which over the years spread his descendants through the towns and cities of southeastern Ontario. In Hamilton, Georgiana lived on to the age of ninety-three, and on January 25, 1898, she was laid to rest beside her husband in the Hamilton cemetery.

Patrick Walker was a man altogether unlike John Caddy, and the careers of the two men were equally different. On his return from Palenque, Walker had once more taken up the staggering plurality of offices, becoming a councillor of the Executive Council as well, and in 1841, serving as magistrate, he began to be referred to as The Honorable Patrick Walker. By dint of his energy and application, his star was clearly on the rise. In May of 1841 he was appointed to proceed to Jamaica (carrying with him the much-traveled account of Palenque expenses) to discuss with the governor of Jamaica proposed changes in the government of The Settlement.

This occasioned the only public comment unfavorable to Walker during his career in British Honduras. It was in the form of a letter to the governor of Jamaica, written by local merchants, at least one of whom had been a defendant in a lawsuit brought by Walker some time before. After averring that they had no wish to state anything disrespectful of any party, the gentlemen go on to comment: "We regret that H.M. Superintendent should have deemed it adviseable to appoint Mr. Walker for this mission as no Individual less qualified by general experience or local knowledge or from the whole tenor of his public conduct more obnoxious to the Inhabitants could possibly have been selected . . . ." One can only be grateful that the gentlemen said nothing which they thought disrespectful of Walker.

Others in The Settlement, from the Superintendent down, seemed to hold Walker in high esteem, suggesting that the five signers of the Jamaica letter were simply seizing an opportunity to grind their private, and probably well-worn, axes. There was some feeling on the part of the citizenry that Walker might be spreading his talent a trifle too thin, and a Select Committee appointed to review salaries of public officers took the occasion to comment on Walker's efforts:

> . . . your Committee have come to the conclusion that it will be unwise to continue in one individual such a plurality of offices—they consider it quite incompatible with the duties of Secretary of H.M. Superintendent that he should at the same time hold the Office of Queen's Advocate, as well as that of Keeper of Militia Arms and Clothing. Our present Superintendent may be pleased to permit his Secretary to hold these Offices, but his immediate successor may at once disapprove of the time of that Officer being occupied in any but his legitimate duties and as it is certain that the Public interests do materially suffer from want of attention in some of the departments, your Committee recommend the Meeting to address His Excellency Her Majesty's Superintendent on the subject, requesting that the person holding in future the situation of Keeper of Militia Clothing shall receive the appointment at the recommendation of the Officer Commanding the Militia, satisfied that the person held responsible by that Officer will be more likely to perform well the duties of the appointment than one over whom he has no control and who considers this Office as a sinecure.

Perhaps it is more than coincidence that the chairman of the Select Committee was the first signer of the Jamaica letter as well. In any case, the committee's recommendation seems to have had no effect, except possibly the reverse of that desired; for Walker was soon appointed commissioner and treasurer of the Mosquito Nation, also serving as mediator in disputes between that nation and the surrounding countries of Central America. Shortly thereafter he was proposed for the post of adviser to the Mosquito King; this and the myriad other positions he continued to hold until May of 1843, when he was granted nine months' leave to enable him to visit England. Later Walker, never one to miss an opportunity, entered a claim for half-salary during the period of his leave, in which claim he was successful.

Walker's stay in England was marked by two important events. First, on January 18, 1844, at St. John's Church, Fulham, Middlesex, he was married (or as he put it in a letter the following week, "committed matrimony") to Elizabeth Barron, daughter of an army agent whom Walker had known for several years. Less than three months later, Walker was appointed Her Majesty's agent and consul general to the Mosquito Shore, severing his connection with British Honduras. The appointment may have been partly the result of a letter which Walker had written to Lord Stanley in November of 1843 in the hope of obtaining promotion in the Colonial Service. In the letter, Walker laid before Lord Stanley, with scarcely a trace of modesty or self-effacement, the high points of his career in British Honduras, including wherever possible quotations of praise heaped upon him by various officials. Walker apparently had tired of his pluralistic endeavors in The Settlement, for he noted in the introductory paragraph of his plea that he was "seeking a less exhausted field" for his future career.

In 1844, Walker proceeded to the Mosquito Shore, on what is now the eastern coast of Costa Rica and Nicaragua. His only known reappearance in The Settlement took place in April and May of 1845, when he, his wife, and suite accompanied the Mosquito King on the H.M. *Hyacinth* for the King's coronation at St. John's Church, Belize.

Walker and his new wife settled in Bluefields and raised the new Mosquitian flag, which rather closely resembled the Union Jack. From 1844 to 1848, Walker's activities were directed primarily at preventing Nicaragua and private individuals from appropriating the territory of the Mosquito Indians and administering the funds provided by the British government for the support of the kingdom. In late 1847 and early 1848, Nicaraguan encroachment on Mosquitian lands included hoisting of the Nicaraguan flag at San Juan; on two occasions, a display of British might brought about withdrawal of Nicaraguan forces and replacement of their flag with that of Mosquitia.

Following the second flag incident, Nicaraguan forces which had evacuated San Juan returned, capturing officials left in command by Walker. Accordingly, an expedition consisting of the British ships H.M. *Alarm* and H.M. *Vixen* was dispatched from Bluefields on February 7, 1848, with Patrick Walker on board his own ship. Vice Admiral Sir F. Austen, writing to the Secretary of the Admiralty while on board the *Vindictive* at Jamaica, March 5, 1848, reported on the expedition:

> . . . Capt. Loch, with Mr. Walker in his own boat, proceeded to Serapaqui & anchored there on the 11th.
> It was there that the melancholy death of Mr. Walker occurred. He was unfortunately drowned whilst attempting to save the life of a friend who had accompanied him in his boat, and had fallen overboard in the night. They both lost their lives.

The *London Times* of April 6, in addition to giving more details on the fighting prior to the eleventh of March, altered the story of the disaster considerably. It stated that Walker's boat was surprised by canoes, and that Walker and another gentleman fell overboard while the seamen were busy arming themselves, adding that the other man was picked up, but Walker could not be found.

Thus, in the space of a few minutes, ended the promising career of Patrick Walker. His devotion and zeal in public service were of no avail at the last, and his accomplishments were swallowed up by a tropical stream, leaving him no lasting monument such as Caddy built with his paintings. It is a curious coincidence that a member of the more famous Palenque expedition was also to die by drowning. Frederick Catherwood, his fame forever secured through his depiction of the ruined cities of Central America, was listed among the missing in the sinking of the S.S. *Arctic*, which went down with heavy loss of life in the Atlantic in 1854.

The final postscript to the forgotten journey was written in 1923, when Marshall Saville, an archaeologist with a deep interest in the high cultures of Mesoamerica and a member of the staff of the Museum of the American Indian in New York City, briefly exhumed from the dust of time Caddy's paintings and description of Palenque. Through Miss Alice Caddy, daughter of John St. Vincent Caddy and herself an artist and illustrator, Saville obtained Caddy's work, had the plates photographed, and briefly mentioned the report in his "Bibliographic Notes on Palenque," published by the museum in 1928. Saville and the Caddy family hoped to have the report published, but once again, as in the early 1840's, nothing came of the expectations. The plates and text were returned to the Caddys, and while in the possession of Miss Georgianna Caddy, Alice Caddy's sister, they, together with other Caddy paintings, letters, and mementoes, were destroyed in a warehouse fire in Ottawa in 1942. It is to Marshall Saville's interest and to the kindness of the Museum of the American Indian that we owe the opportunity of seeing Palenque as it was in 1840 and reliving the forgotten journey through John Caddy's pictures and words.

appendix i: walker's account of expenditures

THE FOLLOWING ACCOUNT, accompanied by MacDonald's dispatch, was prepared by Walker, presumably from notes, since he could not have obtained receipts for most of the items listed. In fact, the obtaining of receipts for purchases made in the bush is difficult or impossible even today. From the list of items, it is possible to gather something of how such an expedition was outfitted and of the food requirements along the way. A small glossary may be needed for the list: the plantains, purchased on November 21, are a fruit related to the banana, but edible only when cooked; the "Pikari" bought on the same day is the peccary, a piglike denizen of the bush; and the "patakies" mentioned on December 23 are double-walled, lidded burden baskets, carried on the back and supported with a rope.

A word, too, about the values of the various items listed. The silver dollar used in the Settlement in the 1840's was officially worth 4s.2d. Sterling, while the Maccaroni, which was reckoned as a quarter-dollar, was valued at one shilling, which might have confused the merchants of Belize had they not borrowed from Jamaica the simpler, unofficial valuation in which the Maccaroni (a title for the Imperial Shilling which was not well received in England) retained its one-shilling value, while the dollar stood at four shillings even. Thus Walker's indicated advance of $1,000 is the equivalent of £200, the amount drawn from the Military Chest for the expedition, and the total expenditure for the 144 days of the journey, $1,418½, is £83.14s. over the advance.

Persons forming Expedition to Palenque &c

From Belize to Duck Run

1 Mr. P. Walker
1 Lt. Caddy R.A.
___
2

Rationed at the expense of expedition

1 Mr Joseph Nod interpreter with the pay of 6°/Stg per diem
1 ——— Carnick R. A.
18 Soldiers of Q.W.I. Regt with 4 glasses of rum or brandy.
9 Creole Paddlers with do do & two steersmen at 6°/Stg and
the remaining seven at 4°/Stg per diem
___
29

From Duck Run to Peten

1 Mr Nod
1 Carnick R.A.
___
2

4 Soldiers Q.W.I. Regt.
3 Muleteers
6 Indians
___
15

From Peten to Palenque

1 Mr Nod
1 Mr Bartlett English Practico
2 Peteneros
4 Soldiers Q.W.I. Regt
3 Muleteers
2 Indians
and at Palenque
1 Spanish Practico
___
14

From Peten to Laguna, Campeche, Sisal, by Cape Catoche to Ascension Bay and Belize

4 Soldiers Q.W.I. Regt

Part of the expenses incurred by Mr. P. Walker in an expedition to Palenque &c.

				Dollars
1839				
Nov.	13	Received from Commissary		$1,000
"	"	Paid Mr. Walsh Executor on Bennett's estate for 2 azimuth compasses, ornamental jewellery for presents &c per account	$50	
"	"	Paid Mr. Barcla for saddles	15	
"	"	Paid Mr. Guild for knives, pots &c	5	
"	"	Paid for canvas for Tarpaulin, locks for boxes &c	13½	
"	"	Paid Mr. Williamson for brandy	34½	
"	"	Paid Mr. Hampshire for red cloth shirts for soldiers and servants	14	
"	"	Paid Mr. Newport account for medicines &c	6½	
"	"	Paid Mr. Boitias for groceries	13	
"	"	Paid Mr. Savage for do.	13	
"	"	Paid Mr. Welsh for barrels of Pork, flour & rum	71½	
"	"	Paid for paddles	10	
"	"	Paid Lt. Caddy acct for Artillery man making boxes	2	
"	"	Paid do. hat for servant	1	
"	"	Paid Antonio for hat, shirts, &c	6½	
"	"	Paid for bag	1	
"	"	Paid Mr. Aris 12 prs mocasins	15	
"	"	Paid for making tarpaulin	1	
"	"	Paid for cordage	¾	
"	"	Paid for oil and wick	2	
"	"	Paid Mr. Nod in advance	62	
"	"	Paid at Big Haulover for plantains	3	
"	"	Paid at Saturday Creek for do.	1½	
	21	Paid 9 paddlers pr order on Mr. Walsh P. Treasurer	120	
"	"	Paid for baskets for Indians carrying, pig &c	5	

"	Paid for corn	1
"	Paid for sundry articles of provision at Duck Run	3
"	Paid C. Gough for plantains	1½
"	Paid Fonseca for do.	1½
"	Paid for Pikari	1
"	Paid in advance to Indian	1
Decr 12	Paid at Santa Rosa provisions for people	1¾
13	Paid for do. do.	1¼
14	Paid for do. do.	1½
14	Paid —— do. at Titchalic for Commandant's retinue	6
15	Paid for do. at Santa Ana	6
16	Paid for do. at Chatchactun	1½
17	Paid carriers 7 muleteers from Duck Run to Peten	50½
"	Paid Torribios exps for Carnick	5

1839

Dec 19	Paid for provisions for 18th & date	4½
	Paid for hats & shoes for Nod and men	5½
20	Paid for provisions	2¼
21	Paid for do.	1½
23	Paid for Band at San Andreas	1½
"	Paid for mending boxes	½
"	Paid for saddle bags	2½
"	Paid for shoes for people	3
"	Paid for carriage of patakies from Chatclacan	1
24	Paid for provisions	2
25	Paid for do.	2½
"	Paid for candles	2
26	Paid provisions	1
"	Paid Mr. Bartlett purchases for road	10
30	Paid provisions for 27th 8th 9th	4

1840

Jany 2	Paid do. for 30th 31st & 1st Jany.	3½
"	Paid Antonio Q.W.I. Regt	1¼
"	Paid soldiers do.	1½

"	Paid Cure for prayers for Carnick	5
"	Paid Sacristan	1
"	Paid Senor Moralez to pay Valerio a prisoner in jail for mule which died	8
	Paid A. Romero messenger to Belize bastimente for road	6
	Order in favor of A. Romero on Mr. Walsh P. Treasurer	15
"	Paid for repairing sadles	6
3	Paid for provisions	2½
4	Paid Mr. Nod	16
"	Paid for provisions for journey	17
"	Paid soldiers of Q.W.I. Regt. on Christmas day & 1st	3
"	Paid for hire of house in Peten	4
"	Paid debts of Jocko & Crusoe Q.W.I. Regt	1¼
"	Paid Jose	17
6	Paid provisions at Titchalic & Sacluc	1¾
"	Paid for hire of horse for Jose	1
7	Paid for provisions	1½
9	Paid Jose	2
"	Paid for provisions 8th & date	4
19	Expce of provisions & blanco at Tennosique	3
"	Hire of boat to Cabasera	1
20	Provisions this day	1½
22	Do. for 1st, date & tobacco	5¼
"	Paid for soap	½
"	Paid Jose in full for 6 mules from Peten ($60)	20
24	Paid provisions for 23rd & date	4
"	Paid do. for voyage and at Multa & Pita	7
"	Paid for boat hire to Balancan	14
1840		
Jany 27	Paid for boat hire from Balancan to Monte Christi	9
"	Paid for provisions	2½
28	Paid for do.	1¼

	29	Paid for horses at Palenque	12
	"	Paid for provisions on road	1¾
	30	Exps for provisions at Palenque	3
	31	Paid for do.	3
	"	Do. for road, Practico & Indians	3
Feby	1	Paid for provisions	3
	2	Paid for do.	3
	3	Paid for pig	6
	"	Paid for provisions	2
	4	Paid for do.	1
	5	Paid for do.	¼
	6	Paid for do.	¼
	"	Paid for mats, candles, &c	4
	"	Paid Guide	½
	7	Provisions for the Ruins	3½
	"	Paid Indian Carrier	½
	8	Paid for provisions	2
	"	Paid Indian	½
	11	Paid for provisions 9th 10th & (date)	7
	15	Paid do. for 12th 13th 14th & date	13
	18	Paid do. for 16th 17th & date	9
	"	Paid for horses at Palenque	3
	"	Paid for rent of house	6
	"	Paid for horses to Monte Christi	11
	19	Paid for provisions	3½
	20	Paid for canoe & Indians	2
	"	Sheeting given soldiers for trowsers	5
		Paid Nod	15½
		Paid Bartlett and 2 Peteneros their wages	40
	21	Paid provisions &c this day	2¼
	22	Paid at Tinta on the Rio	1½
		Paid provisions for voyage	4
	25	Paid expenses at Palizada	5
Mch	3	Paid for provisions at Laguna &c to date	12
	"	Paid Mr. Shiel's bill for provisions to date	18½
	11	Paid Expenses for provisions & at Campeche 5 days	10

	Paid do. for voyage	8
	Paid Patron hire of Bungay in part payment advance	100
	Paid at Sisal for provisions	5
	Paid at do. for people during voyage	21
28	Paid for provisions &c at Bay of Ascension	2
"	Paid for provisions voyage	3½
Apl 4	Paid Patron in full with $2 p. diem demurrage—8 days—	116
"	Paid Antonio Romero additional charges as messenger	13¾
	Paid Mr. Nod salary in full	101½
		$ 1418½

I certify the above to be a true account.

PATK. WALKER

appendix II: list of documents protected by crown copyright

Section II:

Unnumbered despatch of April 28, 1838, Col. MacDonald to Lord Glenelg. Archives of British Honduras, Records 14: Despatches Outwards, 1837 to 1844.

Despatch of August 28, 1838, Honduras No. 31, MacDonald to Lord Glenelg. Archives of British Honduras, Records 14.

Despatch of February 9, 1839, Honduras No. 2 (881), MacDonald to Lord Glenelg. Colonial Office Records C.O. 123/55.

(Data on Walker's career derived from the following records in the archives of British Honduras: Oaths of Office, 1830–45, Private Records FF, June, 1834–March, 1845, and Meetings of Magistrates, 1837–44.)

Section III:

Despatch of November 9, 1839, Honduras No. 21, MacDonald to Lord Russell. Archives of British Honduras, Records 14.

Section VI:

Despatch of February 19, 1840, Colonial Office No. 14, Lord Russell to MacDonald. Archives of British Honduras, Records 18: Despatches Inwards, 1840 to 1841.

Chatfield letters. Archives of British Honduras, Records 10: Letters Inwards, 1826 to 1848.

Section VII:

Walker's report of the expedition. Colonial Office Records, C.O. 123/57.

Section VIII:

Despatch of May 13, 1840, Honduras No. 40, MacDonald to Lord Russell. Archives of British Honduras, Records 14.

Despatch of February 2, 1841, Colonial Office No. 36, Lord Russell to MacDonald. Archives of British Honduras, Records 18.

Despatch of April 21, 1841, Honduras No. 17 (C.O. No. 2303 Honduras), MacDonald to Lord Russell. Archives of British Honduras, Records 14.

Section IX:

Letter to the Governor of Jamaica, enclosure to despatch of July 3, 1841, Honduras No. 8. Colonial Office Records, C.O. 123/59.

Committee report, included with report of Public Meeting of December 22, 1841. Colonial Office Records, C.O. 123/62.

Walker's appointment as agent and consul general to the Mosquito Shore, Despatch of September 22, 1844, C.O. Reference 1765 Honduras, Colonial Office to The Earl of Elgin, governor of Jamaica. Colonial Office Records, C.O. 123/67. Also, Parliamen tary Papers, 1846, XLIV 118, "List of All the Consuls-General, Consuls, Vice-Consuls, and Consular Agents in Her Majesty's Service."

Vice Admiral Austen's account of Walker's death, Vice Admiral Sir F. Austen to the Secretary of the Admiralty. House of Commons Sessional Papers, or Parliamentary Papers, 1847–48, LXV 104.

inöex

The text for *Palenque: The Walker-Caddy Expedition to the Ancient Maya City, 1839–1840* is set on the Linotype in 11½-point Caslon Old Face, an exact and faithful reproduction of the original letter designed by William Caslon. The paper on which the book is printed bears the University of Oklahoma Press watermark and has an effective life of at least three hundred years.